The Oxford Book of
Welsh Verse in English

Chosen by
Gwyn Jones

OXFORD UNIVERSITY PRESS

OXFORD NEW YORK TORONTO

1977

Oxford University Press, Walton Street, Oxford OX2 6DP

OXFORD LONDON GLASGOW NEW YORK
TORONTO MELBOURNE WELLINGTON CAPE TOWN
IBADAN NAIROBI DAR ES SALAAM LUSAKA ADDIS ABABA
KUALA LUMPUR SINGAPORE JAKARTA HONG KONG TOKYO
DELHI BOMBAY CALCUTTA MADRAS KARACHI

ISBN 0 19 211858 7

*The Publisher wishes to make grateful acknowledgement to
the Welsh Arts Council with whose support
this volume is published.*

*Printed in Great Britain
at the University Press, Oxford
by Vivian Ridler
Printer to the University*

CONTENTS

CONTENTS

CONTENTS

CONTENTS

CONTENTS

CONTENTS

CONTENTS

CONTENTS

CONTENTS

CONTENTS

CONTENTS

xv

CONTENTS

INTRODUCTION

In the majestic phrase of early British story, the Welsh poetic tradition which this anthology seeks to display is the oldest and most enduring known to the 'Three Realms of Britain and its Three Adjacent Islands'. Necessarily it is rooted, leafed, and branched in the oldest and most enduring language of the Three Realms, and for these reasons and its own particular quality and excellence is not only significant, but uniquely so. On a broad view the world's poetry is one and indivisible; but seen closer a true national poetry is itself, and not the reflection or copy of something else. It has grown from a native conception of what a poet is, his role in society, his relationship with his audience, and the nature of that audience; it will have a manner and content distinguishable from those of other nations and societies; and it may have, as Welsh does, its own nationally evolved verse forms. Ideally poetry should be read in the language in which it was composed, but with Babel the ideal turned sour, and it is a tiny minority indeed which now knows Welsh or any other Celtic literature at less than one remove. An *Oxford Book of Welsh Verse*, edited by Dr. Thomas Parry, was published in 1962; but despite its English title and apparatus, its verse (rightly) is in the Welsh tongue (*yr iaith Gymraeg*), and left the way open to this very different volume designed for the English-language reader. Its choice of poems starts where Welsh poetry starts, a very long time ago, in the Heroic Age of Britain. Since then poetry has been composed and recorded uninterruptedly in the Welsh language, and a selection of that poetry, extending to 141 poems in all, by 61 known and 34 unknown authors, is presented here in English translation. The writing of verse by Welshmen in the English language began very much later, in Tudor times, became effective only in the seventeenth century with the Herberts and Henry Vaughan, and some would say struck a Welsh balance only in the twentieth; but for the moment it is enough to say that it is represented here by 97 poems written by 44 authors, of whom only two are without a known name.

The names of the founding fathers of Welsh poetry we owe to Nennius, who in his *Historia Brittonum*, of *c.* 796, after a mention of King Ida of Northumbria, who reigned between 547 and 559, said: 'Then, at that time, Eudeyrn was fighting bravely against the nation of the Angles. Then Talhaearn Tad Awen (i.e. Father of the Muse) won renown in poetry; and Aneirin and Taliesin and Blwchfardd and Cian who is called Wheat of Song (?) won renown at one and the same time in British poetry.'

The kinds of poetry transmitted from these earlier centuries are what we should expect from the Heroic Age of Britain: eulogies of martial and munificent princes during their lives and elegies upon them after their deaths; the verse elements of prose sagas of destruction and defeat whose linking prose narrative has been forgotten (early Welsh verse is lyrical rather than directly narrative), and gnomic wisdom. The work of the early poets, the Cynfeirdd,[1] already exhibits a notable characteristic of Welsh poetry throughout the ages: the poet is accountable to society, and is its spokesman. He is recorder, instructor, and celebrant. *Beirdd byd barnant wŷr o galon*, says the *Gododdin*-poet: 'The bards of the world pass judgement on men of valour.' The bard, we might say, is the poet as public figure. It is his business to maintain a leader's fame, retail tribal triumphs and disasters, persuade and foretell, convey to his hearers that accepted corpus of lore and precept relating to animals, weather, crops, human nature and behaviour which involves man in the visible and palpable world, and to set forth repeatedly and unequivocally in the compressed verse-forms, bare syntax, and

---

[1] The poetical history of Wales before the modern period, which is considered to begin *c.* 1600, is traditionally divided into three periods: the Cynfeirdd, the Early Poets, from the beginnings to *c.* 1100; the Gogynfeirdd, the Next to the Early Poets, *c.* 1100–*c.* 1350; and the Cywyddwyr, the masters of the *cywydd* metre, *c.* 1350–*c.* 1600. The Gogynfeirdd are also called the Poets of the Princes and their work Court Poetry. The Cywyddwyr and their work are also called the Poets and the Poetry of the Nobility.

severely stylized diction common to his kind the cherished beliefs
of a hierarchical and war-waging society: valour, loyalty, service,
reward. Much of the early poetry has not survived, but one would
like to think that the output of the Cynfeirdd was more varied
than appears, and that there were many other poems like 'Dino-
gad's Petticoat' (no. 4), personal, informal, and unconcerned to
prove anything save the permanence of human affection.

A high proportion of the early poetry was obviously produced
by men with professional or at least agreed standards, and on the
whole it was this finished work which won regard and survived.
The professionalizing of the poetic art becomes much more
marked when we reach the Poets of the Princes, c. 1100. The
next two hundred years were a time of national reassertion, con-
stant struggle, bitter warfare, internecine as well as external,
when a succession of famed princes left a deep mark on the
national consciousness, and on poetry. Some of these princes
were themselves poets, and all were patrons of poets, not only
for the poets' sake but also for their own. 'Thou without me',
cried Cynddelw to the Lord Rhys, 'thou hadst no voice; I
without thee, no voice have I.' The poet had his place, including
his place at court, and his place in the Order of Bards; and he
had his duties. There were events, deeds, intentions to be re-
corded, persons like a patron and his wife to be extolled in this
world and lamented on their departure for the next; poets them-
selves must die, and what was the Lord of Heaven but another
patron to be praised and placated? And all these things had to
be done the right way, in set form and by rule. Poetic structure
became regularized, the *awdl* (ode) dominated, with its end-
rhymes, sections, connections, repetitions, vocabulary, figures
and tropes, alliteration and internal rhymes, woven into a
rhetorical or musical pattern of song, sonorous, powerful, and
directed very much at the ear. A poet might be born: he had
also to be made. There was a craft to be learned, and without
mastery of this craft, whatever else you might be, you would not
be a court poet.

It could be expected that among the poetic productions of

more than two centuries, the work of men skilled, dedicated, and disciplined in their craft, there would appear many noble and satisfying works of art, though for today's reader their merits are often obscured by their common form and conventionalized subject-matter, amounting to a poetic academicism. Yet certain of the court poets communicate instantly and fully: Meilyr (*fl.* 1100–37), significantly called the Poet, the first of them in point of time; Hywel ab Owain Gwynedd (d. 1170), who brought a lightness and elegance, a new note of gallantry, into court poetry with his threefold hymning of the splendour of battle, the beauty of one's homeland, and the sexual attractiveness of women; Cynddelw (*fl.* 1155–1200), already in his own day styled the Great Poet, a bard of unfailing technique and power, and master of every genre: eulogy of a person, celebration of an event, *marwnad* for a lost lord, petition for a reconciliation with an offended patron, troubadour-like love song, and the *marwysgafn* or poem composed in readiness for one's own deathbed; and no less surely Gruffudd ab yr Ynad Coch (*fl.* 1280), who transcended the bounds of formal elegy in his stupendous outcry for his dead lord, the prince Llywelyn. These were all men at the heart of affairs, not eaters of broken meats at the outward end of a prince's table. 'Our histories', said the author of Llanstephan MS. 144 (and by histories he means the acts and deeds of the gentry and their ancestors and kinsmen): 'Our histories were not written by schoolmasters that travelled no further for his knowledge than a child's journey from his breakfast to his lesson, nor by any monk that journeyed no further than from mass to meat, nor by any prentice that had no other education but from shop to market, nor by any base person of birth, condition, or calling. But by noble bards, nobly descended barons, and fellows to lords and princes.'

Then yet again a change of national fortune led to new developments in the nation's poetry. The loss of Welsh independence so brutally underlined by the killing of Llywelyn, 'our last Prince', in 1282 and his brother Dafydd the following year, helped make the old, long-established, serious-minded, rigidly formalized court poetry obsolete. The change may not have been as sudden or as complete as it looks to be, but as so often and in so many literatures a poet of genius appeared to divide one age of Welsh poetry from another. This was Dafydd ap Gwilym, one of the most consummate metrists these islands have known. As though out of the blue, Wales had a different kind of poet, versatile in the Ovidian way, capable of self-mockery, swayed by the poetic breezes that blew from England and France, whose professed ambition was less to stand firm in battle with his lord than dally under the birch-bough with his sweetheart of the hour. Ever since the sixth century the Welsh poetic record had shown a dearth of love poetry, either because it was not composed or, more likely, because it was not pre-served. Now it had a plenitude. Gwalchmai and Hywel ab Owain Gwynedd had rejoiced in the green leaves and white blossom of May, but the best flowers of the thornbrake for the archtypal Cynddelw had been the scarlet entrails of the enemy dead. Now, suddenly, Wales had a man with a keen, apprecia-tive eye for every aspect of nature. He sang of stars and sun-shine, trees and birds, summer and winter, with the same zest as he narrated his adventures with girls. And for new wine a new bottle, for new modes a new metre.

Dafydd was pre-emptively the first and best master of the *cywydd*, a metrical composition in general not running to more than sixty or seventy lines, whose unit is a rhymed couplet each of whose lines consists of seven syllables, one line ending with a feminine or unstressed, the other with a masculine or stressed syllable, and each line normally employing the rhythmic devices of *cynghanedd*. Though the *awdl* would continue in use (no. 38 is an example), the new metre, sinewy, masculine, and handsomely controlled, would dominate the formal compositions of Welsh poets for the next three hundred years, engage the skills of many fine poets of the eighteenth century, and in the twen-tieth has by no means fallen into disuse. It served for love poetry, whether pure, merry, or gross; an appeal to a patron or a prayer to the Virgin; poets who described the bright world around them or expressed the ills and rejoicings and serried vicissitudes common to mankind found it unfailingly apt. It was a jousting spear or switch of nettles for poetic rivals; *conte*, homily, beast-fable, social comment, friendly invitation, autobiography, tribute, elegy—whatever the need the *cywydd* supplied it. Stylistically it lent itself perfectly to such poetic devices as description by comparison (*dyfalu*), allegory, the break in syntactic flow (*sangiad*) or between what in English are words so closely related as to be inseparable (*trychiad*).

It was natural enough that the landed gentry or nobility who came to the fore in Welsh society after the destruction of the princes and the sequestration of their territories should look for different qualities in poets no longer resident at courts but itinerant between those houses where they might seek hospitality and reward in return for entertainment. Even so, poetry remained a social art, not much concerned with the inner wrestling of a poet's soul, but instead looking outward to a known audience and its declared requirements. Courtly love was 'in', as was Nature, and often they were in together. The new bards from time to time genuflected to other external fashions, like the mortuary descant or rumination on human wickedness; there was more flyting between bards; and, of course, they continued to speak to and for the community on matters religious and devotional, and to each other about such topics as the poetic function and its abuses.

Just as naturally, since the composition and recitation of poetry in the homes of the nobility was a business, a livelihood, a craft, as well as an art, it was only right that a man should perfect himself in it and receive instruction from his betters both as to the form and content of poetry. He learned history, and ancient story and poetry, and heraldry and genealogy, and metrics and grammar, sometimes through written works, but more significantly through oral instruction. We hear of three orders of bards, or three bardic divisions, though we should probably not press these classifications beyond a general recognition that there were carefully trained bards whose works bear witness to their mastery of the poetic craft, and more popular entertainers who addressed themselves to humbler and less sophisticated hearers. That the 'higher' poets, many of them members of the upper class they composed for, were jealous of their status and met periodically to debate the regulation of their order and the practice of their craft is well attested. During three centuries a long line of gifted poets and their sustaining patrons, with a strikingly effective verse form in the ascendant, and an attuned and receptive audience co-extensive with the entire circle of Welsh literacy, began, maintained, then brought to its conclusion possibly the most brilliant epoch in the history of Welsh literature.

Not surprisingly, the seventeenth and eighteenth centuries were a time for new bearings. In the event Welsh poetry became more like the contemporary poetry of England and western Europe in its themes and their treatment. Already before 1600 there were many poets making use of freer metres (probably these were no new thing, but it was the 'classical' poetry which tended to be written down), and shifting from the strict count of syllables and the elaborations of *cynghanedd* to metres determined by the number of accents in the line. Second, poets and verse-makers were influenced in the later decades of the century by the words and melodies of English popular songs, and in following this fashion produced a variety of unclassical metrical forms. Third, and of a native stamp, were the old stanzas (*hen benillion*) or verses to be sung to the harp (*penillion telyn*), existing largely in manuscripts of the seventeenth century, but many of them older than that. These are true folk poetry, composed for social gatherings and singing competitions, for the most part simple in structure and of an immediately accessible content. The pleasures and pains of country love, rural wisdom, and the unrarefied distillation of common experience, the background of the seasons and the dumb creation, satire and gossip, birth, marriage, and death, our unheroic griefs and longings, doubts and confusions—these and their like inspired the verses, which once heard haunt the ear with their harp-notes of sorrow, sentiment, humour and happiness, and all such echoes of a humble Arcadia.

It was during these same two centuries that the first significant poetry came from the hands of Welshmen writing in English. It was significant in three ways: that it happened when it did (or indeed at all); that its best products were no mere prentice work but the highly wrought masterpieces of George Herbert and Henry Vaughan; and that it was the presage (though not the cause) of what would happen all over again three hundred years later. This new poetry resulted inevitably from a half-century of change and legal enactment in respect of Wales from the accession of the Welsh-descended Henry Tudor to the English throne in 1485 to the Act of Union in 1535, with its consequences for education and religion in Wales, the growth of the professions and the attractions of court, with the social shifts attendant on these. So the literary and linguistic dichotomy developed, strongly weighted on the Welsh-language side, and we shall see the Herbert brothers writing in English while Edmwnd Prys, Thomas Prys, and Huw Llwyd wrote in Welsh, and so Henry Vaughan and Huw Morus, and Christopher Smart and Williams Pantycelyn and Goronwy Owen, and an abundance of lesser poets besides. The two centuries ran their course; fashions rose or were adopted; fashions fell or were adapted; by 1800 the poetic landscape showed a visible shortage of tall trees, and the ninth wave had ceased to roll and thunder. Poetry, as always, needed a rebirth.

It was a long while coming. It was John Morris-Jones (1864–1929) who saw most clearly that he and his fellow-poets must get back to first principles: nobility of style, beauty of language, and purity of diction. The poet must be worthy of his heritage, and to be that he must be aware of the Welsh poetic past. He saw his ideal realized in the work of three remarkable poets, like Morris-Jones all teachers in the new University of Wales: T. Gwynn Jones at Aberystwyth, W. J. Gruffydd at Cardiff, and R. Williams Parry at Bangor. Inevitably, to ponder a nation's poetical past is to sharpen one's awareness of its political past, and this was happening at an accelerating rate in Wales after *c.* 1880. The renaissance of poetry meant a renaissance of thought. Poets who began as the new romantics, well-read in literatures ancient and modern—including their own—conscious of their bardic responsibilities, and masters of their art, lived through a full cycle of literary and moral convictions. It was a long haul from their early warm romanticism to the painful probings of their later, or last, work. All three, humanist and agnostic, in love with the world's beauty, lyrical, rebellious against the fact, and visionaries at their dawning, found their world no sure abiding-place. T. Gwynn Jones and Williams Parry were superb craftsmen, the former the best master of *cynghanedd* since the fifteenth century, the latter with an almost uncanny command of the revealing word or phrase. They are numbered in the first rank of our native poets, and as major poets do— especially major poets who see themselves as the restorers of ancient glory—they established norms of subject-matter and manner which first liberated, but then came to inhibit, their younger contemporaries. Another change was indicated, and this time it was not a long while coming.

The new poets like the old were teachers in the University. T. H. Parry-Williams offered his admirers a less exalted posture and diction than the three giants of the renaissance. After spectacular successes at the Eisteddfod with poems which he never thought fit to include in his published volumes, he turned among other things to his *rhigymau*, which one might translate as 'verses', almost 'jottings', which express in a colloquial, part flippant, part cynical, part despairing way the vulnerability of men who feel and remember as well as think in a world as flippant, cynical, and desperate as ours. Also an altogether more explicit nationalist poetry was now at hand, in the writings of Saunders Lewis and Gwenallt. The great romantics had come to long for a better and different Wales, free of injustice and oppression, and like Argoed (no. 115), true to herself whatever the cost; but it was Saunders Lewis who made the opening doors of nationalism reverberate like beaten bronze. He is that unflagging and unaccommodating man all causes need if they are to succeed, and need no less if they are destined to fail; and the distilled essence of his personality, the force of his political and Christian convictions, and the strength of his commitment to the twofold cause of Welsh nationhood and the Welsh language have made him not only the most notable figure in Welsh public life during the last forty years but also one of the most influential of our poets. There is a passion and affirmation in his poems which makes them 'large utterances' in both a modern and traditional sense. Another teacher in the University, and another ardent Christian, whose best-known though not necessarily best poems are lamentations for the mislaid innocence of the Welsh past, is Gwenallt, a detester of anglicization and industrialism in his own South Wales (and often a confuser of the two), a poet of considerable range, deep feeling, natural innocence, and fine craftsmanship.

All these poets were born in the last thirty years of the nineteenth century, and when we add to them their later contemporaries born before the outbreak of the First World War, Kitchener Davies, Euros Bowen, Waldo Williams, and Alun Llywelyn-Williams, we have traversed (and hopefully are still traversing) the most splendid and sustained period of Welsh poetry since the age of the *cywydd*. For new wine a new bottle, for new modes new metres. In general the poets of the modern renaissance and their successors have found the free accentual metres more congenial to their purpose than the strict. Their note is personal and serious, but though the mannered address and bardic posture have been largely abandoned the poet is still a man speaking to men and commenting on matters of import. This does not mean that *vers libre* and the newer experimentalism are nowhere reflected in modern Welsh literature, but their full effects have yet to be seen and appreciated in a country where the poet has always been expected to say something relevant to the moral, political, social, or personal situation of his hearer rather than be enigmatically exploratory of his own ego or prove, however unjust and question-begging the term, 'incomprehensible' of utterance or unhelpful of counsel to the community around him. Thus, Kitchener Davies's 'The Sound of the Wind that is Blowing' (no. 168) appears to me to stand among the most poignant and authentic statements of the Great Depression, a cry for the streets of Askelon (and Rhondda) at once personal, communal, national, and universal. The Christian religion, ragged as old newspapers on those same streets, remains a major concern of Welsh poets like Euros Bowen and Waldo Williams, whether as a passionately held belief, a creative and regenerative force in a disintegrating human society, or part of that idealized or mystical vision of the past without which some see little hope for the future. And Alun Llywelyn-Williams says much to men of my generation that we dearly wish we could say ourselves about the course and aftermath of wars and depressions, the changing vistas of Wales and Welsh society, the hard-held hopes and ideals that no one else can carry for us, our regrets for good things lost and ploughed-in illusions.

The same fifty years saw a parallel process of creative activity among Welshmen whose literary language was to be English. There is, necessarily, a marked contrast between the unity and homogeneity of the Welsh-language poets and the uncorrelated and sometimes almost tangential nature of their more miscellaneous compatriots. Yet there is more than a coincidence of begetting in the 1871–2 birth dates of T. Gwynn Jones, W. H. Davies, and John Cowper Powys; the 1878–84 grouping of Edward Thomas, W. J. Gruffydd, and R. Williams Parry; and that of 1893–5 for Wilfred Owen, Saunders Lewis, and David Jones. Subsequent outcrops in both languages, more especially between 1902 and 1906 and in 1913–15 (Alun Llywelyn-Williams, R. S. Thomas, Dylan Thomas, and Alun Lewis) offer no surprise. This new onset of Welsh writing in English was certain to come about, and inasmuch as it was the rendering articulate of four-fifths of the nation was intensely desirable. It was money in the long black stocking that the new front-runners (and out-riders), W. H. Davies, Powys, Edward Thomas, Wilfred Owen, and David Jones, were richly gifted men of lasting, and some of them mighty, achievement.

Yet this is by no means the whole of the story. If you define literature in terms of language only, then a Welshman who writes in English is an English author—which should give Americans, Australians, Scotsmen, and West Indians plenty to think about. On the other hand the English, Americans, Scotsmen, West Indians, are clear that Vernon Watkins, Dylan Thomas, and R. S. Thomas are Welshmen and Welsh authors. In Wales English-speaking Welshmen tend to call all Welshmen Welshmen, but when we speak of a Welsh author we usually mean one who writes in Welsh. To get round this muddle of logic and nomenclature the word 'Anglo-Welsh' came into general use in the nineteen-thirties as a term of literary criticism descriptive of the creative work of Welshmen who write in English. It had been heard before but gained validity only then because the thirties saw a sudden flowering, indeed an explosion, of such writing associated with the names (to confine ourselves to poets) of David Jones, Idris Davies, Glyn Jones, Vernon Watkins, Brenda Chamberlain, Margiad Evans, R. S. Thomas, Dylan Thomas, Alun Lewis, and maybe a score of others.

Some of this has by now acquired a world-wide fame. But it was then very much a new movement of new men, owing nothing to the unchildered Adams and inconceivable Eves of remoter centuries, and offering only a distant nod to the immediate past. I don't think I can exaggerate the individualism, the spontaneity of those inaugural years. Everybody appeared to be going his own way, doing his own thing, and building his own poetic monument or mausoleum. But white hairs and many funerals have by now emphasized the tendencies and resemblances more than the differences. One war was over and another about to begin, at home there had been the General Strike and Great Depression, and abroad the rolling-up of democracies and an apparently irreparable assault on the concept of the brotherhood of man. South Wales, ravaged and in rags, was still as idealistic and socially minded as ever, immersed in debate about everything from political ideologies, soup-kitchens, and greyhounds, to the new canons of art forever seeping through from Europe to Europe's western shore. There was also the common denominator of our Welshness: origin, birth, upbringing, residence, sense of identity or affinity, in varying degrees and different combinations; and for most of us a common or similar working-class or lower middle-class background, with the quickening of mind this guaranteed at the hands of the best generation of teachers this country has ever known. There was, and still is, the complicated problem of Anglo-Welsh attitudes towards Wales, the Welsh language, nationalism, themselves and each other, and the consequences of all this for their work. Finally there was the accident of talent or genius. Certainly a deal of splendid poetry resulted from all this activity and turmoil, or rather from the poets who made their mark in the three decades after 1935, some in Wales, some in the Three Realms, and some in the Five Continents.

This Introduction has by design been historical rather than appreciatory, and since the major Anglo-Welsh poets from Herbert and Vaughan to Edward, R. S., and Dylan Thomas may be taken as read, it has been mainly concerned with poetry written in Welsh. I judged it more important, for example, to offer the reader some explanation why Welsh poetry in the ninth, fourteenth, and twentieth centuries is the kind of poetry it is, exhibiting the qualities it does, than to assert or demonstrate the excellence of individual poems. No such demonstration is needed. For I cannot believe that the reader of this book will find even in the early periods significant barriers to his enjoyment and appreciation, despite the absence there of that autumnal English invention, the Celtic Twilight, or the presence of that springtime Celtic innovation, the prosody of the bards. Cynddelw's 'Poem on his Death-bed' (no. 20) belongs to a Celtic genre, but requires no explicator, and speaks triumphantly for itself. 'The Girls of Llanbadarn' (no. 26) is purest Dafydd ap Gwilym, but its two minxes speak for minxes throughout the ages. Just as Lewis Glyn Cothi speaks for all fathers at all times in all places with a poem (no. 39) which is at once a public rehearsal of the *cywydd*-maker's art and a naked cry of private grief. Six hundred years later, 'Miraculous Dawn' (no. 128), 'To the Good Thief' (no. 146), 'Rhydcymerau' (no. 151), 'In Two Fields' (no. 175), and 'Pont y Caniedydd' (no. 199), are poetry in any language; and when we reach our poets of the last pages, who needs assuring that the future is bright?

My presentation of the texts of poems conforms to the practice of the series. They are taken from approved sources and printed verbatim, with two exceptions. English-language poems written before *c*. 1750 have been modernized in spelling, punctuation, and capitalization. A number of the translations of Welsh-language poems have not yet appeared in print, and with the approval of the translators concerned I have reproduced these from their transcripts. The symbol *ọ̦* at the right of a poem's title denotes that it is translated from the Welsh, and refers the reader to the Index of Translators on p. 303. Almost all the translations chosen are modern ones, for the good reason that they are better than those attempted by the pioneers of earlier centuries. A number of poems in both languages have been abbreviated, as shown, not by way of 'improvement', but to allow the reader acquaintance with poems of reputation and significance which just could not be reproduced here in full. I have not supplied the English reader with a guide to the pronunciation of Welsh (but see below for proper names); or to the mysteries of *cynghanedd*, which he will not encounter; or to the rules of Welsh versification, which largely or entirely disappear in translation. Instead, I have offered a wide selection of footnotes elucidatory of places, persons, and the like, mainly in the Welsh-language poems, and a series of more extended notes at the back of the book, some of them supplementary to the Introduction.

In conclusion, I believe my 238 poems form the most comprehensive volume of Welsh poetry of its kind yet to appear in print. It is my hope it may bring its reader a share of the pleasure it has brought me. What it cannot bring him is my sense of privilege in being allowed to prepare it.

GWYN JONES
University College,   *St. David's Day*
Cardiff   *1st March 1977*

EDITOR'S NOTE

It is a pleasure to record the wise and generous help I have enjoyed while preparing this anthology of Welsh poetry. I am particularly indebted to Dr. Thomas Parry, Professor Gwynedd Pierce, Mrs. Mair Jones, and Professor Joseph Clancy; and I have received important gifts of information, judgement, and time from a great many others, among whom I am happy to mention Mr. D. J. Bowen, Mrs. Mair K. Davies, Mr. Raymond Garlick, Mr. Glyn Jones, Mr. Saunders Lewis, Professor Alun Llywelyn-Williams, Mr. Jon Stallworthy, and Mr. Gwyn Thomas. The shape and ordering of the volume owe much to the insight and skills of Miss Catharine Carver at the Oxford University Press. I offer them all my warm thanks and lasting appreciation.

G. J.

ACKNOWLEDGEMENTS

The editor and publishers gratefully acknowledge permission to reproduce copyright poems, and translations as credited at p. 303, in this book.

Dannie Abse: from *Walking under Water* (Hutchinson, 1952). Reprinted by permission of Anthony Sheil Associates Ltd.

C. C. Bell: (translation) from *Poems from the Welsh* (Welsh Publishing Co. Ltd., 1913). Reprinted by permission of Idris Christopher Bell.

H. Idris Bell: (translations) no. 35 from *Dafydd ap Gwilym: Fifty Poems* (Hon. Society of Cymmrodorion, 1942); no. 37 from *Transactions of the Hon. Society of Cymmrodorion*, 1940; nos. 38, 77, 134 from Thomas Parry, *A History of Welsh Literature* (Clarendon Press, 1955); nos. 41, 90, 103, 106, 117 from H. I. Bell, *The Development of Welsh Poetry* (Clarendon Press, 1936); nos. 160–5 from the *Welsh Review*, V, ii (1946). Reprinted by permission of Idris Christopher Bell.

Euros Bowen: nos. 171–2 from *Cerddi* (1958); no. 170 from *Cerddi Rhydd* (1961); both published by Hugh Evans & Sons Ltd. Translations from the author's *Poems* (1974), reprinted by permission of J. D. Lewis & Sons Ltd. (Gwasg Gomer).

Brenda Chamberlain: from *The Green Heart* (Oxford University Press, 1958). Reprinted by permission of Neville Chamberlain.

Joseph P. Clancy: (translations) nos. 3, 5, 9, 10, 15, 18–20, 22, 23 from *The Earliest Welsh Poetry* (Macmillan/St. Martin's Press, 1970); nos. 27, 30, 32–3, 36, 39, 44, 52, 55 from *Medieval Welsh Lyrics* (Macmillan/St. Martin's Press, 1965). Reprinted by permission of the translator.

Anthony Conran: (translations) from *The Penguin Book of Welsh Verse* (1967). Copyright © Anthony Conran, 1967. Reprinted by permission of Penguin Books Ltd.

Aneirin Talfan Davies: (translations) from the *Welsh Review*, III, iv (1944). Reprinted by permission of the translator.

Gareth Alban Davies: from *Balad Lewsyn a'r Môr* (1964). Translated by permission of Gee & Son.

Gloria Evans Davies: from *Her Name Like the Hours* (1974). Reprinted by permission of the author and Chatto & Windus Ltd.

ACKNOWLEDGEMENTS

Idris Davies: 'Do you remember 1926?' and 'Consider famous men, Dai bach' from *Gwalia Deserta* (Dent, 1938); 'Mrs. Evans fach, you want butter again' from *The Angry Summer* (Faber & Faber, 1943). Reprinted by permission of Mrs. Dorothy Morris.

J. Kitchener Davies: from *Cerddi Hir* (Gwasg Gee). Translated by permission of Mrs. Mair K. Davies.

T. Glynne Davies: from *Llwybrau'r Pridd* (1961). Translated by permission of Christopher Davies (Publishers) Ltd.

W. H. Davies: from *The Complete Poems of W. H. Davies* (1963). Copyright © 1963 by Jonathan Cape Ltd. Reprinted by permission of Mrs. H. M. Davies, Jonathan Cape Ltd., and Wesleyan University Press.

Tom Earley: from *A Welshman in Bloomsbury* (Outposts, 1966). Reprinted by permission of the author.

Margiad Evans: from *Poems from Obscurity* (Andrew Dakers, 1948). Reprinted by permission of David Higham Associates Ltd.

Llewelyn Wyn Griffith: from *The Barren Tree* (Penmark Press, 1947). Reprinted by permission of the author.

W. J. Gruffydd: from *Y Llenor* (Hughes & Son). Translated by permission of Christopher Davies (Publishers) Ltd.

Richard Hughes: from *Confessio Juvenis* (Chatto & Windus, 1930). Reprinted by permission of David Higham Associates Ltd.

Emyr Humphreys: from *Ancestor Worship* (1970). Reprinted by permission of Gee & Son.

Rolfe Humphries: (translations) from *Nine Thorny Thickets: Selected Poems of Dafydd ap Gwilym* (1969). Reprinted by permission of Kent State University Press.

Kenneth Jackson: (translations) from *A Celtic Miscellany* (1951). Reprinted by permission of Routledge & Kegan Paul Ltd.

Bobi Jones: 'Portrait of an Engine Driver', 'Spring at Nant Dywelan', 'Portrait of a Nun' from *Y Gân Gyntaf* (1957). Translated by permission of J. D. Lewis & Sons Ltd. (Gwasg Gomer); 'Portrait of a Pregnant Woman' from *Rhwng Taf a Thaf* (1960). Translated by permission of Christopher Davies (Publishers) Ltd.

David Jones: from *In Parenthesis* (1937) and *The Sleeping Lord* (1974). Reprinted by permission of Faber & Faber Ltd. and Chilmark Press.

D. Gwenallt Jones (Gwenallt): 'Rhydcymerau' from *Eples* (1951); 'The Earth' from *Y Coed* (1969); 'Cymru' from *Ysgubau'r Awen* (1938). Translated by permission of J. D. Lewis & Sons Ltd. (Gwasg Gomer).

ACKNOWLEDGEMENTS

Ellis Jones: 'Eaves' translated by permission of the Court of the National Eisteddfod of Wales.

Glyn Jones: (poems and translations) from *Selected Poems* (1975). Reprinted by permission of J. D. Lewis & Sons Ltd. (Gwasg Gomer).

Gwilym R. Jones: from *Cerddi'r Gwilym R* (1969). Translated by permission of The County Press (Gwasg y Sir).

R. Gerallt Jones: (translations) from *Poetry of Wales 1930–1970* (1974). Reprinted by permission of J. D. Lewis & Sons Ltd. (Gwasg Gomer).

T. Gwynn Jones: from *Caniadau* (Hughes & Son, 1926). Translated by permission of Christopher Davies (Publishers) Ltd.

T. H. Jones: 'Difference' from *Enemy in the Heart* (1957); 'The Welshman in Exile Speaks' from *The Beast at the Door* (1963). Reprinted by permission of Rupert Hart-Davis Ltd./Granada Publishing Ltd.

Alun Lewis: 'All day it has rained' from *Raider's Dawn* (1942), 'The Mahratta Ghats', 'In Hospital: Poona', and 'The Jungle' from *Ha! Ha! Among the Trumpets* (1945). Reprinted by permission of George Allen & Unwin (Publishers) Ltd.

Howell Elvet Lewis (Elfed): 'Life's Morning' translated by permission of J. Humphrey Jones.

Saunders Lewis: 'The Deluge' and 'To the Good Thief' from *Byd a Betws* (1941). Translated by permission of J. D. Lewis & Sons Ltd. (Gwasg Gomer); 'Mary Magdalene', 'Ascension Thursday', and 'The Pine' from *Siwan a Cherddi Eraill* (1956). Translated by permission of Christopher Davies (Publishers) Ltd.

D. Myrddin Lloyd: (translations) from *A Book of Wales*, ed. D. M. Lloyd and E. M. Lloyd (1953). Reprinted by permission of William Collins Sons & Co. Ltd.

Alun Llywelyn-Williams: from *Pont y Caniedydd* (1956). Translated by permission of Gee & Son.

Roland Mathias: 'Craswall' from *The Flooded Valley* (Putnam & Co. Ltd., 1960). Reprinted by permission of The Bodley Head; 'Departure in Middle Age' from *Absalom in the Tree* (1971). Reprinted by permission of J. D. Lewis & Sons Ltd. (Gwasg Gomer).

Huw Menai: from *Back in the Return* (1933). Reprinted by permission of William Heinemann Ltd.

Dyfnallt Morgan: (translation) from *D. Gwenallt Jones* (Writers of Wales). Reprinted by permission of the Welsh Arts Council and the University of Wales Press.

ACKNOWLEDGEMENTS

John Morris-Jones: from *Caniadau* (Fox James & Co., 1907). Trans-
lated by permission of the Misses Morris-Jones.

Leslie Norris: 'Water' from *Ransoms* (1970); 'Elegy for Lyn James'
from *Finding Gold* (1967). Reprinted by permission of the author
and Chatto & Windus Ltd.

John Ormond: 'Lament for a Leg' and 'Ancient Monuments' from
Definition of a Waterfall (1973), © Oxford University Press 1973.
Reprinted by permission of the publisher. 'At His Father's Grave'
from the same volume reprinted by permission of Christopher
Davies (Publishers) Ltd.

Wilfred Owen: from *The Collected Poems of Wilfred Owen* (1963).
Copyright Chatto & Windus Ltd. 1946, © 1963. Reprinted by
permission of the Owen Estate, Chatto & Windus Ltd., and New
Directions Publishing Corporation, New York.

R. Williams Parry: 'The Fox' from *Yr Haf a Cherddi Eraill* (Hughes
& Son, 1924). Translated by permission of Christopher Davies
(Publishers) Ltd.; 'Miraculous Dawn', 'The Old Boatman of
Death's River', '"Two Hearts Divided"', 'Branwen's Starling', and
englyn no. 165 from *Cerddi'r Gaeaf* (1952). Translated by permission
of Gee & Son.

T. H. Parry-Williams: from *Datholiad O Gerddi* (Gwasg Gomer).
Translated by permission of J. D. Lewis & Sons Ltd. (Gwasg
Gomer).

John Cowper Powys: from *The Ridge*, reprinted by permission of the
Estate of the late John Cowper Powys and Laurence Pollinger Ltd.

A. G. Prys-Jones: 'St. Govan' and 'A Day which Endures Not'
reprinted by permission of the author.

Ernest Rhys: from *Wales England Wed* (1940). Reprinted by permis-
sion of J. M. Dent & Sons Ltd.

Dylan Thomas: from *Collected Poems* (1952). Reprinted by permission
of J. M. Dent & Sons Ltd. and the Trustees for the Copyrights of
the late Dylan Thomas. Also from (U.S.A.) *The Poems of Dylan
Thomas*. Copyright 1938, 1939, 1946 by New Directions Publishing
Corporation. Reprinted by permission of New Directions Publish-
ing Corporation, New York.

Gwyn Thomas: 'Little Death' from *Y Weledigaeth Haearn* (1965);
'Horses' from *Enw'r Gair* (1972). Translated by permission of Gee
& Son; 'Microscope' from *Cerddi Heddiw* (Gwasg Gomer). Trans-
lated by permission of J. D. Lewis & Sons Ltd. (Gwasg Gomer);
(translations) from *Presenting Saunders Lewis*, ed. Alun R. Jones

and Gwyn Thomas (1973). Reprinted by permission of the University of Wales Press.

R. S. Thomas: 'A Peasant', 'The Hill Farmer Speaks', 'Welsh History', and translation of no. 65 from *Song at the Year's Turning* (1955); 'A Blackbird Singing' from *Poetry for Supper* (1958); 'The Moor' from *Pietá* (1966). Reprinted by permission of Rupert Hart-Davis Ltd./Granada Publishing Ltd.

Thomas Jacob Thomas (Sarnicol): from *Blodau Drain Duon* (Hughes & Son). Translated by permission of Christopher Davies (Publishers) Ltd.

Henry Treece: from *The Haunted Garden* (1947). Reprinted by permission of Faber & Faber Ltd.

Vernon Watkins: 'The Collier' and 'Returning to Goleufryn' from *Selected Poems* (1967). Copyright © Faber & Faber Ltd. 1967; 'The Mare' from *Cypress and Acacia* (1959). Copyright © 1959 by Vernon Watkins; 'Ode to Swansea' from *Affinities* (1962). Copyright © 1962 by Vernon Watkins. All reprinted by permission of Mrs. Gwen Watkins and New Directions Publishing Corporation, New York.

Gwyn Williams: from *Foundation Stock* (1974). Reprinted by permission of J. D. Lewis & Sons Ltd. (Gwasg Gomer); (translations) nos. 4, 83, 127, 196 from *Presenting Welsh Poetry* (Faber & Faber, 1959); nos. 49, 99 from *The Rent that's due to Love* (Editions Poetry London, 1950). Reprinted by permission of Curtis Brown Ltd.; nos. 16, 17, 28, 31, 40, 46, 53, 54 from *Welsh Poems: Sixth Century to 1600* (1973). Reprinted by permission of Faber & Faber Ltd.

Ifor Williams: (translation) reprinted by permission of the Dublin Institute of Advanced Studies.

Rhydwen Williams: from *Barddoniaeth Rhydwen Williams* (1965). Translated by permission of Christopher Davies (Publishers) Ltd.

Waldo Williams: from *Dail Pren* (1956). Translated by permission of J. D. Lewis & Sons Ltd. (Gwasg Gomer).

A NOTE ON THE
PRONUNCIATION OF WELSH PROPER
NAMES

The following generalities will help with the pronunciation of proper names. Variant spellings such as Gereint, Geraint, Mynyddawg, Mynyddog, Pengwern, Penngwern, need not perturb the reader. The accent falls on the penultimate syllable: Cynddýlan, Dinógad, Dywélan, Gwálchmai, Llanbádarn, Mórfudd, Taliésin, etc. Vowels should be given a 'continental' value rather than an English or American one; *w* as a vowel is approximately *oo*. Among consonants, *c* and *g* are always hard, as in cat and garden; *dd* = *th*, as in breathe; *f* = *v*; *ff* = *f*; *r* should be well and truly sounded always; *ch*, as in Scottish loch; *ll* as in Welsh Llanelli; *si* = *sh*. The well-known personal names, Dylan, Gladys, Gwyn, Griffith, Howel(l), Llewelyn, Lloyd, Meredith, Morris, Owen, Preece, are useful straws to clutch at.

G. J.

TALIESIN

6th century

The Battle of Argoed Llwyfain ̧

There was a great battle Saturday morning
From when the sun rose until it grew dark.
The fourfold hosts of Fflamddwyn invaded.
Goddau and Rheged gathered in arms,
Summoned from Argoed as far as Arfynydd—
They might not delay by so much as a day.

With a great swaggering din, Fflamddwyn shouted,
'Are these the hostages come? Are they ready?'
To him then Owain, scourge of the eastlands,
'They've not come, no! They're not, nor shall they be ready!
And a whelp of Coel would indeed be afflicted
Did he have to give any man as a hostage!'

And Urien, lord of Erechwydd, shouted,
'If they would meet us now for our kinsfolk,
High on the hilltop let's raise our ramparts,
Carry our faces over the shield rims,
Raise up our spears, men, over our heads
And set upon Fflamddwyn in the midst of his hosts
And slaughter him, ay, and all that go with him!'

There was many a corpse beside Argoed Llwyfain;
    From warriors ravens grew red,
And with their leader a host attacked.
For a whole year I shall sing to their triumph.

And when I'm grown old, with death hard upon me,
I'll not be happy save to praise Urien.

Fflamddwyn] an English leader, 'Flamebearer'   Rheged] Urien's
kingdom in North Britain   eastlands] the English-held areas of Britain

2 *Death Song for Owain ab Urien* ♩

God, consider the soul's need
   Of Owain son of Urien!
Rheged's prince, secret in loam:
   No shallow work, to praise him!

A strait grave, a man much praised,
   His whetted spear the wings of dawn:
That lord of bright Llwyfenydd,
   Where is his peer?

Reaper of enemies; strong of grip;
   One kind with his fathers;
Owain, to slay Fflamddwyn,
   Thought it no more than sleep.

Sleepeth the wide host of England
   With light in their eyes,
And those that had not fled
   Were braver than were wise.

Owain dealt them doom
   As the wolves devour sheep;
That warrior, bright of harness,
   Gave stallions for the bard.

Though he hoarded wealth like a miser,
   For his soul's sake he gave it.
God, consider the soul's need
   Of Owain son of Urien.

ANEIRIN
6th century

from The Gododdin

1 (VIII)

Men went to Catraeth, keen their war-band.
Pale mead their portion, it was poison.
Three hundred under orders to fight.
And after celebration, silence.
Though they went to churches for shriving,
True is the tale, death confronted them.

2 (XI)

Men went to Catraeth at dawn:
Their high spirits lessened their life-spans.
They drank mead, gold and sweet, ensnaring;
For a year the minstrels were merry.
Red their swords, let the blades remain
Uncleansed, white shields and four-sided spearheads,
Before Mynyddawg Mwynfawr's men.

3 (XXI)

Men went to Catraeth, they were renowned.
Wine and mead from gold cups was their drink,
A year in noble ceremonial,
Three hundred and sixty-three gold-torqued men.
Of all those who charged, after too much drink,
But three won free through courage in strife,
Aeron's two war-hounds and tough Cynon,
And myself, soaked in blood, for my song's sake.

4 (XCV)

Gododdin's war-band on shaggy mounts,
Steeds the hue of swans, in full harness,

Catraeth] Catterick, Yorkshire

ANEIRIN

Fighting for Eidin's treasure and mead.
   On Mynyddawg's orders
   Shields were battered to bits,
   Sword-blades descended
     On pallid cheeks.
They loved combat, broad line of attack:
They bore no disgrace, men who stood firm.

5 (I)

Man's mettle, youth's years,
Courage for combat:
Swift thick-maned stallions
Beneath a fine stripling's thighs,
Broad lightweight buckler
On a slim steed's crupper,
Glittering blue blades,
Gold-bordered garments.
Never will there be
Bitterness between us:
Rather I make of you
Song that will praise you.
The blood-soaked field
Before the marriage-feast,
Foodstuff for crows
Before the burial.
A dear comrade, Owain;
Vile, his cover of crows.
Ghastly to me that ground,
Slain, Marro's only son.

6 (II)

Diademed, to the fore at all times,
Breathless before a maid, he earned mead.
Rent the front of his shield, when he heard
The war-cry, he spared none he pursued.
He'd not turn from a battle till blood
Flowed, like rushes hewed men who'd not flee.

Eidin] a place or region near Edinburgh (Dineidin)

4

At court the Gododdin say there came
Before Madawg's tent on his return
But a single man in a hundred.

7 (XXVII)

Issac, much-honoured man from the South,
Like the incoming ocean his ways,
　　Genial and generous,
　　Well-mannered over mead.
　　Where he buried his weapons
　　　He called it quits.
Not stained, stainless; not faulty, faultless.
His sword rang in the heads of mothers.
A wall in war, Gwydneu's son was praised.

8 (LIII)

A shame the shield was pierced
Of kind-hearted Cynwal.
A shame he set his thighs
On a long-legged steed.
Dark his brown spear-shaft,
Darker his saddle.
In his den a Saxon
Munches on a goat's
Leg: may he seldom
Have spoils in his purse.

9 (LVIII)

Warriors rose together, formed ranks.
With a single mind they assaulted.
Short their lives, long their kinsmen long for them.
Seven times their sum of English they slew:
Their fighting turned wives into widows;
Many a mother with tear-filled eyelids.

10 (LXI)

Because of wine-feast and mead-feast they charged,
Men famed in fighting, heedless of life.
Bright ranks around cups, they joined to feast.

Wine and mead and bragget, these were theirs.
From Mynyddawg's banquet, grief-stricken my mind,
Many I lost of my true comrades.
Of three hundred champions who charged on Catraeth,
It is tragic, but one man came back.

11 (LXXXV)

When thoughts in throngs
Come upon me, mournful of mind,
My breath is faint
As in running, and then I weep.
One dear I mourn,
One dear whom I loved, noble stag,
Grief for the man
Who was ever in Argoed's ranks.
He gave his all
For countrymen, for a lord's sake,
For rough-hewn wood,
For a flood of grief, for the feasts.
Friends about him he bore us to a blazing fire,
And to seats of white skins and to sparkling wine.
Gereint from the South gave the war-cry,
Bright and fair, fair-formed was his face,
Generous spear-lord, praiseworthy lord,
So gracious, well I know his nature,
Well I knew Gereint: kind, noble, he was.

12 (XC)

Three hundred golden-torqued men attacked:
Contending for the land was cruel.
Although they were being slain, they slew;
Till the world ends, they will be honoured.
Of the comrades who went together,
Tragic, but a single man returned.

ANONYMOUS
7th century

4   *Dinogad's Petticoat*   ♀

Dinogad's speckled petticoat
was made of skins of speckled stoat:
whip whip whipalong
eight times we'll sing the song.
When your father hunted the land
spear on shoulder club in hand
thus his speedy dogs he'd teach
Giff Gaff catch her catch her fetch!
In his coracle he'd slay
fish as a lion does its prey.
When your father went to the moor
he'd bring back heads of stag fawn boar
the speckled grouse's head from the mountain
fishes' heads from the falls of Oak Fountain.
Whatever your father struck with his spear
wild pig wild cat fox from his lair
unless it had wings it would never get clear.

7th century

5   *In Praise of Tenby*   ♀

I beg God's grace, guardian of the parish,
Lord of heaven and earth, profound in wisdom.

A splendid fort stands on the sea's surface:
Mirthful at New Year is a bright headland.
And whenever the ocean booms its boast,
Bards are wont to carouse over mead-cups.

4 petticoat] *pais*, tunic, child's dress, petty coat   5 Tenby] in Pem-
brokeshire: i.e. Dinbych, 'the little fortress', presumably the Welsh fortress
on the promontory where a Norman castle was afterwards built

7

Swiftly the wave surges towards it:
They leave the grey-green sea to the Picts.
And may I, O God, for my prayer's sake,
When I keep my pledge, be at peace with you.

A splendid fort stands on the wide ocean,
A sturdy stronghold, sea-encircled.
Ask, Britain, for whom this is fitting:
Head of ab Erbin's house, may it be yours!
There were throngs and songs in the stockade,
And a cloud-high eagle tracking pale faces:
Before a high lord, before a foe-router,
Far-famed and fierce, they fell into line.

A splendid fort stands on the ninth wave:
Splendid its people taking their pleasure.
Their lively life is not based on disdain,
It is not their way to be hard of heart.
I will tell no lie of my welcome:
Better Dyfed's serf than Deudraeth's yeomen.
Its generous comrades, keeping a feast,
Comprise, in each couple, the best in the land.

A splendid fort stands where a throng provides
Pleasure and praise, and the birds are loud.
Merry its melodies on New Year's Eve
For a bountiful lord, bold and brave.
Before he entered the church of oak,
He gave me wine and mead from a crystal cup.

A splendid fort stands on the sea-coast,
Splendid in granting to each his share.
I know in Tenby, glowing its gulls,
The comrades of Bleiddudd, lord of the court.
Mine was the custom on New Year's Eve
Of a place by a lord bold in battle
And a purple robe and high privilege,
Till I was the tongue of Britain's bards.

8

ANONYMOUS

A splendid fort stands that is stirred by songs:
What honours I wished for were mine.
(I do not say 'rights'; I must keep my place:
Who learns not this earns no New Year's gift!)
British writings the foremost concern
In that place where waves make their uproar:
Long may it last, that cell where I stayed.

A splendid fort stands, rising high,
Superb its pleasures, its praise far-famed.
Splendid its bounds, stronghold of heroes,
Withstanding the spray, long are its wings.
Harsh sea-birds rush to the rocky peak.
May wrath, banned, make off over the mountains,
And Bleiddudd's be the highest bliss,
His memory kept in mind over mead.
The Lord of harmonious heaven bless them:
May Owain's great-grandson be one with his men.

9th century

6   *from* Hateful Old Age   ♀

Before my back was bent I was eloquent:
For wonders men acclaimed me,
And Argoed's men maintained me.

Before my back was bent I was confident:
A guest at wassails hailed
In Powys paradise of Wales.

Before my back was bent I was eminent
Of mien. My warspear led the attack;
Now bowbacked, downbent, trouble-racked.

Wooden staff, it is autumn.
Brown the bracken, the stubble yellow;
What once I loved I've said farewell to.

6 Powys] north-eastern Wales

· 9

Wooden staff, it is winter.
Men are loud-tongued over their drink;
None puts in at my bed's brink.

Wooden staff, it is spring.
Cuckoos are hidden, clear their plaintive call;
Girls have no use for me at all.

Wooden staff, it is early summer.
Brown the furrow, curly the young corn;
The sight of your crook makes me groan.

This leaf by the wind rolled,
Alas for its destiny.
Born this year: already old.

What I loved as a lad I now curse:
A girl, a stranger, a young horse;
With none of them can stay the course.

Four ills, of all my hates the chief,
Are met in me together:
Coughing, old age, sickness, grief.

I'm senile, lonely, twisted and cold
After the bed of desire. I'm galled
With misery. My back's thrice-snarled.

No girl wants me, no friend haunts me,
Age daunts and enwalls me.
Ah Death, why don't you call me?

Wretched the doom for Llywarch doomed
The night he left the womb:
Toil upon toil, long pain, unbroken gloom.

ANONYMOUS

9th century

7 *from* The Elegy on Cynddylan ♀

Stand out, maids, and look on the land of Cynddylan; the court of Penngwern is ablaze; alas for the young who long for their brothers! . . .

Cynddylan the bright buttress of the borderland, wearing a chain, stubborn in battle, he defended Trenn, his father's town.

Cynddylan of the bright heart, the stately, wearing a chain, stubborn in the army, he defended Trenn while he lived . . .

How sad it is to my heart to lay the white flesh in the black coffin, Cynddylan the leader of a hundred hosts.

The hall of Cynddylan is dark tonight, without fire, without bed; I shall weep a while, I shall be silent after.

The hall of Cynddylan is dark tonight, without fire, without candle; but for God, who will give me sanity?

The hall of Cynddylan is dark tonight, without fire, without light; longing for you comes over me.

The hall of Cynddylan, its vault is dark after the bright company; alas for him who does not do the good which falls to him!

Hall of Cynddylan, you have become shapeless, your shield is in the grave; while he lived you were not mended with hurdles.

The hall of Cynddylan is loveless tonight, after him who owned it; ah, Death, why does it spare me? . . .

The hall of Cynddylan, it pierces me to see it, without roof, without fire; my lord dead, myself alive . . .

The hall of Cynddylan is still tonight, after losing its chief; great merciful God, what shall I do? . . .

The eagle of Eli, loud is his scream tonight; he swallowed gory drink, the heart's blood of Cynddylan the fair.

Penngwern] Shrewsbury, or the general area of Shrewsbury

11

ANONYMOUS

The eagle of Eli was shrieking tonight, he wallowed in the blood of men; he in the wood, a heavy grief to me.

The eagle of Eli I hear tonight; he is bloodstained, I dare not go near him; he in the wood, a heavy grief upon me . . .

The eagle of Penngwern, grey-created, uplifted is his cry, greedy for the flesh of Cynddylan.

The eagle of Penngwern, grey-crested, uplifted is his claw, greedy for the flesh I love . . .

The chapels of Bassa are his resting-place tonight, his last welcome, the pillar of battle, the heart of the men of Argoed . . .

The chapels of Bassa are a fallow field tonight, the clover has made it; they are red; my heart is full.

The chapels of Bassa have lost their rank after the destruction by the English of Cynddylan and Elfan of Powys . . .

The white town in the breast of the wood, this is its symbol ever— blood on the surface of its grass.

The white town in the land, its symbol is green graves, and blood under the feet of its men.

The white town in the valley, glad is the kite at the bloodshed of battle; its people have perished . . .

After my brothers from the lands of the Severn round the banks of the Dwyryw, woe is me, God! that I am alive . . .

I have looked out on a lovely land from the gravemound of Gorwyn-nion; long is the sun's course—longer are my memories . . .

I had brothers who were not vicious, who grew up like hazel saplings; one by one they have all passed away.

I had brothers whom God has taken from me, it was my ill-luck that caused it; they did not earn fame by fraud . . .

Bassa] Eglwysau Basa, Baschurch

13th-century MS.

8   *from* The Stanzas of the Graves   ♀

1

The graves the rain makes wet and sleek,
Not men who turned the other cheek,
Cerwyd, and Cywryd, and Caw.

2

The graves beneath the thicket's pall,
Not unavenged were seen to fall
Gwrien, Morien, Morial.

3

Long past, long hid, the strife he bred,
Machawy's soil now roofs his head;
Long, white, the fingers of Beidawg the Red.

4

Siawn's grave is on Hirerw Mound,
Between the earth and his oaken shroud,
A treacherous smiler, bitter, proud.

5

After wounds and bloody fields,
And wearing of harness, and white steeds,
This is the grave of Cynddylan.

6

After things blue, and red, and fair,
And taut-necked horses, big and brave,
In Llanheledd Owain's grave.

7

Whose is the grave on yonder scree?
His hand was foe to many.
Battle's bull, may he win mercy!

8

Whose grave is this? Brwyno the Tall,
Whose justice was strong in his land.
No ground was given where he made stand.

9

Whose grave is this? [. . .]
Crazed as a wild boar in mortal strife,
He'd smile on you as he spilled your life.

10

At Camlan the grave of Osfran's son,
After many a bloody fight.
Bedwyr's grave's on Tryfan height.

11

Gwalchmai is in Peryddon ground,
His grave reproaches all mankind;
Cynon in Llanbadarn find.

12

A grave for March, a grave for Gwythur,
A grave for Gwgawn Red-glaive;
The world's enigma, Arthur's grave.

13th-century MS.

9   *Gereint ab Erbin*   𝄐

Before Gereint, foe's affliction,
I saw white stallions red-shinned,
And after battle, bitter death.

Before Gereint, foe left fruitless,
I saw steeds red-shinned from strife,
And after battle, bitter brooding.

Before Gereint, foe's fierce pressure,
I saw steeds, white their trappings,
And after battle, bitter blanket.

At Llongborth I saw fury
And biers, more than abundant,
And men red before Gereint's rush.

At Llongborth I saw slaughter,
Men quaking and heads bloodied,
Before great Gereint, his father's son.

At Llongborth I saw rowels
And men who would not flee from spears
Drinking wine from glittering glasses.

At Llongborth I saw weapons,
Soldiers, and blood being spilled,
And after battle, bitter burial.

At Llongborth I saw Arthur,
Brave soldiers would hew with steel,
The emperor, strife's commander.

At Llongborth was Gereint slain,
Brave soldiers from Devon's lowlands,
And before they were crushed, they had killed.

There were swift stallions under Gereint's thigh,
Long-shanked, raised on wheat-grain,
Roans, spotted eagles' assault.

There were swift stallions under Gereint's thigh,
Long-shanked, grain was theirs,
Roans, black eagles' assault.

There were swift stallions under Gereint's thigh,
Long-shanked, fattened on grain,
Roans, crimson eagles' assault.

There were swift stallions under Gereint's thigh,
Long-shanked, devouring grain,
Roans, white eagles' assault.

There were swift stallions under Gereint's thigh,
Long-shanked, pace of a stag,
Flames' roar on a mountain waste.

There were swift stallions under Gereint's thigh,
Long-shanked, eager for grain,
Grey-tipped their hair like silver.

There were swift stallions under Gereint's thigh,
Long-shanked, worthy of grain,
Roans, grey eagles' assault.

There were swift stallions under Gereint's thigh,
Long-shanked, their nourishment grain,
Roans, brown eagles' assault.

When Gereint was born, heaven's gates were open:
Christ gave what was asked,
A noble form, glory of Britain.

13th-century MS.

10   *from* Winter   ₰

Wind piercing, hill bare, hard to find shelter;
    Ford turns foul, lake freezes.
  A man could stand on a stalk.

  Wave on wave cloaks the land's edge;
Shrill the shrieks from the peaks of the mountain;
    One can scarce stand outside.

Cold the lake-bed from winter's blast;
    Dried reeds, stalks broken;
  Angry wind, woods stripped naked.

Cold bed of fish beneath a screen of ice;
    Stag lean, stalks bearded;
  Short evening, trees bent over.

Snow is falling, white the soil.
Soldiers go not campaigning.
Cold lakes, their colour sunless.

Snow is falling, white hoar-frost.
Shield idle on an old shoulder.
Wind intense, shoots are frozen.

Snow is falling upon the ice.
Wind is sweeping thick tree-tops.
Shield bold on a brave shoulder.

Snow is falling, cloaks the valley.
Soldiers hasten to battle.
I go not, a wound stays me.

Snow is falling on the slope.
Stallion confined; lean cattle.
No summer day is today.

Snow is falling, white the mountain's edge.
Ship's mast bare at sea.
A coward conceives many schemes.

13th-century MS.

11 *Never Tell* ₡

The saplings of the green-tipped birch
Draw my foot from bondage:
Let no boy know your secret!

Oak saplings in the grove
Draw my foot from its chain:
Tell no secret to a maid!

ANONYMOUS

The leafy saplings of the oak
Draw my foot from prison:
Tell no babbler a secret!

Briar shoots with berries on—
Neither a blackbird on her nest,
Nor a liar, are ever still.

13th-century MS.

12   *Sadness in Spring*   ♀

Maytime, loveliest season,
Loud bird-parley, new growth green,
Ploughs in furrow, oxen yoked,
Emerald sea, land-hues dappled.

When cuckoos call from fair tree-tops
    Greater grows my sorrow;
    Stinging smoke, grief awake
    For my kinsfolk's passing.

On hill, in vale, in ocean's isles,
    Whichever way man goes,
Blest Christ there's no evading.

13th-century MS.

13   *On Christians, Mercy Will Fall*   ♀

I sought of bishop and priest and judges
From the west to the east:
'For the good of the soul what course is best?'

Paternoster, beati, and the holy creed
Who chants is well served in his soul's hour of need,
Till Domesday protected in word and deed.

12 When cuckoos call] the cuckoo's call in Welsh is *cw-cw*: 'Where? Where?'

18

Carve out a way and to it hold,
And fashion peace, which is richer than gold:
Mercy will never die or grow old.

Give food to the hungry, and the naked clothe,
And sing your devotions with suppliant lip,
You'll escape the grip of the demons you loathe.

The vain have a craving, the idle no less,
To miss the way and to go to excess;
Impure is the grain they winnow and press.

Oversleep, wild feasting and excess of mead,
And unrestrained passion given its head—
Sweet things—but bitter in the Day of Dread.

Betraying one's lord and false swearing for lands,
For the kind with hardness of heart uncaring,
That Day, all these will mean ill-faring.

From midnight devotions and lauds sung at dawn,
And on saints if we call,
On Christians, mercy will fall.

13th-century MS.

14   *I am Taliesin. I sing perfect metre*   𝄞

I am Taliesin. I sing perfect metre,
Which will last to the end of the world.
My patron is Elphin . . .

I know why there is an echo in a hollow;
Why silver gleams; why breath is black; why liver is bloody;
Why a cow has horns; why a woman is affectionate;
Why milk is white; why holly is green;
Why a kid is bearded; why the cow-parsnip is hollow;
Why brine is salt; why ale is bitter;
Why the linnet is green and berries red;
Why a cuckoo complains; why it sings;

I know where the cuckoos of summer are in winter.
I know what beasts there are at the bottom of the sea;
How many spears in battle; how many drops in a shower;
Why a river drowned Pharaoh's people;
Why fishes have scales,
Why a white swan has black feet. . .

I have been a blue salmon,
I have been a dog, a stag, a roebuck on the mountain,
A stock, a spade, an axe in the hand,
A stallion, a bull, a buck,
A grain which grew on a hill,
I was reaped, and placed in an oven,
I fell to the ground when I was being roasted
And a hen swallowed me.
For nine nights was I in her crop.
I have been dead, I have been alive,
I am Taliesin.

MEILYR BRYDYDD (the Poet)

fl. 1100–1137

15   *Poem on his Death-bed*   ℓ

Rex regum, for whom praise flows freely,
To my Lord above I offer prayer:
Prince of glory's land, pure region on high,
Master, make peace between you and me.
Sickened, saddened in heart that I have
Offended you, remorseful for it,
I have rated rebuke in God's presence,
My true belief left unpractised:
I will practise it yet, for my Prince,
Before I am buried, left strengthless.
True the prediction to Adam's offspring
That has been proclaimed by the prophets:
Jesus within Mary's virgin womb,
Mary joyfully bore her burden.

MEILYR BRYDYDD

A burden have I built of sins heaped high;
    I have lived in fear of its turmoil.
    Lord of all places, how good to praise you!
    May I praise you, be purged before I burn.
King of kings who knows me, deny me not
    Forgiveness for my transgressions.

    I have often had gold and brocade
    From mortal lords for singing their praise,
    And the gift of song gone, powers failing,
    Stripped of wealth my tongue fell silent.
I, Meilyr the Poet, pilgrim to Peter,
    Gate-keeper who gauges true value,
    At the time set for us to arise
    Who are in the grave, make me ready.
May I dwell while awaiting the summons
    In the cell with the tide beside it:
    Secluded it is, undimmed its fame,
    With its graves in the breast of the sea,
Fair Mary's isle, saintly isle of her saints,
    Resurrection's scene, it is splendid.
Christ, his cross foretold, will know me, lead me
    Past the pains of hell, exile's dwelling.
    The Maker who made me will meet me
    In the fair parish of Enlli's faithful.

HYWEL AB OWAIN GWYNEDD
d. 1170

16   *Exultation*   ǭ

A foaming white wave washes over a grave,
the tomb of Rhufawn Pebyr, regal chieftain.
I love today what the English hate, the open land of the North,
and the varied growth that borders the Lliw.
I love those who gave me my fill of mead

15 Enlli] Ynys Enlli: the island of Bardsey off Llŷn, famed in tradition as
the close-packed graveyard of twenty thousand saints

21

where the seas reach in long contention.
I love its household and its strong buildings
and at its lord's wish to go to war.
I love its strand and its mountains,
its castle near the woods and its fine lands,
its water meadows and its valleys,
its white gulls and its lovely women.
I love its soldiers, its trained stallions,
its woods, its brave men and its homes.
I love its fields under the little clover,
where honour was granted a secure joy.
I love its regions, to which valour entitles,
its wide waste lands and its wealth.
O, Son of God, how great a wonder,
how splendid the stags, great their possessions!
With the thrust of a spear I did splendid work
between the host of Powys and lovely Gwynedd.
On a pale white horse, a rash adventure,
may I now win freedom from my exile.
I'll never hold out till my people come;
a dream says so and God wills so.
A foaming white wave washes over a grave.

A white wave, near the homesteads, foams over,
coloured like hoar-frost in the hour of its advance.
I love the sea-coast of Meirionnydd,
where a white arm was my pillow.
I love the nightingale in the wild wood,
where two waters meet in that sweet valley.
Lord of heaven and earth, ruler of Gwynedd,
how far Kerry is from Caer Lliwelydd!
In Maelienydd I mounted on a bay
and rode night and day to Rheged.
May I have, before my grave, a new conquest,
the land of Tegeingl, fairest in the world.
Though I be a lover of Ovid's way,
may God be mindful of me at my end.
A white wave, near the homesteads, foams over.

Gwynedd] north-western Wales   Tegeingl] a district in north-eastern
Wales, corresponding to much of modern Flintshire

The Poet's Loves ǫ

I salute the most high lord,
the most worthy one, because he's a king.
I compose a poem in the first place,
a song of praise like Merlin sang,
my skill in verse to the women who own it
(how hesitant their virtue makes them!),
the best in all the country west
of Chester gates to Porth Ysgewin.

One is a girl who must be chiefly praised,
    Gwenllian, summer-weather-hued;
  the second is the one in the mantle and gold collar;
  my lips are far from her.

Fair Gweirfyl, my gift, my mystery, whom I never had;
    whom not one of my kin won;
  though I be killed with double-edged blades,
  it grieves me for the wife of a king's foster-brother.

For seemly Gwladus, shy, childish young woman,
    beloved of the people,
  I'll compose a secret sigh,
  I'll praise her with the yellow of the gorse.

Soon may I see, with my vigour far removed from his,
    and with my sword in my hand,
  bright Lleucu, my love, laughing;
  her husband won't laugh before the onrush.

I am involved in the strife that has come to me
    and longing, alas, is natural,
  for pretty Nest, like apple blossom,
  my golden passion, heart of my sin.

For the virgin Generys who does not relieve my passion;
    may she not insist on chastity!
  For Hunydd there's matter till Doomsday,
  for Hawis my chosen ritual.

I had a girl of the same mind one day;
I had two, their praise be the greater;
I had three and four and fortune;
I had five, splendid in their white flesh;
I had six without concealing sin;
a bright girl from above the white fort came to me;
I had seven and an arduous business it was;
I had eight, repaying some of the praise I sang;
   teeth are good to keep the tongue quiet!

CYNDDELW BRYDYDD MAWR
(the Great Poet)
fl. 1155–1200

18   *Petition for Reconciliation*   ǫ

To Rhys ap Gruffudd

I beseech God's favour, faultless your gift,
   Your gifted man am I,
   For your men, eagle of wars,
   For your land, lord of the South.

I beseech, I beg, great suit to the Lord
   Who made heaven and earth,
   Favour from your rage, song's friend,
   For your gates, for your sentry.

I beseech, I beg, suitor they see me,
   Favour, true tranquil bond,
   For your golden-trimmed portals,
   For your porter, fair land's lord.

I beseech your favour, bar not your aid,
   Since respite is fitting.
   Court-heralds, call for silence:
   Be silent, bards—hear a bard!

I beg full favour, kind men of the South,
   Sure support of singers,
  For your host, your shield-bearers,
  For your band, for your king's sons.

I beg full favour, rank's benevolence,
   Kings cannot withstand you,
  For your host, corps of combat,
  For your men, worthy of mead.

Mead-supper their drink, mead-horns strengthen them,
   And gold deeds defend them,
  And mighty bright drinking-bouts,
  And a brave lord and bold king.

Britain's regal hawks, I chant your high song,
   Your high honour I bear,
  Your bard, your judge I shall be,
  Your assistance is due me.

Answer what I sing, what I may sing, lord:
   Hear me, since I have come.
  Lord of Lleisiawn, bold lion:
  Ease your wrath, your bard am I.

I am my lord's singer, green sea-swell's sway,
   Roadways' sway, song's welcome.
  Peaceful prayer, long hard exile,
  I beseech a lord's favour.

19   *In Praise of Owain Gwynedd*   ♩

I praise a patron high-hearted in strife,
   Wolf of warfare, challenging, charging,
  Singing the pleasure of his presence,
  Singing his power, mead-nourished worth,
  Singing his fervour, swift-winged falcon,
  Singing a lofty soul's lofty thoughts,
  Singing daring deeds, lord of war-hounds,

Singing of one who inspires high praise,
Singing a song for my lavish lord,
Singing words of praise to praise Owain.
In arms against Angles in Tegeingl's lands,
　Blood spilling in streams, blood pouring forth.
　Dragons encountered, rulers of Rome,
　A prince's heir, red their precious wine.
　In strife with the Dragon of the East,
　Fair Western Dragon, the best was his.
　Ardent the lord, sword bright above sheath,
　Spear in strife and outpouring from sword,
　Sword-blade in hand and hand hewing heads,
　Hand on sword and sword on Norman troops,
And constant anguish from the sight of death,
　And spilling of blood and revelling,
　Blood covering men, their skulls bloodied.
　For flesh I heard a pledge to the birds,
　In the piercing thrust of spear in hand,
　In the blood-trail inviting ravens.
　They rode on corpses for a thousand crows,
　Brynaich's riders, Owain's war-ravens,
　Slaughter by the barrel, carcasses stiff,
　A tidbit for them, dead men's entrails.
In hosts we went, for his prize, for his praise,
　Many minstrels for Owain's bounty,
　To Cadell Hiriell Hiriein's bold offspring,
　To Coel's line's guardian, for their reward.
　Battlefield's spear-thrust, lavish with praise,
　Buckler-bearing, onrushing eagle,
　Court's courageous, alert defender,
　Three-coloured his spear, savage assault.
At Aberteifi they cut through falling spears
　As at Badon Fawr, valiant war-cry.
　I saw war-stags and stiff red corpses,
　It was left to the wolves, their burial;
　I saw them routed, without their hands,
　Beneath birds' claws, men mighty in war;

Dragon of the East] Henry II of England　　　Aberteifi] Cardigan
Badon Fawr] Arthur's victory over the English in 516 took place, by
tradition, at Mount Badon, its site unknown

I saw their ruin, three hundred dead,
I saw, battle done, bowels on thorns;
I saw strife cause a dreadful uproar,
Troops contending, a rout collapsing.
I saw struggle, men falling from sea-cliffs,
I saw their fortress, enemy slain,
I saw soldiers' spears round a stone wall,
I saw lances red from Owain's rush,
I saw for Saxons sorry corpses,
Long day at an end, princes' reaping.
Battle won, prince of his country's sons,
Battle dear-bought, he may scorn pursuit.
I saw at Rhuddlan a bright red tide,
Hero's host, for man, for glory,
I saw in Penfro a flawless ruler,
I saw in Penardd a lord roving,
I saw their brave slaughter, brave troops down
That a brave land bears, seagull's bounty.
I saw fierce throngs, I saw scurrying,
I saw zeal cry, resounding signal,
I saw a rout of troops, of comrades,
I saw strife round Caer, round Coed Llwyfain.
They were not, Gwynedd's valour, mere boys:
You were fearless, shepherd of Britain.

20 *Poem on his Death-bed* ǭ

I salute God, asylum's gift,
To praise my Lord, bounteous, benign,
Sole Son of Mary, source of morn and eve
And teeming river-mouths,
Who made wood, and mead, and true measure,
And harvests, and God's overflowing gifts,
Who made grass and grove and mountain heather,
Made one man joyful, righteous judgement,
And another in need, ungifted,
Impoverished and bitter-tempered.

19 Penfro] Pembroke   Caer] Chester

CYNDDELW BRYDYDD MAWR

I pray God's Son, for He has power,
To forgive our sin, sinning is wrong,
And welcome us in heaven's haven:
May we go to the land we long for.

I salute God, I solicit acclaim
    For the piece I perform:
    There are thousands praise you, High Prince,
    And your hosts to the highest bounds.
I would beseech, my Lord, with your blessing,
    In your love I believe,
    You, song-renowned, I celebrate,
    Grant a gift, let me not be lost.
    More than needful, the greatest grace,
    Lord, was saving the strong at last.
    The thought terrifies me, thinking
    Of the sinning that Adam sinned.
Vile exile, I, if I shun your fair land,
    And your fair host around me.
    The bards of the glorious church,
    Their support has been my portion,
    Pleasant the path to the place I search for,
    Hope in the High Judge, fellowship I seek:
    Monarch of all, salvation for me,
    After leaving the world, my reward,
    By the Father's favour, most royal,
    And the Son's, and the Spirit's, pure splendour.
    In sanctified glory I shall be,
    In angels' charge, innocent, gentle,
    In a fair land, Lord, heaven I beg for.

Almighty Ruler, when you were born,
Came mercy for us, came redemption,
Came Adam's sons from faithless faction,
From soiled lawlessness, from slavery,
Came to our anguish and our longing,
There came valour, plentiful power,
Came Christ incarnate, mainstay, master,
Came in Mary's womb the wished-for Son,
Came the world's five ages from torment,

CYNDDELW BRYDYDD MAWR

From deceit, from darkness, fraud's abode,
From lasting sorrow, from strong affliction,
   From the foe's prison, whence they were freed.
   And He is our helm and our haven
   Who judges our deeds by our doing,
   And He, heaven's Lord, portion of peace,
   Brought us forth from perdition when pierced,
And He rose for us, and won His reward,
   And the Lord will not deny us His help.
   And as a reward He was seated
   In full might, the sun's road His domain.
The man whose hand will give his tithe to God,
   He is not thwarted of his reward.
   I am a bard, flawlessly fashioned:
   In my Creator's hold, legion's Lord,
   I, Cynddelw the singer, grace I ask;
   Michael, who knows me, welcome be mine!

Almighty Ruler, when of you I sang,
   Not worthless the piece that I performed,
   No lack of fine style in His lyric,
   No little largesse have I obtained,
   Not fashioned was I by changeless God
   For devising folly, fraud, or force.
No unfaithful man may have faith in God,
   Not he foulness dwells with, sewer's filth,
   Not he whose heart is slow to waken,
   Not for him, heaven, who will not seek.
   Not easy the form I have fashioned,
   No excessive reward have I earned,
No bearing of boldness has my heart dared,
   No bearing of penance have I craved.
   For the Lord's asylum have I longed,
   My soul's freedom, this need have I sought.

   Almighty Ruler, deign to receive,
   Reverent request, harmonious,
   Flawless in formation of language,
   My song in your praise, fair land's candle.
Since you are master, since you are monarch,

Since you are prophet, since you are judge,
Since you are kind, since you are benign,
Since you are my teacher, banish me not,
In your wrath, from your fair land.
Refuse me not your grace, exile's Lord,
Scorn me not amidst the wretched crew,
Spill me not from your hand, vile dwelling,
Throw me not to the black loveless throng.

DAFYDD BENFRAS
d. 1257

21   *From Exile*   ♩

It's bright the icy foam as it flows,
It's fierce in January great sea tumult,
It's woe's me the language, long-wished-for speech
For the sake of tales, would be sweet to my ear.

Ability in English I never had,
Neither knew phrases of passionate French:
A stranger and foolish, when I've asked questions
It turned out crooked—I spoke North Welsh!

On a wave may God's son grant us our wish
And out from amongst them readily bring us
To a Wales made one, contented and fair,
To a prince throned, laden nobly with gifts,
To the lord of Dinorwig's bright citadel land,
To the country of Dafydd, where Welsh freely flows!

GRUFFUDD AB YR YNAD COCH
(son of the Red Judge)
fl. 1280

     Lament for Llywelyn ap Gruffudd   ♭

Heart cold in the breast with terror, grieving
  For a king, oak door, of Aberffraw.
    Bright gold was bestowed by his hand,
    A gold chaplet befitted him.
A gold king's gold cups come not to me, mirth
  Of Llywelyn; not for me free raiment.
I grieve for a prince, hawk free of reproach,
  I grieve for the ill that befell him,
I grieve for the loss, I grieve for the lot,
  I grieve to hear how he was wounded.
Cadwaladr's stronghold, sharp-drilling safeguard,
  Lord of the red lance, gold-handed lord,
He showered riches, arrayed each winter
  Around me the raiment around him.
  Lord rich in herds, he aids us no more,
  Life everlasting is left for him.
  Mine, rage at the Saxon who robbed me,
  Mine, before death, the need to lament,
Mine, with good reason, to rave against God
    Who has left me without him,
  Mine to praise him, unstinting, unstilled,
  Mine to be ever mindful of him,
Mine all my lifetime sorrowing for him,
  Since mine is the woe, mine the weeping.
  A lord I have lost, long will I fear,
  A lord, high court's, was killed by a hand,
A lord constant and true, listen to me—
  How loudly I keen, wretched keening!
    A lord thriving till eighteen died,
    A lord of gifts, low is he laid,
A lord like a lion leading his land,
  A lord chafing for devastation.

Aberffraw] in Anglesey: the royal seat of the rulers of Gwynedd

A lord who prospered, till he left Emrais
   No Saxon would venture to strike him,
A lord, stone is his roof, Welshmen's monarch,
    Of the right line to rule Aberffraw.
      Lord Christ, how I sorrow for him:
      Lord who is faithful, redeem him.
   From a heavy sword-stroke his downfall,
   From long sword-blades came his suppression:
   From my ruler's wound comes my distress,
   From word of Bodfaeo's lord's collapse.
Perfect the lad killed by hostile men's hands,
   Perfect his forebears' honour in him.
Candle of kings, strong lion of Gwynedd,
    Throne of honour, there was need of him.
    From Britain's death, Cynllaith's defender,
    From Nancoel's lion slain, Nanco's mail,
Many a tear sliding swift down a cheek.
   Many a side made red with slashes,
   Many a foot in a pool of blood,
   Many a widow wailing for him,
   Many a heavy heart in pieces,
   Many a son reft of his father,
Many a home black in the firebrand's track,
   And many a place pillage lays waste,
Many a wretched cry as at Camlan,
   Many a tear rolling down a cheek.
    With my prop cut down, gold-handed prince,
    With Llywelyn's death, gone is my mind.
    Heart frozen in the breast with terror,
    Desire decays like dried-up branches.
    See you not the rush of wind and rain?
    See you not the oaks lash each other?
See you not the ocean scourging the shore?
    See you not the truth is portending?
See you not the sun hurtling the sky?
    See you not that the stars have fallen?
Have you no belief in God, foolish men?
    See you not that the world is ending?

Camlan] Arthur's disastrous last battle, its site unknown

GRUFFUDD AB YR YNAD COCH

Ah God, that the sea would cover the land!
  What is left us that we should linger?
  No place to flee from terror's prison,
  No place to live; wretched is living!
No counsel, no clasp, no path left open
    One way to be freed from fear's sad strife.
      All retainers were true to his trust,
      All warriors were his defenders,
      All stern men would swear by his hand,
      All leaders, all lands were his own.
  All counties, all towns are now troubled,
  All households, all clans are collapsing.
  All the weak, all the strong he kept safe:
  All children now cry in their cradles.
  Little good it did me to dupe me,
  Leaving me a head, with him headless.
      Head that slain made fear unhateful,
      Head that slain made surrender best,
      Head of a soldier, head of praise,
      Head of a duke, a dragon's head,
Head of fair Llywelyn, sharp the world's fear,
      An iron spike through it,
      Head of my lord, harsh pain is mine,
      Head of my spirit left speechless,
Head that had honour in nine hundred lands,
      Nine hundred feasts for him,
  Head of a king, his hand hurled iron,
  Head of a proud hawk, he forced a breach,
  Head of a kingly wolf thrust foremost,
  Head of kings, heaven be his haven!
Blest king, great deeds were his, blest company,
    Who longed to reach Llydaw,
    King right royal of Aberffraw,
    May heaven's fair land be his home.

DAFYDD BACH AP MADOG WLADAIDD
fl. 1340–1390

23   *A Christmas Revel*   ♀

I have seen a court, and a dozen courts,
  And no court have I seen as gracious
As the court I love for its chieftain's sake,
  Not weak is my praise, like Celliwig:
Heaven's bounty on earth in Bachelldref,
  Where there is a revel each Christmas,
A crowd of kinsmen, a lake of liquor,
  Bright the honour of Meurig's homeland,
Many a minstrel and merry fiddler,
  And much the mirth on a polished floor,
And a sound of strings, a deluge of drinks,
  And the constant cadence of singing,
And a red-hued lance of Cadwaladr's line,
  A blood-gushing blade, promise of meat,
And minstrels' swaying, and children chirping,
  And the bustle of boys bringing food,
The cup-bearer weary, kitchen sore-tried,
  And three kinds of wine for the thirsty.
Three customs there are, a merry country,
  At Dafydd's high court, blameless boldness:
Whoever you are, whatever you sing,
  And whatever the thing you're known for,
Come whenever you wish, take what you see,
  And once come, stay as long as you like.

DAFYDD AP GWILYM
fl. 1340–1370

24   *The Seagull*   ♀

Gracing the tide-warmth, this seagull,
  The snow-semblanced, moon-matcher,

23 Dafydd] Dafydd ap Cadwaladr, lord of Bachelldref in eastern mid-Wales

The sun-shard and sea-gauntlet
Floating, the immaculate loveliness.
The feathered one, fishfed, the swift-proud,
Is buoyant, breasting the combers.

Sea-lily, fly to this anchor to me,
Perch your webs on my hand.
You nun among ripples, habited
Brilliant as paper-work, come.
Girl-glorified you shall be, pandered to,
Gaining that castle mass, her fortalice.
Scout them out, seagull, those glowing battlements,
Reconnoitre her, the Eigr-complexioned.
Repeat my pleas, my citations, go
Girlward, gull, where I ache to be chosen.
She solus, pluck up courage, accost her,
Stress your finesse to the fastidious one;
Use honeyed diplomacy, hinting
I cannot remain extant without her.
I worship her, every particle worships!

Look, friends, not old Merlin, hot-hearted,
Not Taliesin the bright-browed, beheld
The superior of this one in loveliness.
Cypress-shapely, but derisive beneath
Her tangled crop of copper, gull,
O, when you eye all Christendom's
Loveliest cheek—this girl will bring
Annihilation upon me, should your answer
Sound, gull, no relenting note.

25   *In Morfudd's Arms*   ♀

Praised beyond all Enids be
Lady Morfudd, my lovely.
I burn with more than a fire
From the torch-light of her hair,

24 Eigr] the mother of Arthur, famed for her beauty   Taliesin] 'Beauti-
ful Brow'

And yet, her touch as it fell
Was almost-virgin-gentle.

Around my neck white arms went;
Her red lips were impatient.
That kind of kissing has come,
So more than mild, most seldom.
Her poet-prisoner, frail
In her wine-sweet body-gaol,
So I, though I do not tell
All truth of the miracle.

So, in the bonds of the bright
Of her arms, all snow-drift white,
She was imprisoning me
All courtly, lightly, gently.
Who would want to stir
Out of her hold and halter?
Who would want to move
Out of that lock-up love?

And how could a man do better
Than submit to this fetter,
These gyves, this white-snow-gentle
Link and loop of the circle,
Chain and charm of the shackle,
Feather-threat of the throttle,
Wrist-hold, kiss-bold tether
Keeping us close together?

Each man thinks he knows best
Of Arthur's loveliest—
Tegau of the golden breast,
Dyfyr of the golden hair,
Enid, the radiant girl,
Daughter of Yniwl the Earl.

But I, Dafydd the dark,
The swarthy one, soot-sallow,
The too black crow-skin fellow
Rise over them all, and follow

Companioned only with
My marvel, my Morfudd,
So follow, and so fare
Towards that wider air
Rimmed by the gold-white arc.

How bountiful! How blest!

The Girls of Llanbadarn ọ

I am one of passion's asses,
Plague on all these parish lasses!
Though I long for them like mad,
Not one female have I had,
Not a one in all my life,
Virgin, damsel, hag, or wife.
What maliciousness, what lack,
What does make them turn their back?
Would it be a shame to be
In a bower of leaves with me?
No one's ever been so bitched,
So bewildered, so bewitched
Saving Garwy's lunatics
By their foul fantastic tricks.

So I fall in love, I do,
Every day, with one or two,
Get no closer, any day,
Than an arrow's length away.
Every single Sunday, I,
Llanbadarn can testify,
Go to church and take my stand
With my plumed hat in my hand,
Make my reverence to the altar,
Find the right page in my psalter,

26 Garwy] a famed lover   Llanbadarn] Llanbadarn Fawr, near
Aberystwyth. The church there is about six miles from Dafydd's childhood
home at Brogynin, and about twelve from his burial place at Strata Florida

Turn my back on holy God,
Face the girls, and wink, and nod
For a long, long time, and look
Over feather, at the folk.
Suddenly, what do I hear?
A stage whisper, all too clear,
A girl's voice, and her companion
Isn't slow at catching on.

'See that simple fellow there,
Pale and with his sister's hair
Giving me those leering looks
Wickeder than any crook's?'

'Don't you think that he's sincere?' ‘
Asks the other in her ear.
'All I'll give him is *Get out!*
Let the Devil take the lout!'

Pretty payment, in return
For the love with which I burn.
Burn for what? The bright girl's gift
Offers me the shortest shrift.
I must give them up, resign
These fear-troubled hopes of mine:
Better be a hermit, thief,
Anything, to bring relief.
Oh, strange lesson, that I must
Go companionless and lost,
Go because I looked too long,
I, who loved the power of song.

27   *The Wind*   ℺

Welkin's wind, way unhindered,
Big blusterer passing by,
A harsh-voiced man of marvels,
World-bold, without foot or wing,

DAFYDD AP GWILYM

How strange that sent from heaven's
Pantry with never a foot,
Now you can race so swiftly
Over the hillside above.
No bridge over stream, no boat;
Forewarned, you remain undrowned,
A free and easy crossing.
Winnowing leaves, you steal nests,
None charge you, you're not halted
By armed band, lieutenant's hand,
Blue blade or flood or downpour.
No sheriff or troop takes you,
Pruner of the treetop plumes.
No mother's son slays, crime's tale,
Fire burns, deceit undoes you.

Unspied, in your wide bare bed,
Nest of storms, thousands hear you,
The sky's swift signatory,
Fine leaper of nine wild lands.
Godsent you skim over ground,
Roar of an oak-top broken,
A thirsty creature, sharp-set,
A great sky-trampling progress,
Huntsman in lofty snow-fields
Loudly heaping useless husks.
Tell me, incessant hymn-tune,
Your course, north-wind of the glen,
Tempest fettering the sea,
Lad romping on the seastrand,
Rhetorician, magician,
Sower, pursuer of leaves,
Hurling, laughter on hillsides,
Wild masts in white-breasted brine.

You fly the length of the world,
Hover tonight, hill's weather:
O wind, go to Uwch Aeron,
A bright beauty, a clear tune.
Do not stay, do not steer clear,

39

Do not fear Bwa Bach's poisoned
Complaints and accusations;
Closed is that country to me.
Sad day for me when I set
My heart on golden Morfudd:
A girl has brought me exile;
Run above her father's home.
Pound the door, make it unlock
Before day to my envoy.
If there is a way, find her
And moan the sound of my sigh.

You come from the zodiac;
Tell my great-hearted darling
For as long as I may live
I am her faithful plaything.
Sad-faced am I without her
If truly she's not untrue.
Fly high, you'll see a beauty,
Fly low, find a road of sky.
Go to my pale blonde maiden,
Bounty of the sky, fare well.

28   *The Woodland Mass*   ọ

A pleasant place I was at today,
under mantles of the worthy green hazel,
listening at day's beginning
to the skilful cock thrush
singing a splendid stanza
of fluent signs and symbols;
a stranger here, wisdom his nature,
a brown messenger who had journeyed far,
coming from rich Carmarthenshire
at my golden girl's command.
Wordy, yet with no password,
he comes to the sky of this valley.
It was Morfudd who sent it,

27 Bwa Bach] the Little Hunchback, Morfudd's husband

this metrical singing of May's foster son.
About him was a setting
of flowers of the sweet boughs of May,
like green mantles, his chasuble
was of the wings of the wind.
There was here, by the great God,
nothing but gold in the altar's canopy.
I heard, in polished language,
a long and faultless chanting,
an unhesitant reading to the people
of a gospel without mumbling;
the elevation, on the hill for us there,
of a good leaf for a holy wafer.
Then the slim eloquent nightingale
from the corner of a grove nearby,
poetess of the valley, sings to the many
the Sanctus bell in lively whistling.
The sacrifice is raised
up to the sky above the bush,
devotion to God the Father,
the chalice of ecstasy and love.
The psalmody contents me;
it was bred of a birch-grove in the sweet woods.

29   *The Ruin*   ǫ

Nothing but a hovel now
Between moorland and meadow,
Once the owners saw in you
A comely cottage, bright, new,
Now roof, rafters, ridge-pole, all
Broken down by a broken wall.

A day of delight was once there
For me, long ago, no care
When I had a glimpse of her
Fair in an ingle-corner.
Beside each other we lay
In the delight of that day.

Her forearm, snowflake-lovely,
Softly white, pillowing me,
Proffered a pleasant pattern
For me to give in my turn,
And that was our blessing for
The new-cut lintel and door.

Now the wild wind, wailing by,
Crashes with curse and with cry
Against my stones, a tempest
Born and bred in the East,
Or south ram-batterers break
The shelter that folk forsake.

Life is illusion and grief;
A tile whirls off, as a leaf
Or a lath goes sailing, high
In the keening of kite-kill cry.
Could it be, our couch once stood
Sturdily under that wood?
Pillar and post, it would seem
Now you are less than a dream.
Are you that, or only the lost
Wreck of a riddle, rune-ghost?

'Dafydd, the cross on their graves
Marks what little it saves,
Says, *They did well in their lives.*'

LLYWELYN GOCH AP MEURIG HEN
(the Red, son of Meurig the Old)
fl. 1360–1390

30   *Lament for Lleucu Llwyd*   ◊

For gay bard, barren summer,
Barren the world for a bard.
I was stripped bare, grief's comrade,

For choosing this month to tryst.
Today in Gwynedd remains
No moon, no light, no colour,
Since they placed, sorry welcome,
Beauty's moon in the hard ground.

Fair girl in the chest of oak,
I'm bent on wrath, you left me.
Lovely form, Gwynedd's candle,
Though you are closed in the grave,
Arise, come up, my dearest,
Open the dark door of earth,
Refuse the long bed of sand,
And come to face me, maiden.
Here is, heavy cost of grief,
Above your grave, sun's radiance,
A sad-faced man without you,
Llywelyn, bell of your praise.
Wailing bard, I am walking
A foul world, priest of lust's bliss.
Dear one, whose worth grew daily,
Yesterday over your grave
I let tears fall in torrents
Like a rope across my cheeks.

But you, mute girl's fair image,
From the pit made no reply.
Sadly silent, lacking love.
You promised, speechless maiden,
Mild your manner, silk-shrouded,
To stay for me, pure bright gem,
Till I came, I know the truth,
Strong safeguard, from the southland.
I heard nothing, straight-spoken,
But the truth, slim silent girl,
Measure of maidens, Indeg,
Before this, from your sweet mouth.
Hard blow, why care where's my home,
You broke faith, and it grieves me.

Indeg] a beautiful woman of Welsh romance, and a love of Arthur's

43

You are, my cywydd is false,
Truthful, words sweetly spoken:
It's I, grief's spilled-out language,
Who lie in sad harmonies;
I'm lying, skimping prayer,
Lying the words I have cried.
I will leave Gwynedd today,
What care I where, bright beauty,
My fine flowering sweetheart:
If you lived, by God, I'd stay!
Where shall I, what care I where,
See you, fair moon's pure flower,
On Mount, Ovid's passion spurned,
Olivet, radiant maiden?
You've secured my place surely,
Lleucu, fair comely-hued wave,
Beautiful bright-skinned maiden,
Sleeper too long under stone.

Rise to finish the revels,
See if you thirst for some mead,
Come to your bard, whose laughter
Long ended, golden diadem.
Come, with your cheeks of foxgloves,
Up from the earth's dreary house.
A wayward trail the footprints,
No need to lie, my feet leave,
In faltering from passion
About your house, Lleucu Llwyd.
All the words, Gwynedd's lantern,
I've sung, complexion of snow,
Three groans of grief, gold-ringed hand,
Lleucu, praised you, my precious.
With these lips, deft my praise-craft,
What I'll sing, life-long, in praise,
My dear, foam's hue on rivers,
My love, will be your lament.

Lucid, sweet-spoken Lleucu,
My sweetheart's legacy was:

Her soul, Merioneth's treasure,
To God the Father, true vow;
Her slender, fine flour's colour,
Body to sanctified soil;
Girl mourned far, flour-white favour,
World's wealth to the proud dark man;
And yearning, lyric of grief,
This legacy she left me.

Two equal gifts, sad custom,
Pretty Lleucu, snow-spray's hue,
Earth and stone, bitter grief's gem,
Cover her cheeks, and oakwood.
Ah God, so heavy's the grave,
The earth on beauty's mistress.
Ah God, a coffin holds you,
Between us a house of stone,
Church chancel and stone curtain
And earth's weight and gown of wood.
Ah God, fair girl of Pennal,
A nightmare, buried your brow.
Hard lock of oak, bitter grief,
And earth, your brows were lovely,
And heavy door, heavy clasp,
And the land's floor between us,
A firm wall, a hard black lock,
A latch—farewell, my Lleucu.

IOLO GOCH (the Red)

c. 1320–*c.* 1398

31   *The Labourer*   ○̷

When the world's folk, one day of freedom,
the lively host of Christendom,
show their works before God
the beloved Lord (fine true words)

on the great mountain of Olivet,
where they will all be judged,
the labourer, the meadow traveller,
will tell a simple, cheerful tale.

The lively God is generous;
if a man has given God offering and tithe,
then a good soul directly
he'll pay to God and merit bliss.
The worker in the bright meadow
easily trusts to the Lord God.
Most properly his almsgiving
and hospitality are for all.
He'll speak his mind only on ploughs;
he hates dissension where he works.
He'll make and follow no war,
he'll oppress no one for his goods,
he's never brutal with us
nor will he pursue false claims.
Suffering is his seemly way,
yet there's no life without him.
He finds it many times pleasanter,
and I think no worse of him,
to grip in his placid way
the crooked plough and the goad
than if he were wrecking a tower
in the guise of a ravaging Arthur.

Without his work there's no
Christ's sacrifice to feed our faith,
and without him no pope
or emperor can keep alive,
no wine-giving, sprightly king
of notable prudence, no living man.

The useful old Elucidarium
put it thus happily,
'Blessed is he who through his youth
holds in his hands the plough.'
It's a cradle tearing the smooth long broom,

a fishing basket lacing the field,
a holy image of dear praise,
a heron opening a quick furrow,
a basket for the wild earth, now to be tamed
in honoured, coultered order;
a gander of the wild acres,
grain will come of its true skill.
It fetches crops from the rich earth,
it's a good beast biting the ground.
It must have its knife and its board
and its food right under its thigh.
It goes unwillingly through stones,
it skins the field with leg outstretched.
Its head is ever employed
on a fair way beneath oxen's feet.
It has often sung its hymn,
it loves to follow the plough chain.
A root-breaker of valley growth,
it stretches a stiff neck out;
tough-headed train-bearer,
its wooden shank scatters the earth.

Hu Gadarn, lord of a lively people,
a king who gave wine for verse,
emperor of land and seas,
Constantinople's golden constable,
after defeat took up
the nimble, fine-beamed plough,
for this hale, host-scattering lord,
this great leader never sought bread
but, so well instructed was he,
by his own labour. This gifted eagle
wished to show to the proud
and to the wisely humble that
in the sight of the Father of the holy relic
one craft was best, a sign of triumph,
that ploughing is a scholarship.

Hu Gadarn] Hugh the Strong, Emperor of Constantinople in the twelfth-
century *Pélerinage de Charlemagne*, translated into Welsh in the fourteenth
century

Where there's belief and baptism
and everyone upholding the faith,
the Lord God's hand on this best of men
and Mary's hand on every labourer.

ANONYMOUS

15th century

32   *The Virgin Mary*   ǫ

We pray to life's source, Mary,
Lady goldsmith of true health.
She is rightly named the queen,
Through her grace, heaven listens.
To hell her power reaches,
Above and across the world.
Right, fearing pain, fearing wreck
In the Channel, to name her.
Right for Mary, whom I name,
To be named a light-bearer.

Gabriel, through bright heavens,
Addressed to this holy saint
Ave, for sinful Eva;
Mary bore that, great her grace.
Blessed was the conception,
Her Father's word, of her womb.
Good was the maid, hope's dwelling,
Her flesh bore heaven for you,
In goodness bearing her Son,
And the Father who made her.
The Three, below the sun's round,
In the bright sun were dwelling.
Humbly we'll go in prayer,
As God He was born, as man.
Mary sang God lullabies
And bore Him, a pure virgin.

ANONYMOUS

As the prophecy foretold
To Egypt she brought Jesus;
The lions were light-hearted,
And the snakes, with the pure saint.
Great blessings, Mary noticed
One day when the sun was strong
A tall tree with luscious fruit
On its crest, which she craved for.

His gold love asked of Joseph
Some from the top, a bright gift.
Then angrily, in few words,
Joseph replied to Mary:
'Ask the one, fair slim maiden,
Who made you pregnant, pure saint.'
It bowed to the level earth,
That tree, by the Son's wonders;
She had from the top her fill
Of fruit, she and her household.

None could briefly tell her Son's
Wonders worked to help Mary.
O that I, as is fitting,
Knew a hundred works to sing,
And could sing them with fine art,
And each word praising Mary.
Let us seek our lands, praying,
And 'Mary' our only word.
The Virgin does much pleading,
She will not leave men behind.
She plucks us from the briers,
And after this life, with her
Bliss for us, singing to her,
Heaven, we'll sing to Mary.

15th century

33　　　　　　　　　　　*The Tryst*　　　　　　　　　ộ

Cause of this stab in my side,
Girl I love, and have long loved,
Your colour God created,
Like the daisy is your brow.
Your red-gold is God's giving,
Your hair like a tongue of gold,
Your neck grows straight and slender,
Your breasts are full balls of yarn.
Your cheeks a charming scarlet,
Your brows, maid, are London black;
Your eyes like two bright brooches,
Your nose, it's on a dear girl.
Your smile, five joys of Mary;
Your flesh filches me from faith.
You are white as Saint Anne's child,
Fair colour and fine figure.

So sweet, under fine-spun hair,
So fair, come to the hillside.
Make our bed on a hill's breast,
Four ages under fresh birches,
The dale's green leaves its mattress,
And its fine curtains of fern,
And trees for a coverlet
To shield us from the showers.

I shall lie there like David,
Zealous prophet, for a tryst,
Solomon's father, who made
Seven psalms, for the dawnlight.
I will make, if she greets me,
Psalms of the kisses of love,
Seven the maiden's kisses,
Seven birches by the grave,
Seven vespers and masses,

Seven sermons from the thrush,
Seven leaf-covered lyrics,
Seven nightingales and boughs,
Seven strokes of ecstasy,
Seven gems, seven lyrics,
Seven songs to slim Morfudd's
Firm flesh, twenty times seven.
She will lock up no longer
The reckoning owed to love.

15th century

34   *The Saxons of Flint*   ǫ

A man, like others, formed by God,
On Sunday morning last I trod
The streets of Flint; an ill built maze—
I wish the whole were in a blaze!
An English marriage feast was there,
Which, like all English feasts, was spare.
Naught there revealed our mountain land,
The generous heart—the liberal hand—
No *hirlas* there was passed around
With richly foaming mead high crowned.
The reason why I thither came
Was something for my art to claim—
An art that oft from prince and lord
Had won its just—its due reward.
With lips inspired I then began
To sing an ode to this mean clan:
Rudely they mocked my song and me,
And loathed my oft praised minstrelsy.
Alas! that through my cherished art
Boors should distress and wound my heart.
Fool that I was to think the muse
Could charm corn dealers—knavish Jews;

34 *hirlas*] lit. a 'long blue' festive drinking-horn

My polished ode forsooth they hissed,
And I midst laughter was dismissed.
For William Beisir's bag they bawl,
'Largess for him' they loudly squall;
Each roared with throat at widest stretch
For Will the piper—low born wretch!
Will forward steps as best he can,
Unlike a free ennobled man:
A pliant bag 'tween arm and chest,
While limping on he tightly prest.
He stares—he strives the bag to sound;
He swells his maw—and ogles round;
He twists and turns himself about,
With fetid breath his cheeks swell out.
What savage boors! his hideous claws
And glutton's skin win their applause!
With shuffling hand and clumsy mien
To doff his cloak he next is seen;
He snorted; bridled in his face,
And bent it down with much grimace.
Like to a kite he seemed that day,
A kite, when feathering of his prey!
The churl did blow a grating shriek,
The bag did swell, and harshly squeak,
·As does a goose from nightmare crying,
Or dog, crushed by a chest when dying;
This whistling box's changeless note
Is forced from turgid veins and throat;
Its sound is like a crane's harsh moan,
Or like a gosling's latest groan;
Just such a noise a wounded goat
Sends from her hoarse and gurgling throat.
His unattractive screeching lay
Being ended, William sought for pay;
Some *fees* he had from this mean band,
But *largess* from no noble hand;
Some pence were offered by a few,
Others gave little halfpence too.
Unheeded by this shabby band
I left their feast with empty hand.

ANONYMOUS

A dire mischance I wish indeed
On slavish Flint and its mean breed,
Oh! may its furnace be the place
Which they and piper Will may grace!
For their ill luck my prayer be told,
My curses on them young and old!
I ne'er again will venture there,
May death all further visits spare!

15th century

35   *A Snowy Day*   ♀

I cannot sleep or take the air—
Of a truth this load is hard to bear!
Ford or slope is none to be found,
Nor open space, nor bare ground.
No girl's word shall tempt me now
Out of my house into the snow.
The plaguey feathers drifting down
Like dragon's scales cling to the gown,
And all I wear would soon be
White as miller's coat to see.
True 'tis, the Winter Calends gone,
Ermine's the wear for everyone;
In January's month, first of the year,
God makes hermits everywhere.
Everywhere, the country round,
He has whitewashed the black ground,
Clothed in white each woodland glade,
On every copse a white sheet spread.
To every stump clings heavenly meal,
Like the white blossoms of April.
A cold veil on the forest lies,
A load of chalk crushes the trees.
Like wheaten flour the drifts appear,
A coat of mail that the plains wear,

34 its furnace] there was a noted iron foundry at Flint in the fifteenth century

53

ANONYMOUS

A cold grit on field and fallow,
On earth's whole skin a thick tallow,
Foam-flakes flying thick and fast,
Fleeces big as a man's fist,
White bees of heaven on the wing,
Through all Gwynedd wandering.
Will God's plenty never cease—
So many feathers of holy geese,
Like winnowed chaff, heaped together,
A robe of ermine above the heather?
There in deep drifts the fine dust stays,
Where song was and the winding ways.
Who can tell me what folk they are
On the wintry earth spit from afar?
Heaven's white angels they must be
Busy about their carpentry.
The plank is lifted from the flour bin,
And down floats the flour within;
Silver cloaks of ice that pass,
Quicksilver, the coldest ever was,
A hampering chimer, white and chill,
Cement on hollow, ditch, and hill,
Earth's mail corslet, cold and hard,
A pavement vast as the sea's graveyard.
On all my land what monstrous fall,
From sea to sea a grey wall!
Who dare affront its rude domain?
A cloak of lead!—where is the rain?

SIÔN CENT
fl. 1400–1430

36 *The Vanity of the World* ♀

Mortal flesh is full of grief,
The world, cold thing, 's a sermon.

35 chimer] Welsh *simwr*, French *simar(re)*, a gown

SIÔN CENT

Today a gay man of gold
Has brooches, rings, and jewels,
Heaps of scarlet and camlet,
And fine silk, if it's in vogue,
Splendid drinking-horns of gold,
Wine and kestrels and falcons.
Mounted on Gascon stallions
He rides before, and all bow.
To ask for a good farmhold
On his lands is an offence;
He gets a weak man under
His thumb, and seizes his place,
Takes his farm from one who's blind,
And takes another's acres,
Takes the grain under ashtrees,
Takes an innocent man's hay,
Collects two hundred cattle,
Gets the goods, and jails the man.

Futile the frantic plotting
Of weak clay, dead in a day.
From bare earth he came, dark cold,
Coldly he goes in ashes.
Two cows he'd not surrender
Yesterday, for two from God!
Today in earth he's worthless,
Of all his goods he has none.
Pain fills him, when he goes there,
Covered with gravel and grit;
His bed will be much too base,
His forehead next the roof-beam;
His tight-belted robe the shroud,
His cradle earth and gravel;
The porter above his head
Earth black as a nightmare;
His proud flesh in an oak-chest,
His nose a pale sorry grey;
His coat of mail black with grime,
Its fringes all have rusted;
His robe wood, grief's constriction,

55

His shirt without sleeves or shape;
His sure road into this earth,
His arms across his bosom;
His walks vacant, gone the wine,
His cook deserts his kitchen;
His hounds, in the empty hall,
His steeds, in doubt about him;
His wife, from the drinking hall,
Quite rightly, weds another;
His stately whitewashed mansion
A small coffin the world spares;
The wealth of the world leaves him
Down below with empty hands.

When in his honoured coffin
He's speeded from court to church,
No pretty girl will follow,
No healthy man, past the grave.
No slender wanton will slide
Her hand beneath that blanket.
No grief will long continue
Nor lie a month on his grave.
When for an hour he's lain there,
This man with long yellow hair,
Should he notice, dark the house,
A toad will tend his bedside.
Under the neck of the stone
More fat worms than fair branches.
Around him in earth's sad house
More coffins than great stallions.
The choir priests detest dealing
With the three executors:
Three hundred pounds in payment
Received for their services;
His kin above will be proud
If they complete three masses.
There the spirit will possess
No mansion, rank, or favour,
No ornament, no idols,
Only what it did for God.

SIÔN CENT

Where are the towers? the town?
The many courts? the singers?
The gabled houses? the land?
The high places for merit?
Where's the morsel? the new dish?
The roast? the cook who serves it?
Where's the wine? the birds? the boughs
Carried throughout the country?
The wine-cellar? the kitchen
Under the hill? Where's the mead?
The trip to England? the gear?
The splendid bards? the dais?
Where are the huge gentle hounds?
The flock of swans? the stallions?
The full wardrobe? the treasure?
Possessions on land and sea,
The great hall newly enclosed,
The palaces, the mansions?
There remains no small holding,
Only seven feet, man's end.

The flesh, once wrapped in purple,
Lies in a chest next the choir,
And there the soul does not know,
Dim-witted, where it's going.
For the wrongs and heresies
Committed in his lifetime,
That dark day, as I'm a man,
Is too late for repentance.
There not one of his hundred
He'll reward, that sleep's too long;
Not one fellow will follow,
He'll not conquer, nor bear arms,
Nor love girls, nor be greeted,
Nor pace through council and court;
He'll have no mead for a spree,
Nor leave the grave to revel.
I'd not give a head of leek
For his corpse in the coffin.

The soul, shuttled shamefully,
Between ice and fire, freezes,
Where he's compelled, no shelter,
To a close compact with cold.
What help in a hall of ice?
Beware, the pit is frightful.
Pools and infernal ovens,
Cauldrons, dragons, devils' shapes;
See each beast, Christ is mighty,
Horned and tusked and glowering;
The hand of every devil
Holds a crooked cooking fork;
And a smoky blackness like
Flood-tide's treacherous onslaught.
May Christ, that place is dreadful,
Preserve men from going there!

Learn that there's a worldly state
Leads many to the devil.
Holy Saint Benedict says
God gives only one heaven.
Just one may, eloquent words,
Be won, though helped by Mary.
Let no man in the pleasure
Of lust find his heaven here,
Lest he lose, say the masters,
Eternal heaven through sin:
Day without night is displayed,
Health without drawn-out illness,
The gaily coloured face of
Heaven's land, better than wealth.
This world fails, a nest of twigs,
But heaven lasts for ever,
Without end, all men as one,
Amen, O Son of Mary!

LLYWELYN AB Y MOEL

d. 1440

37   *The Battle of Waun Gaseg*   ọ̇

A happy band on the hill slope
Were we that day, in high hope,
All at stretch and in good heart,
Resolute to play our part
With doughty deeds in winning fame
In men's mouths for Owain's name.
And there before the fray began,
In keen debate our talk ran
What part of profit each should gain
In booty when the foe was slain;
And ere a foeman hove in sight
Each averred, come what might,
Never yielding, he'd be found
Standing gloriously his ground.

While thus, after mirth and song,
We with our God debated long,
Beside us suddenly we espied
Through the bracken—woe betide!—
Into our midst in full course
Charging, more than a hundred horse.
And with them came—and 'pon my word
More piercing din was never heard—
A whippersnapper, spruce and trim
—French badgerward would blush at him—
Whose monkey mouth from his bugle blew
Sounds ruder than cannon ever knew.

We, alack! the sorry host,
Never thought, for all our boast,
To stand our ground there on the moor
And face the foe, no, not for an hour;
No test of arms or harness made,
In wild defenceless haste we fled,

D

And the foe in angry mood
Unremitting our flight pursued.
Hard they drove us from place to place,
Across nine dingles went the chase,
As goats are driven they drove us then
With the wild rush of Usk's picked men.
A rude turn to our pride had we,
And bitter was it there to see,
Flung on Waun Gaseg's grassy green,
Our bloodless lances, bright and clean.

For me—ah! poor pre-eminence—
The sole advantage I had thence
Was but that with surpassing haste
I ran, my fellows far out-paced,
Across the gorge in full view
Of foes who knew me—too well they knew!
Dull fool is he who in white coat strays,
Courting ill hap, on the mountain ways.
Then let who will, when the call they hear,
Prompt at the mustering place appear,
But ill befall me if I be seen
In my white coat by the Waun ravine!

DAFYDD NANMOR

fl. 1450–1480

38   *Ode to Rhys ap Maredudd of Tywyn*   ọ̀

Genau'r Glyn, Tywyn, each day from these   to Rhys's halls
    Men flock in companies.
   May plenty reign there, may rich peace
   Through endless ages never cease!

Long age, as of an oak, be his; may he   no end
    To Fortune's favour see
   Till every star shall numbered be,
   Earth's dust and blossoms of each tree.

Like the pied blossoms which the trees adorn,   like snow,
   Like birds that haunt the corn,
  Like rain, like dew that decks the morn,
  To him be so my blessing borne.

Blessing like dew, I pray, each valley fill;   may Rhys
   At Tywyn have all that he will
  While stand the ancient heavens still,
  And, earth and stone, the nearby hill.

Liquor he'll buy; vineyards their bounteous store   of wine
   Will send the south seas o'er,
  Eighteen stout merchantmen and more
  With freight of wine-vats by the score.

Wine-vats and weapons, store enow   at his command
   Now and for evermo,
  Good meinie wheresoe'er he go
  Of weaponed men, like trees a-row.

Like trees a-row, a thousand, stout and bold: to each,
   Aye, thousands more, is told
  Largesse of silver and of gold,
  Of wine and mead ten thousandfold.

Thousand, two thousand to his hest repair,
A thousand ever his gay livery wear,
  Thousand, two thousand poets rare   his greatness greet,
Songs honey-sweet a thousand minstrels sing.

Many as snowflakes on Rhydodin shed,
Many as leaves on ash boughs overhead,
  As seeds o'er fertile furrows spread   each first of May,
So lavish is the pay his hands will fling.

A hundred halls are his if he demand,
Acres and men to match at his command,
  Estates a hundred of good land   are his each one,
Houses and farms a hundred at his whim.

Nine score of chargers in the year he buys,
Nine score of breastplates 'gainst the shaft that flies,
   Nine score of gleaming lances rise   in stalwart hands,
At need nine score of lands will follow him.

Nor Italy nor Scotland boasts a knight,
Nor Calais, proof against all foemen's might,
   Nor on wide-nostrilled charger white   a lord of Wales,
Nor England, who less quails at sight of foe.

Eye never saw in hall with holly gay,
Tongue hath not told on great lord's mustering day,
   No host hath heard so far away   as distant Llŷn
Of one e'er seen good fare to lavish so.

No foam-flecked courser half so swiftly hies,
No hart from ford or buck from bracken flies,
   No salmon through the water plies   at turn of tide
As, when the feast is cried, men to Tywyn.

Not so far yet hath journeyed bird or star,
Nor sun nor moon nor all the waves that are,
   Nor the wide cirque of heaven so far,   since first he came,
As Rhys's fame hath spread beyond the Glyn.

LEWIS GLYN COTHI
1447–1486

39   *Lament for Siôn y Glyn*   ọ̀

One boy, Saint Dwyn, my bauble:
His father rues he was born!
Sorrow was bred of fondness,
Lasting pain, lacking a son.

39 Lewis Glyn Cothi] Lewis of the Valley of the Cothi, in north Carmarthen-
shire   Siôn y Glyn] Siôn (pron. Shone = English John) of the Valley
Dwyn] or Dwynwen, a fifth-century female saint, in favour with lovers

My two sides, dead is my die,
For Siôn y Glyn are aching.
I moan everlastingly
For a baron of boyhood.

A sweet apple and a bird
The boy loved, and white pebbles,
A bow of a thorntree twig,
And swords, wooden and brittle;
Scared of pipes, scared of scarecrows,
Begging mother for a ball,
Singing to all his chanting,
Singing 'Oo-o' for a nut.
He would play sweet, and flatter,
And then turn sulky with me,
Make peace for a wooden chip
Or the dice he was fond of.

Ah that Siôn, pure and gentle,
Cannot be a Lazarus!
Beuno once brought back to life
Seven who'd gone to heaven;
My heart's sorrow, it's doubled,
That Siôn's soul is not the eighth.

Mary, I groan, he lies there,
And my sides ache by his grave.
The death of Siôn stands by me
Stabbing me twice in the chest.
My boy, my twirling taper,
My bosom, my heart, my song,
My prime concern till my death,
My clever bard, my daydream,
My toy he was, my candle,
My fair soul, my one deceit,
My chick learning my singing,
My Iseult's chaplet, my kiss,
My strength, in grief he's left me,

Beuno] a seventh-century saint

My lark, my weaver of spells,
My bow, my arrow, my love,
My beggar, O my boyhood.
Siôn is sending his father
A sword of longing and love.

Farewell the smile on my mouth,
Farewell to my lips' laughter,
Farewell sweet consolation,
Farewell the begging for nuts,
Farewell, far-off the ballgame,
Farewell to the high-pitched song,
Farewell, while I stay earthbound,
My gay darling, Siôn my son.

DAFYDD AB EDMWND
fl. 1450–1480

40   *A Girl's Hair*   Ǫ

He who could win the girl I love
would win a grove of light,
with her silken, starry hair
in golden columns from her head,
dragon fire lighting up a door,
three chains like the Milky Way.
She sets alight in one bush
a roof of hair like a bonfire.
Yellow broom or a great birch tree
is this gold-topped girl of Maelor.
A host coloured like angels,
her armour's many-branched,
a peacock-feather pennon,
a tall bush like the golden door,
all this lively looking hair
virtued like the sun, fetter of girls.
Anyone would know, were he a goldsmith,

who owns this fine strong hair.
In summer she has on her head
something like the Golden Hillside.
This fair growth is the girl's garment,
a tent for the sun, or harp strings,
ears of corn closed in above,
reed peelings as ornaments for the breast;
a peahen constantly carrying
hair of broom from head to ground,
a noose of woven amber,
the gold of corn like twig-chains;
her hair's a tree-high woodland,
a twig-crown of new wax.
Labour of bees has ripened
the seeds of warmth from a girl's flesh,
saffron on the herb eyebright,
cherries of gold, like the stars of night.
A good band round its coming growth,
fresh water-grass, golden water-hair,
lye water wets it like sweet herbs;
yellow-hammer head, bush of silk;
a sheaf of Mary Magdalen's broom
is the gold band that binds her hair.
If we let it down all glowing,
she'll wear a gown of golden hair.
It covers her two breasts
from its roof of gold in two fathoms,
fair ringlets, load of a girl's head,
flax before bush of yellow.
If spread out, the bush is gold:
was ever bush so yellow?
In order that from the christening font
the oil of faith should mark her head,
giving life to the sun's bush,
there's no such bush now under the sun.

GWERFYL MECHAIN
fl. 1460–1500

41   *The Hostess of the Ferry Inn*   ♀

I keep the custom of the Ferry, a tavern none can blame, a white-
robed moon giving sweet welcome to him that comes with silver.
'Tis my desire to be, to all men's content, a faultless world to my
guests, and to sing among them in familiar converse as I pour out
the mead.

42   *The Snowfall*   ♀

White flour, earth-flesh, a cold fleece on the mountain, small snow of
the chill black day; snow like a platter, bitter cold plumage, a softness
sent to entrammel me.
White snow on the cold hill above has blinded me and soaked my
clothes. By the blessed God! I had no hope I should ever get to my
house.

LLAWDDEN
c. 1460

43   *No Place like Home*   ♀

True-blue the salmon—from his sally
Back to the redds he'll roam.
When weary of the towns' stale tally
Lovely to look to home.

TUDUR ALED
fl. 1480–1525

44

The Stallion   ♀

Petition to the Abbot of Aberconwy on behalf of Lewis ap Madog

With one who safeguards Gwynedd
I would feast on Conwy's bank,
Abbot over eight districts,
Aberconwy, field of vines,
A lord who gives feasts gladly,
Twice the custom, at his board:
Spices in the one man's dish,
An orange for these others.
Thrice a prince's kitchen's worth,
His cook works hard at turning.

Conwy, in a warm valley,
White stream where I'd have fresh wine,
Wine-rich house, shrine of honey,
Passage and pantry below:
In choosing his wines at once
He was best of all nations,
Glyn Grwst and fair Austin's fort,
Green glen of wine in gallons.
Where seek I saints in session?
With him and his fellow monks,
Men numbered with the Romans,
White and red the robes they wear.
If his breast and cope were white,
So dressed he'd pass for bishop.
Under miniver he'd pass,
Should he try, as Rome's Pontiff.
Troublesome task, foolish men,
Competing for position:
For the place he won, this man,
Aberconwy, was leader.

They'd have a thousand small rents,
He wished the rent of Maenon.
For him on Merioneth's face
A band like woodland blossoms,
Soldiers from Maelor to Rhos,
Tegeingl, his close relations.

Lewis ap Madog's trustful,
Steed begged and bestowed for long,
Choosing by the month of May
Fair girl and steed to bear her.
A stag's form, for a cywydd,
Dimple-nosed, loose in his skin,
Nose that will hold my bridle,
Wide muzzle like a French gun,
Bear's muzzle, jaw in motion,
Bridle's loop holding his nose.
Keen eyes that are like two pears
In his head lively leaping,
Two slender and twitching ears,
Sage leaves beside his forehead.
A glazier's glossed his crupper
As if he polished a gem,
His skin like silk new-woven,
Hair the hue of gossamer,
Silken robe of a skylark,
Camlet upon a young stag.

Like the deer, his eye frenzied,
His feet weaving through wild fire,
He was spinning without hands,
Weaving of silk, moved nearer.
Pursuing the thunder's path
And trotting when he chooses
He loosed a leap at heaven,
Sure of his power to fly.

Stout colt chewing the highway,
A fair-bell, flee from his path!
Stars from the road or lightning

68

Whenever his fetlocks lift,
Frisky on thirty-two nails,
Sparks they are, every nailhead,
A spinner on a hilltop,
Holds the nailheads to the sun,
Sparks flash from each one of them,
Each hoof sewn with eight stitches.
His vigour I'd compare to
A red hind before the hounds:
His mind was fixed on floating,
A most lively beast he was;
If driven to the hayfield,
His hoof will not break eight stalks.

He was a river-leaper,
A roebuck's leap from a snake;
He'd face whatever he wished:
If rafter, try to clear it;
There's no need, to make him leap,
For steel against his belly.
With a keen horseman, no clod,
He would know his intention.
If he's sent over a fence,
He will run, the lord's stallion,
Bold jumper where thorns grow thick,
Full of spikes, in Llaneurgain.
Best ever, when set running,
Fine steed to steal a fair girl.
Here awaits me a maiden,
Fair girl, if I have a horse.

For a hind's form what payment
Betters praise of the slim foal?

45   *Trystan and Esyllt*   ♀

Then Trystan and Gwalchmai went to Arthur, and Arthur made peace there between Trystan and March ap Meirchion. And Arthur talked to the two of them in turn, but neither was willing to be without Esyllt. Whereupon Arthur adjudged her to the one of them while the leaves would be on the trees, and to the other while the leaves would not be on the trees, the husband to choose. And he chose when the leaves would not be on the trees, because the nights would be longest during that season. And Arthur reported that to Esyllt. And she said, 'A blessing on the judgement and on him that uttered it forth!' And Esyllt sang this englyn:

> 'Three trees there are, and good are they,
> The holly, the ivy, the yew;
> They put forth leaves for ever and aye,
> And Trystan shall have me his whole life through.'

And in this fashion March lost Esyllt for ever.

16th century

46   *Glyn Cynon Wood*   ♀

> Aberdare, Llanwynno through,
> all Merthyr to Llanfabon;
> there was never a more disastrous thing
> than the cutting of Glyn Cynon.

> They cut down many a parlour pure
> where youth and manhood meet;
> in those days of the regular star
> Glyn Cynon's woods were sweet.

45 Trystan, Esyllt, Gwalchmai, March ap Meirchion] Tristan, Iseult, Gawain, King Mark

ANONYMOUS

If a man in sudden plight
took to flight from foe,
for guest-house to the nightingale
in Cynon Vale he'd go.

Many a birch-tree green of cloak
(I'd like to choke the Saxon!)
is now a flaming heap of fire
where iron-workers blacken.

For cutting the branch and bearing away
the wild birds' habitation
may misfortune quickly reach
Rowenna's treacherous children!

Rather should the English be
strung up beneath the seas,
keeping painful house in hell
than felling Cynon's trees.

Upon my oath, I've heard it said
that a herd of the red deer
for Mawddwy's deep dark woods has left,
bereft of its warmth here.

No more the badger's earth we'll sack
nor start a buck from the glade;
no more deer-stalking in my day,
now they've cut Glyn Cynon's shade.

If ever a stag got into a wood
with huntsmen a stride behind,
never again will he turn in his run
with Cynon Wood in mind.

If the flour-white girl once came
to walk along the brook,
Glyn Cynon's wood was always there
as a fair trysting nook.

Rowenna's children] Rowenna, the sister of Hengist and Horsa, and wife
of Vortigern, was known to the Welsh triadically as Alis Ronwen, and her
progeny of English kings as *plant Alis*, 'Alice's children'

71

ANONYMOUS

If as in times gone by men plan
to span the mountain river;
though wood be found for house and church
Glyn Cynon's no provider.

I'd like to call on them a quest
of every honest bird,
where the owl, worthiest in the wood,
as hangman would be heard.

If there's a question who rehearsed
in verse this cruel tale,
it's one who many a tryst has kept
in the depth of Cynon Vale.

16th century

47   *The Shirt of a Lad*   ♀

As I did the washing one day
Under the bridge at Aberteifi,
And a golden stick to drub it,
And my sweetheart's shirt beneath it—
A knight came by upon a charger,
Proud and swift and broad of shoulder,
And he asked if I would sell
The shirt of the lad that I loved well.

No, I said, I will not trade—
Not if a hundred pounds were paid;
Not if two hillsides I could keep
Full with wethers and white sheep;
Not if two fields full of oxen
Under yoke were in the bargain;
Not if the herbs of all Llanddewi,
Trodden and pressed, were offered to me—
Not for the likes of that I'd sell
The shirt of the lad that I love well.

16th century

48   *He whose Hand and Eye are Gentle*   ọ̀

To tell you from the start, I have lost him whose hand and eye are gentle; I shall go to seek him of the slender eyebrows, wherever the most generous and fairest of men may be.

I shall go to the midst of Gwent without delaying, to the south I shall go to search, and charge the sun and the moon to seek for him whose hand and eye are gentle.

I shall search through all the lands, in the valley and on the mountain, in the church and in the market, where is he whose hand and eye are gentle.

Mark you well, my friends, where you see a company of gentlemen, who is the finest and most loving of them; that is he whose hand and eye are gentle.

As I was walking under the vine the nightingale bade me rest, and it would get information for me where was he whose hand and eye are gentle.

The cuckoo said most kindly that she herself was quite well informed, and would send her servant to inquire without ceasing where was he whose hand and eye are gentle.

The cock-thrush advised me to have faith and hope, and said he himself would take a message to him whose hand and eye are gentle.

The blackbird told me she would travel to Cambridge and to Oxford, and would not complete her nest till she found him whose hand and eye are gentle.

I know that he whose speech is pleasant can play the lute and play the organ; God gave the gift of every music to him whose hand and eye are gentle.

Hunting with hawks and hounds and horses, catching and calling and letting slip, none loves a slim dog or a hound like him whose hand and eye are gentle.

Gwent] south-eastern Wales; once an extensive kingdom, now approximating to modern Monmouthshire

16th century

49   *from* Against Women   ♀

Woman is by aptitude
destined to servitude;
extremely cruel and proud
she's by no reason bowed
by law nor governance cowed;
of her dowry boastful
of each good way neglectful
of idle paths she's heedful.

She'll do nothing in its day
observes no middle way;
she lies down if she's stroked
and leaps up if provoked;
a white hot flame in ferment
like ice in disappointment,
she'll do no wanted thing,
she's storm without ending.

    .   .   .   .   .

Woman is full of devil's prattle
and her tongue of empty tattle;
and her distaff as a rattle
she'd beat Arthur in a battle.

Lewd she is and prodigal,
fickle, vain and cruel,
clattering complaints perpetual,
yet she grants what isn't legal.

Full of disdain and violence,
ostentation, arrogance,
envy and covetance,
caprice and instability;
she's eager to do injury,
revels in lies and luxury
and takes revenge extempore.

    .   .   .   .   .

She'll elevate Eve's throne
higher than Snowdon's crown;
she'll boast the thing she knows not
and what she knows she shows not.

.   .   .   .   .

If you'll but attend
to the tales I append
you will understand
that there's no deed unplanned
by a woman's hand.

.   .   .   .   .

Helen caused the stitching
of new sails, the rigging
of Greek ships to destroy
the citizens of Troy.

Berenice her brother loved,
of all deeds most disapproved,
for she lay at his side,
her girdle's knot untied.

Her sire was Myrrha's only joy,
Semiramis' her eldest boy
whom she did destroy.

You've all heard of the Danaids
those most murderous newly-weds
who killed their husbands in their beds.

No better were those dames of Thrace
who did the greatest poet deface;
nor can I relate for shame
the wrong linked with Pasiphae's name.

We've heard about the deeds of Phaedra
and the trickery of Rebecca
and the bane of Deianira;
nor has witnessed any era

since the days of Adam
than Eve a naughtier madam.

    .   .   .

No arms ever employed,
no fire, no sea has yet destroyed
as many heroes strong
as fall to woman's tongue.

A girl can make her face
shine brighter in a glass;
she'll set her hair and know
how to make it flow;
she'll prink and preen until
she's trimmed with weapons ill
and ready for the kill.

She'll use the wanton gesture,
the languorous eye corner
and each lascivious move
to kill a man with love.

And when comes the moment
for her to give consent,
to avoid the name
of being too easy game,
she'll weep throughout the skirmish
and yet laugh at the finish.

Her bosom she devests,
the groove between her breasts
will fill the eyes with bane
and make you lust again.
It's dangerous for lads
to know her tricks and fads.

For they are the sea monsters,
they are the deep sea dangers,
the ubiquitous destroyers;
for there's no town or city,
temple or cemetery,
no island and no country,

ANONYMOUS

no meadow or mountain side,
no land or ocean wide,
but there bad girls abide.

They are doomed with the art
which the fates impart
of turning men to stone
with a glance alone.
So young and old take care,
don't fall into love's snare.

Sitting on mountain sward
this satire from a bard
of honeyed muse I heard,
and in the shepherds' cote
I got it all by rote.

17th century

50 *The Slender Lad* &

As I was walking in the fields last Tuesday of all days, in a hollow
under the quiet wood I heard two talking together. I drew nearer to
them until I was at the very place, and who should be there conversing
but my sweetheart with her mother.

'My dear daughter, here you are by me with your hands free, your
costume fair, handsomely set up—and I mean to marry you off. You
shall mount your horse, my delicate maiden, with obsequious grooms
to curry it, and you shall have worldly wealth of yellow gold and
bright silver at your side.'

'Though I had a share in the lands of India, the silks of Persia, the
gold of Peru, I prefer the lad I love, and shall stand true to him.' 'Oh
is it so? and that's your purpose? Then you shall make your bed
among thorns; unless you mark my words, it will be a bitter play if
you trust yourself to the Slender Lad.'

'To the Slender Lad I will trust myself, mother, to tell you true; I shall
leave wealth to misers, and trust myself to him who is the flower of

the shire, with his white face and his yellow hair, and in his cheeks are two roses—happy is the girl who sleeps the night in his arms.

'If my love has gone far over the seas, if he has gone and left me on the shore, yet may St. David give him good fortune and guide him in every place. I shall not weep, no, nor fret, nor cry out after him; for if it is so fated for me, my dear love will come back yet.

'With his own hand he wrote a letter, and on its back was a wax seal, and nothing broke my heart like reading it morning and evening. In it there are three letters which are taking away my looks and figure; and unless he comes back to spell them out they will bring me down to my grave.'

?17th century

51 *Mary's Dream* ♀

'Mary mother, dost thou sleep?'
'Yes, my child, and dream of thee.'
'Mother dear, but thou dost weep,—
Mother dear, what dost thou see?'
'Child, I see thee compassed round,
See thee taken, see thee bound,
On a cross I see thee tied,
See a spear-head pierce thee through,
See the blood break from thy side'—
'Mother dear, the dream is true!'

Whosoe'er these words aright
Three times o'er shall say each night,
No ill dreams shall vex his bed,
Hell's dark land he ne'er shall tread.

50 St. David] the patron saint of Wales

SIÔN PHYLIP
d. 1620

The Seagull

Fair gull on the water's bank,
Bright-plumed breast, well-provided,
Hawk does not seize or pursue,
Water drown, nor man own you.
Nun feasting on the ocean,
Green sea's corners' coarse-voiced girl,
Thrusting wide through the lake's neck;
And then shaking a herring,
Salt water's clear white sunlight,
You're the banner of the shore.
The blessed godchild are you,
Below the bank, of Neptune:
A sorrow for you, the change
Of your life, cold your christening,
Brave white bird in rough waters,
Once a girl in a man's arms.

Halcyon, fair slim-browed maiden,
You were called in your kind land,
And after your man, good cause,
To the waves then you ventured,
And to the wild strait's seagull
You were changed, weak-footed bird.
You live, quick fish-feeding girl,
Below the slope and billows,
And the same cry for your mate
You screech loudly till doomsday.

Was there ever on the sea
A more submissive swimmer?
Hear my cry, wise and white-cloaked,
The hurt of the bare sea's bard:
My breast is pained with passion,
Pining for love of a girl.

SIÔN PHYLIP

I have begged from my boyhood
That she'd make one tryst with me,
And the tryst was for today:
Great was grief, it was wasted.
Swim, forget not my complaint,
To the dear maiden's region;
Fly to the shore, brave brightness,
And say where I was held fast
By the mouth, no gentle wave,
Of rough Bermo, cold foaming,
In all moods a sorry spot,
A cold black sea for sailing.

I rose, I travelled as day was
Breaking towards that dear bright face.
Dawn came on a thorny seastrand,
A cold day from the south-east.
A foul wind winnowed gravel,
Stripping stones, the whirlwind's nest.
The signs grew darker with dawn,
Twrch Trwydd drenching the beaches.
Inky was the wind's gullet
Where the western wind draws breath.

Harsh is the shore in conflict
If the western inlet's rough:
The sea spews, turning rocks green,
From the east spews fresh water.
Deep heaves from the ocean-bed,
In pain the pale moon's swooning.
The green pond is heaved abroad,
A snake's heave, sick from surfeit.
Sad heave where I saw tide ebb,
Rain's drivel that came pouring,
Cold black bed between two slopes,
Salt-filled briny sea-water.
Furnace dregs, draff of hell-spit,
Mouth sucking drops from the stars,

Bermo] Y Bermo, Barmouth, Meirionydd   Twrch Trwydd] the Other-
world Boar hunted by Arthur in the Mabinogion

SIÔN PHYLIP

A winter night's greedy mouth,
Greed on the face of night-time,
Crock-shaped wet-edged enclosure,
A ban between bard and girl,
Foul hollow gap, raging pit,
Foggy land's filthy cranny,
Cromlech of every sickness,
Narrow pit of the world's plagues.
The pit was the sea-pool's haunt,
High it leaped, pool of prickles.
As high as the shelf it climbs,
Spew of the storm-path's anguish.
It never ebbs, will not turn:
I could not cross the current.

Three waters could flow eastwards,
Three oceans, these are the ones:
The Euxin, where rain wets us,
The Adriatic, black look,
The flood that runs to Rhuddallt,
Ancient Noah's flood turned salt.
The water-gate at Bermo,
Tide and shelf, may it turn land!

EDMWND PRYS
1544–1623

53   *A Welsh Ballad*   ℺

upon the measure *About the Bank of Helicon*

A shout came from the loquacious ones
whom we heard yesterday under green trees,
   holy and church-like place,
three lives to those gentle poets,

52 The flood that runs to Rhuddallt] the storm-heaped sea that floods the
river Mawddach at Barmouth

grove linnet, innocent nightingale,
    pensive and paradisal,
sweet thrush of pure oration,
the blackbird greater in desire
and the lascivious siskin
who net the song of the lark,
    singing,
    plucking
    so much poetry,
    so lively,
    so clearly,
  and in their true lusting.

A near-by grove with notes increasing,
an April grove and primrose-full,
    place of fine song and daisies;
a dale full of the spring clover
and the green clothes of true delight
    filling with happiness,
with flowers on the thorn points,
the slim birch and the fresh leaves;
fair is the fountain, sweet the spot,
from under boughs there springs
    the clear water,
    the fresh water;
    fair, fortunate place,
    a place to sleep,
    a place to learn
  all knots of descanting.

I'd have all sweetness in my house,
both the song of Gwynedd's darling
    to some sprightly music
and an Irish girl called Eurwedd,
unyoked pair of laughing girls
    in shining green tree mansion,
to sing loud of happy summers
all with bird song entwined;
profitably to sing to God
a golden cycle of great praise;

        a tuning up
        of psalmody
        in varying notes;
        devices,
        turning voices
    for unnumbered ages.

Many tree-clusters, open woodlands,
many a column deeply fashioned,
        many a clear knot of praise;
a peaceful place full of sweet chords
of the plentiful praise that's made
        by the meadow-dwellers;
each bird in its own voice,
each tree in bright green tunic,
each plant in its own virtue,
each bird with a poet's lips,
        not suffering
        but sprightly
        in heavenly notes;
        not troubled
        but in treble;
    the place is Venus's.

Delight is good for all mankind
and merriment for maidens,
        Sunday is good for men;
this is fair and not odious for age,
fair, not unpleasant, for youth.
        Sunday is good for men,
planned fair by the true God Father,
his gift and notable grace.
Each voice is fair, every turn,
as long as there's no sin.
        On earth
        how gentle;
        early on the wheat
        and on the grove;
        how mild the land
    where the great blessing's given!

THOMAS PRYS
c. 1564–1634

54 *A Poem to show the Trouble that befell him*
when he was at Sea

I followed, o splendid season,
the water over the world to Spain,
thinking that, taking to the sea,
I should come by all treasure.
Wandering, sieving the waters
needily, is the seaman's fate.
I bought a ship, stripped the land
for money for the venture;
victualled it fitly and fair,
victualled where butlers abounded.
I gathered men, a gloomy task,
for utterly vain sea-faring,
some vicious dark-hued Jews,
hell-bellied and abusive.
I took ship to train the men,
then came the need for cursing.
There was a roaring on board,
the master calling muster.
'*Turn the capstan,*' he howled an order,
'*Weigh anchor, all you younkers!*'
A question, '*Where is Meyrick?*'
Then the words, '*Coil the cable quick!*'
Deubott the carpenter's diligent,
'*Assay the pump, you see the pit.*'
'Turn you to fire and be damned!'
'*Trim the ship, whip* to it, yare!
Make haste there, haste, you waster!
Bring in the bowline, you boor!
Bear hard up to throw off plague;
bear aloof if it rain toads!
You, Bunny, fast the bonnet,
sound fine with the line and lead.

84

THOMAS PRYS

Veer the sheet, impotent booby;
about again, if a hundred times!'
Farewell England and dry sand
and Scilly, lovely island.
Roll away with royal wings
to parley off the Burlings.

'*Here's Atkins. Where is Woodcock?*
Bear all night right to the Rock.
Beware of any mishap;
our course is the southern cape.
Take height in all good sense.
Thou Poyns, yonder is the Pole.'

Today we hold in dark tides,
we'll veer away tomorrow.
'You, *Hulling, loose the halliard!*
Off you go along the yard!
Bring near the timber, tomboy!
What cheer? A can of beer, boy!
Munson, hoist up the mainsail.
Be merry, I see a sail.
Give chase, for all I've got!
Out topsail, you lout tipsy!
Give way!' In the winter storm
we mustered and mastered the wind,
starboard and larboard labouring.
'*Clear abaft*, keep clear of trouble!
Port hard the helm, bastard one!
Steady thus, man! Do you hear?
Keep the prize (look out wisely,
hear thou, lad) under thy lee.
Now fire a piece in order.'
Instead, he shot three into her.
'*Shoot again a broadside, gunner!*
We'll be brave if we have her.
Fight for store and leave sorrow,
fear not, shoot the wild fire now!
Lay her aboard!' In all the din,
'*Now enter*, venture over!'

Whilst fighting, open discredit,
we lost our men on the vessel in smoke.
'Give back, lest all be taken!
Is there a means *to save some men?'*
We took an unfortunate day,
we find we mind this Monday,
loudly bewailing fortune's blow,
'O Lord, here is too hard luck!'
Foulk Harry, awkward booby,
is drowned in the battle's din;
Brown Robin Austin withal
is dead, and so is Duddal,
Wenford, Rowland and Winfield,
William and Cobham are killed.
Tom, Meyrick, Dick, each one
is hurt, and so is Horton.
Our ship in grappling so
is *weak and full of leak below,*
and if a storm now takes us
we'll be in too hard a state.
'Go to, pain; let's get to port!
Barris, the beer is sour.'

Thus I got a sleep of care
in payment for this venture.
I doubt if Thomas from here
will get home safe from the green sea.
Before I will pillage or part
buy a ship, I'll be a shepherd.

HUW LLWYD

c. 1568–1630

55   *The Fox's Counsel*   ỻ

Good morning, fox of the cave,
Every tame fowl's arch-foeman,

HUW LLWYD

Your ripple I recognize,
Welcome to fertile country.
Describe, in the fair meadow,
Your life, bold soft-bellied beast.

Fair and clean, you are noted,
And shapely in every part:
You were dyed with dark colour,
Red and gold that will not fade;
Your narrow nose is savage,
Your teeth, they are marvellous,
Strange pincers, swiftly gripping,
And able to crunch through bones;
And your eye's glowering look
You turn like an old traitor.
On your head, fine beast, always,
Is the semblance of stiff stumps;
Your neck beneath was well-dressed,
Shaped like a ridge, you're splendid;
Bulging belly in coarse cloth,
A belly full of malice!
Short leg, bold through thick-branched grove,
Keen trotter towards weak lambkins.
Your tail, the length of mid-day,
Thick coarse cloth, is your pillow;
That tail is a yard-long brush,
A roll extremely swollen.
Kindling on the cairn's summit,
Kindled lad in a stout den,
Well-designed is your dwelling,
A hide-out from terriers.

Sorry scheme, you live yonder,
Paunchy lad, by plundering,
Pilfering, when it's quiet,
And strolling through leaves all day:
Kid's meat, when it's to be had,
Ewes, if they're for the taking;
A fine life, when there are lambs,
Blameless for you to tithe them.

HUW LLWYD

Take hereafter, yours freely,
A goose and hen, unrebuked:
Clever you are, bird-snatching,
Hillside or bog, wild and tame.

All accomplishments your gift,
When closed in, you're a lion.
And if you come with twilight
Is there one so full of sense,
Or any with tricks slicker
Than yours, savage-snarling fox?
Nowhere, I know, in the grove,
Will I find shrewder judgement.
I am a man unwelcomed,
Disheartened, speechless, unloved,
No malice, no violence,
Strengthless in every struggle:
Yours, today, well-earned honours,
Teach me, a gift, how to live;
If you will give good counsel,
Forever I'll sing your praise.

'Be still, sound man, no clamour,
No search for help, no complaint.
See that there are, and take heed,
Two paths for your protection:
One true path, straight is its course;
Another one through falsehood.

'Seeking success, preferment?
I'd wish you to live like me.
One who's simple and peaceful,
Without malice, he'll not mount,
And integrity today,
In the world's view, is foolish.
Pillage or hazard the world,
Try cunning for the moment;
Learn to keep watch, look for faults,
Spare not one nor the other.
Remember, basic lesson,

88

HUW LLWYD

Remember gain, the world's rule.
Devise, beware of a frown,
Traps for all, know all evil.
Do a kindness to no one
All your life, lest life be lost.
Make yourself known where you go,
From fear, cause much gift-giving.

'Hard to live, no denying,
Today by what's gained from love.
If you wish to live for long,
Go with praise, learn to flatter,
And by lauding each small thing
Learn the art of deception.
Speak sweetly on each errand,
Let no profit slip your hand.
Speak nothing but pious words,
Your malice in your belly.
Let not a man who's been born
Know any place your purpose:
That's the way a fool is known,
He reveals what he's thinking.
To prey on the weak's the way;
Treat the strong with smooth talking.
Do wrong, make no amendment:
To you, man, a good day comes.
Do all this, you'll not founder,
With deception as your guide.

'I have nothing more to tell:
The other path, consider.
I see the hounds in pursuit,
Hard for me to speak further
Or stay here on the hillside.
Farewell, I must flee above.'

Folk Verses

56   *Death*   ♀

One night as I lay on my bed,
And sleep on fleeting foot had fled,
Because, no doubt, my mind was heavy
With concern for my last journey:

I got me up and called for water,
That I might wash, and so feel better;
But before I wet my eyes so dim,
There was Death on the bowl's rim.

I went to church that I might pray,
Thinking sure he'd keep away;
But before I got on to my feet,
There sat Death upon my seat.

To my chamber then I hied,
Thinking sure he'd keep outside;
But though I firmly locked the door,
Death came from underneath the floor.

Then to sea I rowed a boat,
Thinking surely Death can't float;
But before I reached the deep,
Death was captain of the ship.

57   *Two-Faced Too*   ♀

A North Wales girl was once my passion.
She'd got two costumes, both in fashion,
Two matching hats as well, the peach,
And two false faces under each.

58   *Grief*   𝄞

My heart is just as heavy
    As the horse on yonder hill;
When trying to be happy,
    I can't, try as I will.
The little shoe it pinches,
    On a spot you would not guess;
My heart with bitter grieving
    Is breaking 'neath the stress.

59   *Unfair to Men*   𝄞

Happy the wild birds that can soar
To sea and mountain, freely roaming;
Wing where they will, and what is more,
No awkward questions after homing.

60   *Unfair to Women*   𝄞

I thought if only I could marry,
I'd sing and dance and live so gaily;
But all the wedded bliss I see
Is rock the cradle, hush the baby.

61   *Song and Poetry*   𝄞

Those men who love the *crwth* and harp,
Cynghanedd, song, the englyn's art,
They love the best things God has given
To please his angel-hosts in heaven.

61 *crwth*] crowd, a kind of fiddle, violin   cynghanedd] the harmonious
congruence of sound-patterns, employing consonants and vowel sounds in
prescribed sequences, with alliteration, stress, and internal rhyme, character-
istic of, and peculiar to, Welsh poetry   englyn] a strictly regulated,
four-lined, thirty-syllabled, cynghanedd-patterned, rhymed Welsh verse form

62 *Good Counsel* ♀

Good for good is only fair;
Bad for bad soon brings despair;
Bad for good is vile and base;
Good for bad shows forth God's grace.

63 *The Shearing* ♀

When my life was thrifty, thrifty,
Soon my one sheep grew to fifty;
After that I lived for fun
And found my flock was back to one.

64 *My Heart is in Merioneth* ♀

Low ye hills in ocean lie,
That hide fair Meirion from my eye;
One distant view, Oh! let me take,
Ere yet my longing heart shall break.

65 *Night and Morning* ♀

One night of tempest I arose and went
Along the Menai shore on dreaming bent;
The wind was strong, and savage swung the tide,
And the waves blustered on Caernarfon side.

But on the morrow, when I passed that way,
On Menai shore the hush of heaven lay;
The wind was gentle and the sea a flower,
And the sun slumbered on Caernarfon tower.

66 *Hiraeth* ̧q

Tell me, men with wisdom gifted,
How hath *hiraeth* been created?
Of what stuff hath it been made,
That it doth not wear nor fade?

Gold and silver wear away,
Velvet too, and silk they say;
Weareth every costly raiment:
But *hiraeth* is a lasting garment.

Now a great and cruel *hiraeth*
In my heart all day endureth,
And when I sleep most heavily,
Hiraeth comes and wakens me.

Hiraeth, *hiraeth*, O! depart!
Why dost thou press upon my heart?
O! move along to the bed side,
And let me rest till morning tide.

67 *Desolation* ̧q

Sun on hillsides, wind on seas,
And grey crags instead of trees;
Instead of men, the gulls' lament—
God! how should not my heart be rent?

   66 *hiraeth*] longing, nostalgia

HUGH HOLLAND
1569–1635

68   *Upon the Lines and Life of the Famous Scenic*
      Poet, Master William Shakespeare

Those hands which you so clapt, go now and wring,
You Britons brave; for done are Shakespeare's days:
His days are done, that made the dainty plays
Which made the Globe of heaven and earth to ring.
Dried is that vein, dried is the Thespian spring,
Turned all to tears, and Phoebus clouds his rays:
That corpse, that coffin, now bestick those bays
Which crowned him Poet first, then Poets' King.
If Tragedies might any Prologue have,
All those he made would scarce make one to this:
Where Fame, now that he is gone to the grave
(Death's public tiring-house), the Nuncius is.
  For though his line of life went soon about,
  The life yet of his lines shall never out.

LORD HERBERT OF CHERBURY
1583–1648

69   *Elegy over a Tomb*

Must I then see, alas! eternal night
    Sitting upon those fairest eyes,
And closing all those beams, which once did rise
    So radiant and bright,
That light and heat in them to us did prove
    Knowledge and Love?

Oh, if you did delight no more to stay
  Upon this low and earthly stage,
But rather chose an endless heritage,
    Tell us at least, we pray,
Where all the beauties that those ashes owed
      Are now bestowed?

Doth the sun now his light with yours renew?
  Have waves the curling of your hair?
Did you restore unto the sky and air
    The red, and white, and blue?
Have you vouchsafed to flowers since your death
      That sweetest breath?

Had not Heaven's lights else in their houses slept,
  Or to some private life retired?
Must not the sky and air have else conspired,
    And in their regions wept?
Must not each flower else the earth could breed
      Have been a weed?

But thus enriched may we not yield some cause
  Why they themselves lament no more?
That must have changed the course they held before,
    And broke their proper laws,
Had not your beauties given this second birth
      To Heaven and Earth?

Tell us—for oracles must still ascend,
  For those that crave them at your tomb—
Tell us, where are those beauties now become,
    And what they now intend:
Tell us, alas, that cannot tell our grief,
      Or hope relief.

GEORGE HERBERT

1593–1633

The Collar

I struck the board, and cried, 'No more!
     I will abroad.
 What? shall I ever sigh and pine?
My lines and life are free; free as the road,
  Loose as the wind, as large as store.
    Shall I be still in suit?
  Have I no harvest but a thorn
  To let me blood, and not restore
  What I have lost with cordial fruit?
     Sure there was wine
Before my sighs did dry it: there was corn
   Before my tears did drown it.
  Is the year only lost to me?
   Have I no bays to crown it?
No flowers, no garlands gay? all blasted?
    All wasted?
  Not so, my heart: but there is fruit,
     And thou hast hands.
  Recover all thy sigh-blown age
On double pleasures: leave thy cold dispute
Of what is fit, and not. Forsake thy cage,
    Thy rope of sands,
Which petty thoughts have made, and made to thee
  Good cable, to enforce and draw,
    And be thy law,
 While thou didst win, and wouldst not see.
    Away, take heed:
    I will abroad.
Call in thy death's head there: tie up thy fears.
    He that forbears
   To suit and serve his need,
    Deserves his load.'
But as I raved and grew more fierce and wild
    At every word,
 Methoughts I heard one calling, 'Child!'
  And I replied, 'My Lord'.

GEORGE HERBERT

71   *Love*

Love bade me welcome; yet my soul drew back,
        Guilty of dust and sin.
But quick-eyed Love, observing me grow slack
        From my first entrance in,
Drew nearer to me, sweetly questioning,
        If I lacked anything.

'A guest', I answered, 'worthy to be here.'
        Love said, 'You shall be he.'
'I, the unkind, ungrateful? Ah, my dear,
        I cannot look on thee.'
Love took my hand, and smiling did reply,
        'Who made the eyes but I?'

'Truth, Lord, but I have marred them; let my shame
        Go where it doth deserve.'
'And know you not', says Love, 'who bore the blame?'
        'My dear, then I will serve.'
'You must sit down', says Love, 'and taste my meat.'
        So I did sit and eat.

72   *Prayer*

Prayer, the Church's banquet, Angels' age,
  God's breath in man returning to his birth,
The soul in paraphrase, heart in pilgrimage,
  The Christian plummet, sounding heaven and earth;
Engine against the Almighty, sinner's tower,
  Reversèd thunder, Christ-side-piercing spear,
The six-days' world transposing in an hour,
  A kind of tune, which all things hear and fear:
Softness, and peace, and joy, and love, and bliss,
  Exalted manna, gladness of the best,
  Heaven in ordinary, man well drest,
The milky way, the bird of Paradise,
    Church-bells beyond the stars heard, the soul's blood,
    The land of spices; something understood.

73 *Jordan*

When first my lines of heav'nly joys made mention,
Such was their lustre, they did so excel,
That I sought out quaint words and trim invention:
My thoughts began to burnish, sprout and swell,
Curling with metaphors a plain intention,
Seeking the sense, as if it were to sell.

Thousands of notions in my brain did run,
Off'ring their service, if I were not sped:
I often blotted what I had begun;
This was not quick enough, and that was dead.
Nothing could seem too rich to clothe the sun,
Much less those joys which trample on his head.

As flames do work and wind, when they ascend!
So did I weave myself into the sense,
But while I bustled, I might hear a friend
Whisper, 'How wide is all this long pretence!
There is in love a sweetness ready penned:
Copy out only that, and save expense.'

JAMES HOWELL

1594–1655

74 *Upon Dr Davies's British Grammar*

To Mr Ben. Jonson

Father Ben, you desired me lately to procure you Dr Davies's Welsh Grammar to add to those many you have. I have lighted upon one at last and I am glad I have it in so seasonable a time that it may serve for a New-year's gift, in which quality I send it you: And because 'twas not you, but your Muse, that desired it of me, for your letter runs on feet, I thought it a good correspondence with you to accompany it with what follows.

74 Dr Davies's British Grammar] the *Antiquæ Linguæ Britannicæ . . . Rudimenta*, 1621, of Dr John Davies of Mallwyd

JAMES HOWELL

'Twas a tough task, believe it, thus to tame
A wild and wealthy language, and to frame
Grammatic toils to curb her, so that she
Now speaks by rules, and sings by prosody:
Such is the strength of Art rough things to shape,
And of rude commons rich Enclosures make.
Doubtless much oil and labour went to couch
Into methodic rules the rugged Dutch;
The Rabbis pass my reach, but judge I can
Something of Clenard and Quintilian;
And for those modern dames, I find they three
Are only lops cut from the Latian tree;
And easy 'twas to square them into parts,
The tree itself so blossoming with arts.
I have been shown for Irish and Basquence
Imperfect rules couched in an accidence:
But I find none of this can take the start
Of Davies, or that prove more men of art,
Who in exacter method and short way,
The idioms of a language do display.

This is the tongue which Bards sung in of old,
And Druids their dark knowledge did unfold:
Merlin in this his prophecies did vent,
Which through the world of fame bear such extent:
This spoke that Son of Mars and Briton bold
Who first 'mongst Christian worthies is enrolled;
This Brennus, who to his desire and glut
The Mistress of the World did prostitute.
This Arviragus, and grave Catarac,
Sole free when all the world was on Rome's rack.
This Lucius, who on angels' wings did soar
To Rome, and would wear diadem no more;
And thousand heroes more, which should I tell,
This New-year scarce would serve me. So farewell.

—Your Son and Servitor   J.H.
   Cal. Apr. 1629.

those modern dames] Italian, Spanish, French   that Son of Mars and
Briton bold] Arthur

99

75 *An Elegy upon his Tomb in Herndon-Hill
Church, erected by his Wife, who speaks*

Take, gentle marble, to thy trust,
And keep untouched this sacred dust:
Grown moist sometimes, that I may see
Thou weep'st in sympathy with me;
And when by him I here shall sleep,
My ashes also safely keep.
And from rude hands preserve us both, until
We rise to Sion Mount from Herndon-Hill.

ROWLAND WATKYNS
d. 1664

76 *Upon Christ's Nativity or Christmas*

From three dark places Christ came forth this day:
First from his Father's bosom, where he lay
Concealed till now; then from the typic Law,
Where we his manhood but by figure saw;
And lastly from his Mother's womb he came
To us a perfect God and perfect man.
Now in a Manger lies the eternal Word,
The Word he is, yet can no speech afford.
He is the Bread of Life, yet hungry lies,
The living Fountain, yet for drink he cries.
He cannot help or clothe himself at need,
Who did the lilies clothe and ravens feed.
He is the Light of Lights, yet now doth shroud
His glory with our nature as a cloud;
He came to us a little one, that we
Like little children might in malice be;
Little he is, and wrapped in clouts, lest he
Might strike us dead if clothed with majesty.

Christ had four beds, and those not soft, nor brave,
The Virgin's Womb, the Manger, Cross, and Grave.
The Angels sung this day, and so will I,
That have more reason to be glad, than they.

WILLIAM PHYLIP

d. 1670

77   *Farewell to Hendre Fechan*   Ǫ

Farewell now, poesy's secret cell,   thy ordered grace,
   Hendre Fechan, farewell.
  Ye books which of song's mysteries tell,
  Songs radiant fair, to you farewell.

A house was mine wherein secure   my life to lead,
   That should till death endure,
  Food, drink, and fire, provision sure—
  God's grace did all my needs procure.

In place of Hendre's hampering business vain,   in place
   Of this world's moil and pain,
  A Homestead new I shall attain
  In Heaven, nor earthward turn again.

Farewell, my trees, ye lovely woodland throng   of birds
   That sang with lucent tongue,
  Groves where ye carolled loud and long,
  And all ye paths, the haunt of song.

  77 Hendre Fechan] the Little Old Homestead

THOMAS VAUGHAN
1621-1666

78   *The Stone*

Lord God! this was a stone,
As hard as any one
Thy laws in Nature framed:
'Tis now a springing well,
And many drops can tell,
Since it by Art was tamed.

My God! my heart is so,
'Tis all of flint, and no
Extract of tears will yield:
Dissolve it with thy fire,
That something may aspire,
And grow up in my field.

Bare tears I'll not entreat,
But let thy Spirit's seat
Upon those waters be:
Then I, new formed with light,
Shall move without all night
Of eccentricity.

HENRY VAUGHAN
1621-1695

79   *The Retreat*

Happy those early days, when I
Shined in my angel-infancy!
Before I understood this place
Appointed for my second race,

Or taught my soul to fancy aught
But a white celestial thought;
When yet I had not walked above
A mile or two from my first love,
And looking back, at that short space,
Could see a glimpse of his bright face;
When on some gilded cloud, or flower,
My gazing soul would dwell an hour,
And in those weaker glories spy
Some shadows of eternity;
Before I taught my tongue to wound
My conscience with a sinful sound,
Or had the black art to dispense
A several sin to every sense,
But felt through all this fleshly dress
Bright shoots of everlastingness.

O how I long to travel back,
And tread again that ancient track!
That I might once more reach that plain
Where first I left my glorious train;
From whence the enlightened spirit sees
That shady City of Palm-trees.
But ah! my soul with too much stay
Is drunk, and staggers in the way.
Some men a forward motion love,
But I by backward steps would move,
And when this dust falls to the urn
In that state I came, return.

80   *The Night*

Through that pure Virgin-shrine,
That sacred veil drawn o'er thy glorious noon
That men might look and live as glow-worms shine,
        And face the moon,
    Wise Nicodemus saw such light
    As made him know his God by night.

Most blest believer he!
Who in that land of darkness and blind eyes
Thy long-expected healing wings could see,
    When thou didst rise,
  And what can never more be done,
  Did at midnight speak with the Sun!

    O who will tell me where
He found thee at that dead and silent hour!
What hallowed solitary ground did bear
    So rare a flower,
  Within whose sacred leaves did lie
  The fullness of the Deity.

    No mercy-seat of gold,
No dead and dusty cherub, nor carved stone,
But his own living works did my Lord hold
    And lodge alone;
  Where trees and herbs did watch and peep
  And wonder, while the Jews did sleep.

    Dear night! this world's defeat;
The stop to busy fools; care's check and curb;
The day of spirits; my soul's calm retreat
    Which none disturb!
  Christ's progress, and his prayer time;
  The hours to which high Heaven doth chime.

    God's silent searching flight:
When my Lord's head is filled with dew, and all
His locks are wet with the clear drops of night;
    His still soft call;
  His knocking time; the soul's dumb watch,
  When spirits their fair kindred catch.

    Were all my loud, evil days
Calm and unhaunted as is thy dark tent,
Whose peace but by some angel's wing or voice
    Is seldom rent,
  Then I in Heaven all the long year
  Would keep and never wander here.

But living where the sun
Doth all things wake, and where all mix and tire
Themselves and others, I consent and run
        To every mire,
    And by this world's ill-guiding light,
    Err more than I can do by night.

        There is in God, some say,
A deep, but dazzling darkness, as men here
Say it is late and dusky, because they
        See not all clear.
    O for that night! where I in him
    Might live invisible and dim.

81   *The Waterfall*

With what deep murmurs through time's silent stealth
Doth thy transparent, cool, and watery wealth
        Here flowing fall,
        And chide and call,
As if his liquid loose retinue stayed
Lingering, and were of this steep place afraid,
        The common pass
        Where, clear as glass,
        All must descend
        Not to an end;
But quickened by this deep and rocky grave,
Rise to a longer course more bright and brave.

    Dear stream! dear bank, where often I
    Have sat, and pleased my pensive eye,
    Why, since each drop of thy quick store
    Runs thither, whence it flowed before,
    Should poor souls fear a shade or night,
    Who came, sure, from a sea of light?
    Or since those drops are all sent back
    So sure to thee, that none doth lack,

Why should frail flesh doubt any more
That what God takes, he'll not restore?
O useful Element and clear!
My sacred wash and cleanser here,
My first consigner unto those
Fountains of life, where the Lamb goes,
What sublime truths, and wholesome themes
Lodge in thy mystical, deep streams!
Such as dull man can never find,
Unless that Spirit lead his mind,
Which first upon thy face did move,
And hatched all with his quickening love.
As this loud brook's incessant fall
In streaming rings restagnates all,
Which reach by course the bank, and then
Are no more seen, just so pass men.
O my invisible estate,
My glorious liberty, still late!
Thou art the channel my soul seeks,
Not this with cataracts and creeks.

82   *Abel's Blood*

Sad, purple well! whose bubbling eye
Did first against a murderer cry;
Whose streams still vocal, still complain
    Of bloody Cain;
And now at evening are as red
As in the morning when first shed.
    If single thou
(Though single voices are but low)
Could'st such a shrill and long cry rear
As speaks still in thy Maker's ear,
What thunders shall those men arraign
Who cannot count those they have slain,
Who bathe not in a shallow flood
But in a deep wide sea of blood?
A sea, whose loud waves cannot sleep
But deep still calleth upon deep:

HENRY VAUGHAN

Whose urgent sound like unto that
Of many waters, beateth at
The everlasting doors above,
Where souls behind the altar move,
And with one strong, incessant cry
Inquire *How Long* of the Most High.
                    Almighty Judge!
At whose just laws no just men grudge;
Whose blessèd, sweet commands do pour
Comforts and joys and hopes each hour
On those that keep them; O accept
Of his vowed heart, whom thou hast kept
From bloody men! and grant I may
That sworn memorial duly pay
To thy bright arm, which was my light
And leader through thick death and night!
        Aye, may that flood,
That proudly spilt and despised blood,
Speechless and calm as infants sleep!
Or, if it watch, forgive and weep
For those that spilt it! May no cries
From the low earth to high heaven rise,
But what (like his whose blood peace brings)
Shall (when they rise) speak better things
Than Abel's doth! May Abel be
Still single heard, while these agree
With his mild blood in voice and will,
Who prayed for those that did him kill!

HUW MORUS

1622–1709

83   *In Praise of a Girl*   ọ̀

Slip of loveliness, slim, seemly,
freshly fashioned, modest maiden, star serene,
sage and queenly, gracious, granting heart;

paragon, look upon
this grave song, growing sign
that I pine, my constant moon.
No beauty clear so dear I'll hold,
not till I'm old, foam of the sea,
loveliest lily of the land,
soft of hand, white-breasted, brisk, bright, flower-crested;
who'd not be charmed whose blood is warmed?
Moon of my nature, it was you
I viewed in my desire,
because your brow is like the snow,
able, notable, gifted, gay, flawless,
laughing, skilful, peerless pearl of girls.

If from all lands girls came in bands
and from a tree one could see
that sweet society of all loveliest ones,
the paragons of town and country,
dazzling, shapely, stately, fair, I declare,
Moon of Wales, your loveliness prevails.
Your praise and glory, peerless girl,
now impel me to applaud
your sweet looks, your subtle tongue,
dawn-sweet dearest, purest, prettiest, many-beautied,
unpolluted and reputed spotless rose;
there's none to make comparison,
wave sparkling in the darkling,
with your parabling of sweet peace,
piece of goodness, fond enchantress, blithesome dove,
lucent, laughing, blameless slip of love.

From love's curse who'll be my nurse?
Will you listen, light of dawn, to my dole?
Deal me charity, slip of beauty;
if I win not your good will
it will kill me, girl of worth; under earth
there's sad dearth of space for a person, in that prison;
low there my share of ash and loam.
That's my legacy from your beauty
unless, daybreak, for my sake

my love-ache you'll relieve, grant reprieve,
properly gentle, fluent, generous girl.
Cure my illness, dawn of sweetness,
shapely, lissom lass;
and bestow, for my woe,
a sweet lotion; maiden, listen
and endorse whilst I rehearse this true verse.

My sweetly woven, only chosen,
if my triumph makes you mine only,
life will be fine, flesh of the lily.
On this journey, soft of parley,
you'll find endless perfect heaven, morn and even,
swift mirth and soft ease on this earth:
I'm the most faithful man yet made,
eggshell maid, still to you.
Where you dwell it will be well
for me to love, luscious, lively slip, so sprightly,
following freely your trim tread;
in spite of all, I expect
to be your fellow, fine of eyebrow;
it's my aim, in God's good name,
nights and days in faithful ways to live
always in the solace of your love.

O, it's bitter, beauteous girl,
a true body can't escape from its sickness,
cruel harshness that I suffer for your sake!
You shall see, rarity,
who adores you ceaselessly; pity me,
cherish me charitably.
If kindly you'll my days extend
and send ending to my pain,
you shall be gloried till I'm buried:
come to greet me, set me free, let there not be
open hurting of my diligent, good heart.
O, take my part in this story
of my weary, stark lament;
don't augment my suffering,
ease my unsparing, gloomy faring,
my sweet darling, with swift loving.

84   *from* The Men that Once Were

Old, old
To live on, wretched to behold,
My hair is white, my smile is cold,
    All inspiration slack:
My two hands miss dexterity,
Their strength is twisted out of me,
To work exact and skilfully—
    Though bounty feed me, still they lack
And worsen in their shape and plight
Until they disappear from sight
    And I to brittle dust go back.

Harsh stroke
To the old when the cold weather broke!
His poor fiddle's a shrivelled oak
    That no one now will play;
Longing a dull ache in my side
For the kind chieftains that have died,
God's gracious works, who now must hide,
    Many a face I know, in clay;
I'm cold for all those generous men,
I'm doubting if I'll find again
    Such lords as in my memory stay.

Hard pain
That they have gone, makes me complain
For their love and true respect again
    And bounty of their weal—
Alas, the breakdown of that race
Of generous power and famous grace,
My pure support in many a place
    Bestowed with love's good-humoured zeal!
Today my frozen cheek lacks cheer,
I don't see any that call me near,
    Nor banquet, nor profit, nor a full meal.

It pays
Ill to have office nowadays,
Unthieving givers are gone, and my ways
   Are heavy and cold and long;
And as I go, not a house I've seen
Ready for praise, as it once had been—
Serious song has gone from the scene,
   There wants to hear me not one of the throng!
Pure Welsh they do not willingly use:
Twice better than the cywydd's muse
   Is the pampered note of the English tongue.

   Betrayed
To wander the world in search of aid,
I have to keep my poet's trade
   Hidden in my despair.
Alas for the broken strength of the earth,
True profit for the Muse of worth!
To follow her now means fear and dearth,
   Every hour a life of care.
To tedious dust I'll soon belong:
Farewell, dear Welsh and kindly song—
   I may not take you with me there!

JOHN DYER
1699–1757

85   *Grongar Hill*

Silent Nymph, with curious eye!
Who, the purple evening, lie
On the mountain's lonely van,
Beyond the noise of busy man;
Painting fair the form of things,
While the yellow linnet sings;
Or the tuneful nightingale
Charms the forest with her tale;

Come with all thy various hues,
Come, and aid thy sister muse;
Now, while Phoebus riding high
Gives lustre to the land and sky!
Grongar Hill invites my song,
Draw the landskip bright and strong;
Grongar, in whose mossy cells
Sweetly-musing Quiet dwells;
Grongar, in whose silent shade,
For the modest Muses made,
So oft, I have the evening still,
At the fountain of a rill,
Sate upon a flowery bed,
With my hand beneath my head;
And strayed my eyes o'er Towy's flood,
Over mead, and over wood,
From house to house, from hill to hill,
'Till contemplation had her fill.

About his chequered sides I wind,
And leave his brooks and meads behind,
And groves, and grottoes where I lay,
And vistas shooting beams of day:
Wide and wider spreads the vale,
As circles on a smooth canal:
The mountains round, unhappy fate,
Sooner or later, of all height,
Withdraw their summits from the skies,
And lessen as the others rise:
Still the prospect wider spreads,
Adds a thousand woods and meads,
Still it widens, widens still,
And sinks the newly-risen hill.

Now, I gain the mountain's brow,
What a landskip lies below!
No clouds, no vapours intervene,
But the gay, the open scene
Does the face of nature show,
In all the hues of heaven's bow;
And, swelling to embrace the light,
Spreads around beyond the sight.

JOHN DYER

Old castles on the cliffs arise,
Proudly towering in the skies!
Rushing from the woods, the spires
Seem from hence ascending fires!
Half his beams Apollo sheds
On the yellow mountain-heads!
Gilds the fleeces of the flocks,
And glitters on the broken rocks!
  Below me, trees unnumbered rise,
Beautiful in various dyes:
The gloomy pine, the poplar blue,
The yellow beech, the sable yew,
The slender fir that taper grows,
The sturdy oak with broad-spread boughs.
And beyond the purple grove,
Haunt of Phillis, queen of love!
Gaudy as the opening dawn,
Lies a long and level lawn,
On which a dark hill, steep and high,
Holds and charms the wandering eye!
Deep are his feet in Towy's flood,
His sides are clothed with waving wood,
And ancient towers crown his brow,
That cast an aweful look below;
Whose ragged walls the ivy creeps,
And with her arms from falling keeps.—
So both a safety from the wind
On mutual dependence find.
  'Tis now the raven's bleak abode;
'Tis now th' apartment of the toad;
And there the fox securely feeds;
And there the poisonous adder breeds,
Concealed in ruins, moss, and weeds:
While, ever and anon, there falls
Huge heaps of hoary mouldered walls.
Yet time has seen that lifts the low,
And level lays the lofty brow,
Has seen this broken pile complete,
Big with the vanity of state;
But transient is the smile of fate!

A little rule, a little sway,
A sunbeam in a winter's day,
Is all the proud and mighty have,
Between the cradle and the grave.

   And see the rivers how they run
Through woods and meads, in shade and sun,
Sometimes swift, and sometimes slow,
Wave succeeding wave, they go
A various journey to the deep,
Like human life, to endless sleep!
Thus is nature's vesture wrought,
To instruct our wandering thought;
Thus she dresses green and gay,
To disperse our cares away.

   Ever charming, ever new,
When will the landskip tire the view!
The fountain's fall, the river's flow,
The woody valleys, warm and low;
The windy summit, wild and high,
Roughly rushing on the sky!
The pleasant seat, the ruined tower,
The naked rock, the shady bower;
The town and village, dome and farm,
Each give each a double charm,
As pearls upon an Aethiop's arm.

   See, on the mountain's southern side,
Where the prospect opens wide,
Where the evening gilds the tide;
How close and small the hedges lie!
What streaks of meadows cross the eye!
A step methinks may pass the stream,
So little distant dangers seem;
So we mistake the future's face,
Eyed through hope's deluding glass;
As yon summits soft and fair,
Clad in colours of the air,
Which, to those who journey near,
Barren, and brown, and rough appear.
Still we tread tired the same coarse way,
The present's still a cloudy day.

O may I with myself agree,
And never covet what I see;
Content me with an humble shade,
My passions tamed, my wishes laid;
For while our wishes wildly roll,
We banish quiet from the soul:
'Tis thus the busy beat the air,
And misers gather wealth and care.

Now, even now, my joy runs high,
As on the mountain-turf I lie;
While the wanton Zephyr sings,
And in the vale perfumes his wings;
While the waters murmur deep,
While the shepherd charms his sheep;
While the birds unbounded fly,
And with music fill the sky.
Now, even now, my joy runs high.

Be full, ye courts; be great who will;
Search for Peace, with all your skill:
Open wide the lofty door,
Seek her on the marble floor,
In vain ye search, she is not there;
In vain ye search the domes of care!
Grass and flowers Quiet treads,
On the meads, and mountain-heads,
Along with Pleasure, close allied,
Ever by each other's side:
And often, by the murmuring rill,
Hears the thrush, while all is still,
Within the groves of Grongar Hill.

LEWIS MORRIS
1701–1765

86   *Poem of the Frost and Snow*   ?

Ere I freeze, to sing bravely
By Mary, is best for me;

I will make a new canto
To the terrible mist and snow,
Steel ground, grass short and withered,
The black month, the shiver-stirred.
I'm not hale here, nor wisely
Sing nor well, alas for me!
Better the awkward Muse might
Run in May or June's sunlight,
When a sweet bird in the thick
Of leaves charms with its music,
And under a birch like heaven
A fool enjoys hugging Gwen,
And his voice in a greenhall
Is found, and a poem's soul.
But not like this, I dare swear,
Does winter stay for ever.
How old it looks, white snowdrift
Hiding every slope and rift,
Everywhere cold, white each tree,
And no stream in the valley.
Water locked, no genial day,
Black frost along the footway;
Birds of the world, sad deadlock—
God's put their food under lock:
The key let Him take home then
Rightly to be kept in heaven!

ANONYMOUS

Early 18th century

87   *In Honour of St. David's Day*

When good St. David, as old writs record,
Exchanged his sacred Crosier for a sword,
Nor drum nor standard kept his men together,
Each smelt his neighbour's vegetable feather.
In heart and stomach stout they turned not crupper:
The Foe their breakfast was, the Leek their supper.

SIR CHARLES HANBURY WILLIAMS
1709–1757

88   *Verses,*
Written on seeing a Man with a heavy Load on his Back and an
Oak Leaf in his Hat on the 29th of May

> Poor fellow, what is it to you,
>   Or King, or Restoration?
> 'Twill make no difference to you,
>   Whoever rules the nation.
>
> Still must thy back support the load,
>   Still bend thy back with toil;
> Still must thou trudge the self-same road,
>   While great ones share the spoil.

EVAN THOMAS
c. 1710–*c.* 1770

89   *To the Gentlewoman of Llanarth Hall*   ⚬
(On the occasion of her shutting the Author's goat indoors for two
    days for the crime of browsing too near the mansion)

> You black-maned, horse-haired, long-faced creature,
>   What have you done to the goat, your sister?
> She's got your father's horns, got your mother's beard,
>   Why durance vile for her, you twister!

88 29th of May] King Charles II was born on 29 May 1630

WILLIAM WILLIAMS (PANTYCELYN)

1717–1791

I gaze across the distant hills   ̭

I gaze across the distant hills,
    Thy coming to espy;
Beloved, haste, the day grows late,
    The sun sinks down the sky.

All the old loves I followed once
    Are now unfaithful found;
But a sweet sickness holds me yet
    Of love that has no bound!

Love that the sensual heart ne'er knows,
    Such power, such grace it brings,
Which sucks desire and thought away
    From all created things.

O make me faithful while I live,
    Attuned but to thy praise,
And may no pleasure born of earth
    Entice to devious ways.

All my affections now withdraw
    From objects false, impure,
To the one object which unchanged
    Shall to the last endure.

There is no station under heaven
    Where I have lust to live;
Only the mansions of God's house
    Can perfect pleasure give.

Regard is dead and lust is dead
    For the world's gilded toys;
Her ways are nought but barrenness,
    And vain are all her joys.

91   *Guide me, O thou great Jehovah*   ♩

Guide me, O thou great Jehovah,
Pilgrim through this barren land;
I am weak, but thou art mighty,
Hold me with thy powerful hand:
Bread of heaven, bread of heaven,
Feed me till I want no more.

Open now the crystal fountain,
Whence the healing stream doth flow;
Let the fire and cloudy pillar
Lead me all my journey through:
Strong deliverer, strong deliverer,
Be thou still my strength and shield.

When I tread the verge of Jordan,
Bid my anxious fears subside;
Death of deaths, and hell's destruction,
Land me safe on Canaan's side:
Songs of praises, songs of praises
I will ever give to thee.

Musing on my habitation,
Musing on my heavenly home,
Fills my soul with holy longing:
Come, my Jesus, quickly come;
Vanity is all I see;
Lord, I long to be with thee!

92   *from* A View of Christ's Kingdom   ♩

THE MARRIAGE IN EDEN

And then, without his knowing, sweet sleep descended down
On all of Adam's senses, heaven's grace so girt him round;
No sense, no feeling knew he, and yet his spirit brought
Awareness that he saw what God now wrought.

WILLIAM WILLIAMS (PANTYCELYN)

For in this sleep of Adam's he thought he saw the Lord,
With whom he held such sweet converse before,
Make an incision in his breast, the left side split apart,
There opposite the root of Adam's heart.

And then draw forth a bone with his celestial hand,
And give it its own human shape, in woman's likeness planned;
And as he pressed and moulded, flesh it became and blood,
He saw she was alive; she breathed, she rose, she stood.

A human form most perfect he saw her drawing near,
Nothing seen by him till now in beauty was her peer;
His wound was closed, the blood-flow sealed,
The pain he thought he suffered, that too was quickly healed.

So lovely and so lovable, so heavenly and so fair,
The very flower of flowers, the fruit of all fruits there,
That all those blessings crowding round through all that smiling place,
As he beheld her countenance lost savour, hue, and grace.

For the beauty of each creature shone in her queenly face,
With a thousand other beauties here gathered in one place;
In her cheeks the rose of love, and splendour in her mien,
Her person and her presence delightful as serene.

So that a glow of human love, that pure and faultless flame,
Till now no part of Adam's make, into his heart's core came;
And in his soul an aching: nothing might please him more,
Save in that longed-for presence to dwell for evermore.

And so when he awoke from that sweet slumbrous spell
(The sweetest from that hour to this that ever man befell),
He looked about on every side; she must, he knew, be found,
Or to see, and then to lose her, deal a sevenfold deeper wound.

He saw her coming towards him, at her Creator's side:
Who now his manly joy may tell, his love's hot genial tide?
After the Fall how *can* we tell? And what knows lust's sick fire
Of love conceived in Paradise, its nature and its power?

Her form, which so possessed his mind, was fair as the morning's
   dawn,
That self-same woman's likeness his recent dream had drawn;
Attired in every loveliness of heaven and earth complete,
And all those traits of elegance for man's true consort meet.

She knew that to be joined with him in the holy marriage-tie
She now approached God's regent in the world;
Earth's first and foremost nuptials in Eden were at hand,
Uniquely great, uniquely fair, by heaven's great Maker planned.

When he had gazed on her this while, he turned to greet the Lord:
'Speak, speak I must,' said Adam, 'and my perfect bliss record.
O gentle, generous Maker, for mercy's works renowned,
With this dear gift thy promises beyond belief are crowned.

'All objects in the firmament, all objects on the sea,
Each gift of thine is lovely, but far more lovely she.
Now I behold a bone made of my bone arise,
And flesh of my own flesh grow tall before my eyes.

'And woman is her name, formed of a perfect man,
No mother's love shall bind him, no father's precept ban,
But he shall cleave unto his wife, one soul and but one heart,
Henceforth these twain shall be one flesh, and never, never part.

'O rose of the creation, o creature fashioned fair,
The widest bounds of nature hold nothing to compare;
Nought else was there might shape thee, save that one hand alone,
More splendid far than he that gave the bone.'

She heard and recognized his voice, she recognized his power,
In majesty of thought he towered supreme;
And yet a sweet decorum and her ever-shamefast mind
Would rightly have him seek ere he should find.

She turned, her back towards him: fair modesty whose spell
Inheres in pure and perfect grace, throve e'en before man fell:
Reverent her step, and delicate, as softly she withdrew,
Most innocent, and yet, that he would follow she well knew.

WILLIAM WILLIAMS (PANTYCELYN)

He hastened to her joyously, both in their Maker's sight,
He plied her mind with tender pleas and arguments of might;
She weighed his words, she pondered, she kindled with a fire,
The power of love and reason, these conquered Eve entire.

And honourably she yielded. What less could woman say,
Her role explained, accepted, in all things to obey?
Her Maker her bestower, how should she him deny?
And He his blessing gave them, in heavenly majesty.

'Multiply, be fruitful, the world is yours to fill,
So rule it, so possess it, the beasts bend to your will;
And in the sea all fishes, and in the sky each bird,
The quick and the unquickened heed your word.'

Heaven's high vault and each blithe star with happiness now glow,
And pour their sweetest pleasures here below;
The earth rejoiced, the earth gave thanks, the grateful signs abound,
And all the chords of nature in joyous descant sound.

The gums and scented flowers their mingled perfumes shed,
The breeze those mingled perfumes raise up and endless spread;
The trees put forth their blossoms in all their various dyes,
And heaven's zephyrs waft them through the garden paradise.

All things that there surround him, great joy their hearts upbore,
That Adam finds that half of love his world had lacked before:
All things that God had given life, each comely pard, each beast,
As though they carolled, carolled, for earth's first bridal feast.

Until such hour the nightingale began to pour his song,
To usher in those gentlest joys that to man's love belong,
And cause that star to hasten which leads night through her sphere,
A shining marriage lamp on high for earth's first bridal pair.

EDWARD DAVIES
1718–1789

93   *from* Chepstow: A Poem

(i) TINTERN ABBEY

Above Lancaut, in a sequestered dell,
Where monks, in former days, were wont to dwell,
Enclosed with woods and hills on every side,
Stands Tintern Abbey, spoiled of all her pride,
Whose mournful ruins fill the soul with awe,
Where once was taught God's holy saving law;
Where mitred abbots fanned the heavenly fire,
And shook, with hymns divine, the heavenly choir.
Though now the fallen roof admits the day,
She claims our veneration, in decay;
Looks like a goodly matron, drowned in tears,
By friends forsaken, and broke down with years.
Her fine old windows, arches, walls, unite
To fill the mind with pity and delight;
For from her splendid ruins may be seen
How beautiful this desecrated place has been.
Round the old walls observe the ivy twine,
A plant attached to grandeur in decline.
The tottering pile she clasps in her embrace,
With a green mask conceals its furrowed face,
And keeps it standing on its time-worn base.
Learn hence, O man! to act the ivy's part,
Fix deep the bright exemplar in thine heart;
To friendship's sacred call with joy attend—
Cling, like the ivy, round a falling friend!
Who, when she can no longer prop the wall,
Hugs her old friend, and both together fall.

(ii) THE CAMBRIAN SWAIN

Where cider ends there ale begins to reign,
And warms on Brecknock hills the Cambrian swain;

123   F

High on the summit of King Arthur's Chair
He quaffs his ale, and breathes untainted air;
Looks down on Hereford with scornful eyes—
Esteems himself a native of the skies:
Puffed with the thoughts of his exalted birth,
He scorns the humble mushroom sons of earth;
His high descent from time's first dawn can trace,
From Gomer down to Owen Tudor's race;
Thinks none so great on this terraqueous ball—
Himself the ragged emperor of all.
This mountain prince outflies ballooning Kings,
A cloud his car—the winds his whistling wings.

(iii) THE WILY FOX

Here, in the hollow caverns of the rocks,
Skulks, in security, the wily fox:
Snug, in his fronzy kennel, Reynard lies,
And all the snares of men and dogs defies.
In vain the hounds attempt to storm his cave—
Some enter, but, alas! there find a grave;
Some tumble down the rocks, and perish in the wave.
Confusion reigns, enraged, the baying pack,
Loud and more loud renews the vain attack.
In vain the huntsmen shout, and wind the horn—
The fox, triumphant, laughs them all to scorn.

CHRISTOPHER SMART

1722–1771

94   *To the Rev. Mr Powell*

On the non-performance of a promise he made the author of
a hare

Friend, with regard to this same hare,
Am I to hope, or to despair?

CHRISTOPHER SMART

By punctual post the letter came,
With Powell's hand, and Powell's name:
Yet there appeared, for love nor money,
Nor hare, nor leveret, nor coney.
Say, my dear Morgan, has my Lord
Like other great ones kept his word?
Or have you been deceived by squire?
Or has your poacher lost his wire,
Or in some unpropitious hole,
Instead of puss, trepanned a mole?
Thou valiant son of great Cadwallader,
Hast thou a hare or hast thou swallowed her?

But now methinks I hear you say,
(And shake your head) 'Ah, well-a-day!
Painful pre-eminence to be wise,
We wits have such short memories!
Oh, that the Act was not in force!
A horse—my kingdom for a horse!
To love—yet be denied the sport!
Oh, for a friend or two at court!
God knows, there's scarce a man of quality
In all our peerless Principality—'

But hold—for on his Country joking,
To a warm Welchman's most provoking.
As for poor puss, upon my honour,
I never set my heart upon her.
But any gift from friend to friend
Is pleasing in its aim and end.
I, like the cock, would spurn a jewel
Sent by th'unkind, th'unjust, or cruel.
But honest Powell—sure, from him
A barley-corn would be a gem.
Pleased therefore had I been, and proud,
And praised thy generous heart aloud,
If 'stead of hare (but do not blab it)
You'd send me only a Welch Rabbit.

95   *from* Jubilate Agno

FOR I WILL CONSIDER MY CAT JEOFFRY

[For I am the seed of the WELCH WOMAN and speak the truth from my heart.]

For I will consider my Cat Jeoffry.

For he is the servant of the Living God, duly and daily serving him.

For at the first glance of the glory of God in the East he worships in his way.

For this is done by wreathing his body seven times round with elegant quickness.

For then he leaps up to catch the musk, which is the blessing of God upon his prayer.

For he rolls upon prank to work it in.

For having done duty and received blessing he begins to consider himself.

For this he performs in ten degrees.

For first he looks upon his fore-paws to see if they are clean.

For secondly he kicks up behind to clear away there.

For thirdly he works it upon stretch with the fore paws extended.

For fourthly he sharpens his paws by wood.

For fifthly he washes himself.

For sixthly he rolls upon wash.

For seventhly he fleas himself, that he may not be interrupted upon the beat.

For eighthly he rubs himself against a post.

For ninthly he looks up for his instructions.

For tenthly he goes in quest of food.

For having considered God and himself he will consider his neighbour.

For if he meets another cat he will kiss her in kindness.

For when he takes his prey he plays with it to give it chance.

For one mouse in seven escapes by his dallying.

For when his day's work is done his business more properly begins.

For he keeps the Lord's watch in the night against the adversary.

For he counteracts the powers of darkness by his electrical skin and glaring eyes.

For he counteracts the Devil, who is death, by brisking about the life.

For in his morning orisons he loves the sun and the sun loves him.

For he is of the tribe of Tiger.

For the Cherub Cat is a term of the Angel Tiger.

For he has the subtlety and hissing of a serpent, which in goodness he suppresses.

For he will not do destruction, if he is well-fed, neither will he spit without provocation.

For he purrs in thankfulness, when God tells him he's a good Cat.

For he is an instrument for the children to learn benevolence upon.

For every house is incompleat without him and a blessing is lacking in the spirit.

For the Lord commanded Moses concerning the cats at the departure of the Children of Israel from Egypt.

For every family had one cat at least in the bag.

For the English Cats are the best in Europe.

For he is the cleanest in the use of his fore-paws of any quadrupede.

For the dexterity of his defence is an instance of the love of God to him exceedingly.

For he is the quickest to his mark of any creature.

For he is tenacious of his point.

For he is a mixture of gravity and waggery.

For he knows that God is his Saviour.

For there is nothing sweeter than his peace when at rest.

For there is nothing brisker than his life when in motion.

For he is of the Lord's poor and so indeed is he called by benevolence perpetually—Poor Jeoffry! poor Jeoffry! the rat has bit thy throat.

For I bless the name of the Lord Jesus that Jeoffry is better.

For the divine spirit comes about his body to sustain it in compleat cat.

For his tongue is exceeding pure so that it has in purity what it wants in musick.

For he is docile and can learn certain things.

For he can set up with gravity which is patience upon approbation.

For he can fetch and carry, which is patience in employment.

For he can jump over a stick which is patience upon proof positive.

For he can spraggle upon waggle at the word of command.

For he can jump from an eminence into his master's bosom.

For he can catch the cork and toss it again.

For he is hated by the hypocrite and miser.

For the former is afraid of detection.

For the latter refuses the charge.

For he camels his back to bear the first notion of business.

For he is good to think on, if a man would express himself neatly.

For he made a great figure in Egypt for his signal services.

For he killed the Icneumon-rat very pernicious by land.

For his ears are so acute that they sting again.

For from this proceeds the passing quickness of his attention.

For by stroaking of him I have found out electricity.

For I perceived God's light about him both wax and fire.

For the Electrical fire is the spiritual substance, which God sends from heaven to sustain the bodies both of man and beast.

For God has blessed him in the variety of his movements.

For, tho he cannot fly, he is an excellent clamberer.

For his motions upon the face of the earth are more than any other quadrupede.

For he can tread to all the measures upon the musick.

For he can swim for life.

For he can creep.

[Let Bilshan rejoice with the Leek. David for ever!
God bless the Welch March 1st 1761 n.s.]

96   *from* A Song to David

David the Son of Jesse said, and the Man who was raised up on High, the Anointed of the GOD of Jacob, and the sweet Psalmist of Israel, said,

The SPIRIT OF THE LORD spake by Me, and HIS WORD was in my Tongue.—2 Sam. xxiii. 1, 2.

O thou, that sitst upon a throne,
With harp of high majestic tone,
   To praise the King of kings;
And voice of heaven-ascending swell,
Which, while its deeper notes excel,
   Clear, as a clarion, rings:

To bless each valley, grove and coast,
And charm the cherubs to the post
   Of gratitude in throngs;
To keep the days on Zion's mount,
And send the year to his account,
   With dances and with songs:

O Servant of God's holiest charge,
The minister of praise at large,
   Which thou mayst now receive;
From thy blest mansion hail and hear,
From topmost eminence appear
   To this the wreath I weave.

He sang of God—the mighty source
Of all things—the stupendous force
   On which all strength depends;
From whose right arm, beneath whose eyes,
All period, power, and enterprise
   Commences, reigns, and ends.

Angels—their ministry and meed,
Which to and fro with blessings speed,
   Or with their citterns wait;
Where Michael with his millions bows,
Where dwells the seraph and his spouse,
   The cherub and her mate.

Of man—the semblance and effect
Of God and Love—the Saint elect
   For infinite applause—
To rule the land, and briny broad,
To be laborious in his laud,
   And heroes in his cause.

The world, the clustering spheres, He made;
The glorious light, the soothing shade,
   Dale, champaign, grove, and hill;
The multitudinous abyss,
Where Secrecy remains in bliss,
   And Wisdom hides her skill.

Trees, plants, and flowers—of virtuous root;
Gem yielding blossom, yielding fruit,
  Choice gums and precious balm;
Bless ye the nosegay in the vale,
And with the sweetness of the gale
  Enrich the thankful psalm.

Of fowl—e'en every beak and wing
Which cheer the winter, hail the spring,
  That live in peace or prey;
They that make music, or that mock,
The quail, the brave domestic cock,
  The raven, swan, and jay.

Of fishes—every size and shape,
Which nature frames of light escape,
  Devouring man to shun:
The shells are in the wealthy deep,
The shoals upon the surface leap,
  And love the glancing sun.

Of beasts—the beaver plods his task;
While the sleek tigers roll and bask,
  Nor yet the shades arouse:
Her cave the mining coney scoops;
Where o'er the mead the mountain stoops,
  The kids exult and browse.

Of gems—their virtue and their price,
Which hid in earth from man's device,
  Their darts of lustre sheathe;
The jasper of the master's stamp,
The topaz blazing like a lamp
  Among the mines beneath.

—

For ADORATION seasons change,
And order, truth, and beauty range,
  Adjust, attract, and fill:
The grass the polyanthus cheques;
And polished porphyry reflects,
  By the descending rill.

CHRISTOPHER SMART

Rich almonds colour to the prime
For ADORATION; tendrils climb,
    And fruit-trees pledge their gems;
And Ivis with her gorgeous vest
Builds for her eggs her cunning nest,
    And bell-flowers bow their stems.

With vinous syrup cedars spout;
From rocks pure honey gushing out,
    For ADORATION springs:
All scenes of painting crowd the map
Of nature; to the mermaid's pap
    The scalèd infant clings.

The spotted ounce and playsome cubs
Run rustling 'mongst the flowering shrubs,
    And lizards feed the moss;
For ADORATION beasts embark,
While waves upholding halycon's ark
    No longer roar and toss.

While Israel sits beneath his fig,
With coral root and amber sprig
    The weaned adventurer sports;
Where to the palm the jasmin cleaves,
For ADORATION 'mongst the leaves
    The gale his peace reports.

Increasing days their reign exalt,
Nor in the pink and mottled vault
    The opposing spirits tilt;
And, by the coasting reader spied,
The silverlings and crusions glide
    For ADORATION gilt.

Sweet is the dew that falls betimes,
And drops upon the leafy limes;
    Sweet Hermon's fragrant air:
Sweet is the lily's silver bell,
And sweet the wakeful tapers smell
    That watch for early prayer.

Sweet the young nurse with love intense,
Which smiles o'er sleeping innocence;
   Sweet when the lost arrive:
Sweet the musician's ardour beats,
While his vague mind's in quest of sweets,
   The choicest flowers to hive.

Sweeter in all the strains of love,
The language of thy turtle dove,
   Paired to thy swelling chord;
Sweeter with every grace endued,
The glory of thy gratitude,
   Respired unto the Lord.

Strong is the horse upon his speed;
Strong in pursuit the rapid glede,
   Which makes at once his game:
Strong the tall ostrich on the ground;
Strong through the turbulent profound
   Shoots xiphias to his aim.

Strong is the lion—like a coal
His eye-ball—like a bastion's mole
   His chest against the foes:
Strong, the gier-eagle on his sail,
Strong against tide, the enormous whale
   Emerges as he goes.

But stronger still, in earth and air,
And in the sea, the man of prayer;
   And far beneath the tide;
And in the seat to faith assigned,
Where ask is have, where seek is find,
   Where knock is open wide.

Beauteous the fleet before the gale;
Beauteous the multitudes in mail,
   Ranked arms and crested heads:
Beauteous the garden's umbrage mild,
Walk, water, meditated wild,
   And all the bloomy beds.

Beauteous the moon full on the lawn;
And beauteous, when the veil's withdrawn,
   The virgin to her spouse:
Beauteous the temple decked and filled,
When to the heaven of heavens they build
   Their heart-directed vows.

Beauteous, yea beauteous more than these,
The shepherd king upon his knees,
   For his momentous trust;
With wish of infinite conceit,
For man, beast, mute, the small and great,
   And prostrate dust to dust.

Glorious the sun in mid career;
Glorious the assembled fires appear;
   Glorious the comet's train:
Glorious the trumpet and alarm;
Glorious the almighty stretched-out arm;
   Glorious the enraptured main:

Glorious the northern lights astream;
Glorious the song, when God's the theme;
   Glorious the thunder's roar:
Glorious hosanna from the den;
Glorious the catholic amen;
   Glorious the martyr's gore:

Glorious—more glorious is the crown
Of him that brought salvation down
   By meekness, called thy Son;
Thou that stupendous truth believed,
And now the matchless deed's achieved,
   DETERMINED, DARED, and DONE.

The Invitation

Parry, of all my friends the best,
Thou who thy Maker cherishest,
Thou who regard'st me so sincere,
And who to me art no less dear;
Kind friend, in London since thou art,
To love thee's not my wisest part;
This separation's hard to bear:
To love thee not far better were.

But wilt thou not from London town
Journey some day to Northolt down,
Song to obtain, O sweet reward,
And walk the garden of the Bard?
But thy employ, the year throughout,
Is wandering the White Tower about,
Moulding and stamping coin with care,
The farthing small and shilling fair.
Let for a month thy Mint lie still,
Covetous be not, little Will;
Fly from the birth-place of the smoke,
Nor in that wicked city choke;
O come, though money's charms be strong,
And if thou come I'll give thee song,
A draught of water, hap what may,
Pure air to make thy spirits gay,
And welcome from an honest heart,
That's free from every guileful art.
I'll promise—fain thy face I'd see—
Yet something more, sweet friend, to Thee:
The poet's *cwrw* thou shalt prove,
In talk with him the garden rove,

The Invitation] sent from Northolt, in 1745, to William Parry, Deputy
Comptroller of the Mint   *cwrw*] ale

Where in each leaf thou shalt behold
The Almighty's wonders manifold;
And every flower, in verity,
Shall unto thee show visibly,
In every fibre of its frame,
His deep design, who made the same.
A thousand flowers stand here around,
With glorious brightness some are crown'd:
How beauteous art thou, lily fair!
With thee no silver can compare:
I'll not forget thy dress outshone
The pomp of regal Solomon.

I write the friend, I love so well,
No sounding verse his heart to swell.
The fragile flowerets of the plain
Can rival human triumphs vain.
I liken to a floweret's fate
The fleeting joys of mortal state;
The flower so glorious seen today
Tomorrow dying fades away:
An end has soon the flowery clan
And soon arrives the end of man;
The fairest floweret ever known
Would fade when cheerful summer's flown;
Then hither haste, ere turns the wheel!
Old age doth on these flowers steal;
Though pass'd two-thirds of autumn-time,
Of summer temperature's the clime;
The garden shows no sickliness,
The weather old age vanquishes,
The leaves are greenly glorious still—
But friend! grow old they must and will.

The rose, at edge of winter now,
Doth fade with all its summer glow;
Old are become the roses all,
Decline to age we also shall;
And with this prayer I'll end my lay,
Amen, with me, O Parry say;

To us be rest from all annoy,
And a robust old age of joy;
May we, ere pangs of death we know,
Back to our native Mona go;
May pleasant days us there await,
United and inseparate!
And the dread hour, when God shall please
To bid our mutual journey cease,
May Christ, who reigns in heaven above,
Receive us to his breast of love.

98   *Elegy for His Daughter Ellen*   ọ̀

Too sad is the grief in my heart! down my cheeks run salt streams. I have lost my Ellen of the hue of fair weather, my bright-braided merry daughter.

My darling, bright-shaped, beautiful, my warm-smiling angel; a golden speech was the infant talk of her lips, the girl of the colour of the stars (what profit now to speak?), whose form was delicate, whose voice was soft, with a happy cry to welcome her father, that orphaned man. Orphaned is her father, with a crushing wound in his pierced and broken heart, in inconsolable distress—how well I know, bound down with my yearning for her!

Since I lost my neat slender girl, all the time I mourn her sadly and ponder on her ways. When I think of her, anguish springs up and wretched affliction in my breast, my heart is faint for her and broken because of her; it is a pang to speak of her, my trim daughter, of the dear gentle words she uttered, and of her delicate pale white hands.

Farewell, my soul, my joyful gay princess, farewell again, my Nelly, pure of heart, farewell my pretty little merry daughter, my angel, resting in the midst of the graveyard at Walton, until the far assembly of the white Saints and the cry of the clamour of the unfailing Messengers. When the earth shall give up its meek and innocent, when the throngs shall be summoned from the mighty oceans, you shall get, my soul, you too, a fine gold crown and a place in the light of the host of angels.

EVAN EVANS (IEUAN FARDD, the Bard)

1731–1788

The Hall of Ifor Hael

Ifor Hael's hall, poorly it looks,
A cairn it lies in the meadow;
Thorns and the blight of thistles own it,
Briars where once was greatness.

There's no more genius there,
No bards or boards of joy;
No gold within its walls,
No mail, no generous giver.

Cold grief for Dafydd, skilled in song,
The putting of Ifor in earth;
The paths where once was singing
Are now the owl's places.

Despite the brief glory of lords,
Grandeur and walls must end;
Strange place for pride to be
Is houses in the gravel.

Ieuan Fardd] among a people short of surnames Evan Evans further identi-
fied himself as Ieuan Brydydd Hir, Evan the Tall Poet   Ifor Hael] Ifor
the Generous, fourteenth-century lord of Basaleg in South Wales   mail]
largesse   Dafydd] Dafydd ap Gwilym, though it is not certain that Ifor
was ever Dafydd's patron

EVAN LLOYD
1734–1776

100   *from* The Powers of the Pen

HELEN LIKE THE ROSE

Drawn by old Homer's hand, the rose
Still on the cheek of Helen blows.
Her beauty suffers no decay,
Nor moulders for the worm a prey;
Time's chisel cuts no wrinkles in
The velvet smoothness of her skin:
Nor can the thirst of Old Age sip
The dewy moisture of her lip;
And now her eyes as brilliant show,
As Paris saw them long ago.
For though her beauteous body must
Have crumbled into native dust,
Yet still her features live in song,
Like Hebe, ever fair and young.

ANONYMOUS
18th century

101   *The Seven Wonders of North Wales*

Pistyll Rhaeadr and Wrexham steeple,
Snowdon's mountain without its people,
Overton yew-trees, Gresford bells,
Llangollen bridge and St. Winifred's well.

101 Pistyll Rhaeadr] both words mean waterfall: the cataract of Rhaeadr
(Rhayader) in Radnorshire

EDWARD WILLIAMS (IOLO MORGANWG)
1747–1826

102   *The Poet's Arbour in the Birchwood*   ọ̀

Gloomy am I, oppressed and sad; love is not for me while winter lasts, until May comes to make the hedges green with its green veil over every lovely greenwood. There I have got a merry dwelling-place, a green pride of green leaves, a bright joy to the heart, in the glade of dark green thick-grown pathways, well-rounded and trim, a pleasant paling. Odious men do not come there and make their dwellings, nor any but my deft gracious gentle-hearted love. Delightful is its aspect, snug when the leaves come, the green house on the lawn under its pure mantle. It has a fine porch of soft bushes; and on the ground green field clover. There the skilled cuckoo, amorous, entrancing, sings his pure song full of love-longing; and the young thrush in its clear mellow language sings glorious and bright, the gay poet of summer; the merry woodland nightingale plies incessantly in the green leaves its songs of love-making; and with the daybreak the lark's glad singing makes sweet verses in swift outpouring. We shall have every joy of the sweet long day if I can bring you there for a while, my Gwenno.

ANN GRIFFITHS
1776–1805

103   *Lo, between the myrtles standing*   ọ̀

Lo, between the myrtles standing,
  One who merits well my love,
Though His worth I guess but dimly,
  High all earthly things above;
    Happy morning
  When at last I see him clear!

139

Rose of Sharon, so men name Him;
   White and red His cheeks adorn;
Store untold of earthly treasure
   Will His merit put to scorn;
     Friend of sinners,
   He their pilot o'er the deep.

What can weigh with me henceforward
   All the idols of the earth?
One and all I here proclaim them,
   Matched with Jesus, nothing worth;
     O to rest me
   All my lifetime in His love!

EMILY JANE PFEIFFER
1827–1890

104   *A Song of Winter*

Barb'd blossoms of the guarded gorse,
   I love thee where I see thee shine:
Thou sweetener of our common-ways,
And brightener of our wintry days.

Flower of the gorse, the rose is dead,
   Thou art undying, O be mine!
Be mine with all thy thorns, and prest
Close on a heart that asks not rest.

I pluck thee and thy stigma set
   Upon my breast and on my brow;
Blow, buds, and plenish so my wreath
That none may know the wounds beneath.

O crown of thorn that seem'st of gold,
   No festal coronal art thou;
Thy honey'd blossoms are but hives
That guard the growth of wingèd lives.

I saw thee in the time of flowers
   As sunshine spill'd upon the land,
Or burning bushes all ablaze
With sacred fire; but went my ways;

I went my ways, and as I went
   Pluck'd kindlier blooms on either hand;
Now of those blooms so passing sweet
None lives to stay my passing feet.

And still thy lamp upon the hill
   Feeds on the autumn's dying sigh,
And from thy midst comes murmuring
A music sweeter than in spring.

Barb'd blossoms of the guarded gorse,
   Be mine to wear until I die,
And mine the wounds of love which still
Bear witness to his human will.

JOHN CEIRIOG HUGHES (CEIRIOG)
1832–1887

105   *The Mountain Stream*   ò

Mountain stream, clear and limpid, wandering down towards the valley, whispering songs among the rushes—oh, that I were as the stream!

Mountain heather all in flower—longing fills me, at the sight, to stay upon the hills in the wind and the heather.

Small birds of the high mountain that soar up in the healthy wind, flitting from one peak to the other—oh, that I were as the bird!

Son of the mountain am I, far from home making my song; but my heart is in the mountain, with the heather and small birds.

106   *Epilogue to Alun Mabon*   &

Still the mighty mountains stand,
 Round them still the tempests roar;
Still with dawn through all the land
 Sing the shepherds as of yore.
Round the foot of hill and scar
 Daisies still their buds unfold;
Changed the shepherds only are
 On those mighty mountains old.

Passing with the passing years
 Ancient customs change and flow;
Fraught with doom of joy or tears,
 Generations come and go.
Out of tears' and tempests' reach
 Alun Mabon sleeps secure;—
Still lives on the ancient speech,
 Still the ancient songs endure.

ERNEST RHYS
1859–1946

107   *Wales England Wed*

Wales England wed, so I was bred,
 'twas merry London gave me breath.
I dreamt of love—and fame. I strove:
 but Ireland taught me love was best.
And Irish eyes, and London cries,
 and streams of Wales, may tell the rest.
What more than these I asked of life,
 I am content to have from Death.

106 Alun Mabon] The central figure in Ceiriog's pastoral poem of that name

JOHN MORRIS-JONES

1864-1929

108   *The Wind's Lament*   ♩

Sooner tears than sleep this midnight
    Come into my eyes.
On my window the complaining
    Tempest groans and sighs.

Grows the noise now of its weeping,
    Sobbing to and fro—
On the glass the tears come hurtling
    Of some wildest woe.

Why, O wind against my window,
    Come you grief to prove?
Can it be your heart's gone grieving
    For its own lost love?

109   *The North Star*   ♩

There wanders many a lighted star
    That in the high vault burns,
And every star an orbit hath
    And in that orbit turns.

There's one white star, of all the rounds
    That wheel high overhead,
And it is hung on heaven's pole
    And will not rise nor bed.

So too with me: my firmament
    Its own white star reveals,
And every sphere my heaven holds
    Round her fixed axis wheels.

W. H. DAVIES

1871–1940

110

The Kingfisher

It was the Rainbow gave thee birth,
　　And left thee all her lovely hues;
And, as her mother's name was Tears,
　　So runs it in my blood to choose
For haunts the lonely pools, and keep
In company with trees that weep.

Go you and, with such glorious hues,
　　Live with proud Peacocks in green parks;
On lawns as smooth as shining glass,
　　Let every feather show its marks;
Get thee on boughs and clap thy wings
Before the windows of proud kings.

Nay, lovely Bird, thou art not vain;
　　Thou hast no proud, ambitious mind;
I also love a quiet place
　　That's green, away from all mankind;
A lonely pool, and let a tree
Sigh with her bosom over me.

111

The Rat

'That woman there is almost dead,
Her feet and hands like heavy lead;
Her cat's gone out for his delight,
He will not come again this night.

'Her husband in a pothouse drinks,
Her daughter at a soldier winks;
Her son is at his sweetest game,
Teasing the cobbler old and lame.

'Now with these teeth that powder stones,
I'll pick at one of her cheek-bones:
When husband, son and daughter come,
They'll soon see who was left at home.'

112 *The Dumb World*

I cannot see the short, white curls
   Upon the forehead of an Ox,
But what I see them dripping with
   That poor thing's blood, and hear the axe;
When I see calves and lambs, I see
   Them led to death; I see no bird
Or rabbit cross the open field
   But what a sudden shot is heard;
A shout that tells me men aim true,
   For death or wound, doth chill me through.

The shot that kills a hare or bird
   Doth pass through me; I feel the wound
When those poor things find peace in death,
   And when I hear no more that sound.
These cat-like men do hate to see
   Small lives in happy motion; I
Would almost rather hide my face
   From Nature than pass these men by;
And rather see a battle than
A dumb thing near a drunken man.

113 *The Visitor*

She brings that breath, and music too,
   That comes when April's days begin;
And sweetness Autumn never had
   In any bursting skin.

She's big with laughter at the breasts,
   Like netted fish they leap:
Oh God, that I were far from here,
   Or lying fast asleep!

114 *A Bright Day*

My windows now are giant drops of dew,
  The common stones are dancing in my eyes;
The light is winged, and panting, and the world
  Is fluttering with a little fall or rise.

See, while they shoot the sun with singing Larks,
  How those broad meadows sparkle and rejoice!
Where can the Cuckoo hide in all this light,
  And still remain unseen, and but a voice?

Shall I be mean, when all this light is mine?
  Is anything unworthy of its place?
Call for the rat, and let him share my joy,
  And sit beside me here, to wash his face.

T. GWYNN JONES
1871–1949

115 *Argoed* ☉

I

Argoed, Argoed of the secret places . . .
Your hills, your sunken glades, where were they,
Your winding glooms and quiet towns?

Ah, quiet then, till doom was dealt you,
But after it, nothing save a black desert
Of ashes was seen of wide-wooded Argoed.

Argoed, wide-wooded . . . Though you have vanished,
Yet from the unremembering depths, for a moment,
Is it there, your whispering ghost, when we listen—

115 Argoed] not the Argoed of North Britain, nor the Argoed of Powys in
Wales, but an imagined enclave of Gaul confronting the Roman conquest

Listen in silence to the wordless speech
Where the wave of yearning clings to your name,
Argoed, Argoed of the secret places?

2

Away in Gaul, 'mid its splendour and famed
Riches, were the secret solitudes of Argoed;
There, there was inspiration and adventure,
And words, for truth's sake, chosen by the wise;
The heart of her people kept faith; richness
Of her history never lapsed to oblivion,
And sweet there and pure the old tongue continued
And custom as old as her earliest dawn.

Mystery, in that place, kept its repose
Under sleep lingering in her dark shades;
Her oaks and maples, the silent might of ages,
Sunlight, and warmth, and the crystal rain,
World-wonder, the wheel, the miracle of seasons,
Labouring green through innumerable veins;
Old history feeling its way out of them
(As it were) in perfumes and great mounds of colour
And many a murmur, till, being fused,
They became soul and quick of every inspiration,
A force, momentum of dreams half-remembered,
That to the thought of a poet gives form
When tumultuous senses have for long lodged it.

When Winter had fled the country of Gaul
And it was Spring there, come once more,
In the quiet, mysterious forests of Argoed
The old, irresistible miracle quickened;
Under the beating of its wing, slowly,
The countryside over, opened the eyes
Of buds innumerable: life broke forth
In a flood of colour, diversity of kinds,
Till the vigour of it raced in the blood of the beasts
And it rolled like fire through the hearts of men;
Which new vigour and virtue of Nature,

Despite bias of lethargy, grew in strength,
Withering, growing old, and yet renewing—
That inextinguishable flame that was given
To conquer anguish and the power of death.

Yet lovely also was Argoed when, over the trees,
Spread all the magic of autumnal pomp,
Colours innumerable, and sleepy hours,
Hours rounded in unruffled plenty,
Hours untroubled, as if the berries were ripe
On Time's branches, and the splendours of it,
Its sleep, its peace, had all been pressed into them
As the Summer gives to the juicy fruit of the vine
Its virtue and sparkle, and reckless power.

There, in the midst of her knotted oaks
And privet, was a stretch of open ground,
And webs of bright gossamer with dew upon it
Whether in Summer or Springtime, or Winter,
And under the dawn the uncountable dew
Was as if each drop were an opening eye
That glinted an instant, presently closing
As the yellow-gold sunlight rose before it
Like seaspray that dies even as it splashes,
Or sparks of a smithy, fading as they fly;
And on that open ground, a town at the wood's end,
Time out of mind the Children of Arofan
Had sustained their state purely, and never forsaken
The life of blessedness their fathers had known—
Hunting or herding, as there was need of it,
Living and suffering, as life required them,
Fearing no weakness, craving no luxuries,
Nor sought to oppress, nor feared the oppressor;
In such tranquillity, generation to generation,
They raised strong sons and lovely daughters;
Recited their tales of courage of old times,
Attentive to hear, to know the true sentence
Of words of wisdom of men that were good men
And all the mysteries hidden in musecraft;
They listened to the secret learning of Druids,

T. GWYNN JONES

Men with the gods themselves acquainted,
Who kept in the mind, generation to generation,
A wisdom of wonder-lore, not proper to be graved
On stone or wood, or preserved in writing.

Oh then, how joyous were the days
In the quiet, mysterious forests of Argoed!
But she, in her ancient piety, knew not
Gaul was pulled down, under heel of her enemies,
And already the fame of her cities had dwindled
With coming of trickery, foreigner's ways,
To tame her energy, waste an old language
And custom as old as her earliest dawn.

Argoed, Argoed of the secret places . . .
Oh then, was not a poet born in that land,
One inspired to sing her old glory,
Turning the tales of courage of old times,
Words of wisdom of men that were good men,
And all the custom hidden in musecraft,
To fit a new song, whence glory grew
Of his country and its past, and praise of its language?

And Argoed was proud that her poet was gone
To the courts of Gaul and seats of her splendour,
Reciting there of the might and valour
And manners of men, heroes of old times,
Glory and legendary past of his nation
And the gods themselves walking the world.

Argoed, Argoed, of the secret places,
How great would be the day of his homecoming
Back to them, bearing his fill
Of the gifts and honour that rightly rewarded
The new song he had fashioned his nation
In the quiet, mysterious forests of Argoed,
Argoed, Argoed of the secret places!

3

One night, from a court of Alesia city—
A citadel that, in the day of her might,
Had held back the pomp of Roman soldiers
Nor stooped to cherish the yoke of her enemies—
One night, from this court of Alesia city,
From the good cheer of the feasting within,
From the unthinking crowd's dull tumult,
Women half-naked and daintified boys
Of that famed city, that danced therein,
Their flesh and their smiles passionate with wine,
From that tight throng and its wantoning friendship
And many an eye wandering ardent in lust,
Into the air of the night, cold and dark,
A man stepped forth; he was nearing the wall,
His features weary, as if with the knowledge
He was disgraced there, instead of honoured.

In grievous pain he stood for a moment
With a weariness on him like despair,
For in his heart that night he knew
His nation's valour and ancient glory
Was lost for ever, gone from the world—
He, that had sung the chief of that glory,
Turning the tales of courage of old times,
Words of wisdom of men that were good men,
And all the custom hidden in musecraft,
To fit a new song, whence glory grew
Of his country and its past, and praise of its language—
And now, at last, vain was the labour,
For Gaul was pulled down under heel of her enemies
With coming of trickery, foreigner's ways,
To tame her vigour, waste an old language
And custom as old as her earliest dawn;
Now they could grasp neither metre nor meaning,
Nor would his singing earn him aught better
Than the sneer of a slave, awkwardly mocking him
In a patois malformed from wretched Latin—
Ah now, at last, how vain was his labour!

Slaves must be slaves, then? Ay, he that sells
Of his birthright, his be the shame of it . . .
And yet, despite that, in Argoed also
Would there be heard this broken-down Latin
On the lips of slaves, defiled and unworthy?
A generation come there not comprehending
The words of wisdom of men that were good men?
An end in that place of talent and nobleness
And all clean living, oppressed by her enemies?
This jabbering to oust a dignified language,
And vile dishonour, where men had been brave?

Then did the bright fire light in his eyes,
The blood in him boiled as that servile laughter
Again burst from within. He listened, head bent,
For a moment stayed hesitant. Then,
Like a man that can finally see before him
The day of his hopes ended for ever,
With a kind of sob, a catch in his breath,
Did he laugh also, striding on his journey,
His path soon hidden in the cold, wet gloom.

4

And tribute from Argoed was decreed, three times,
And then, three times, Argoed refused it,
For never had Argoed at all given honour
To a foreign might or brutal oppression;
The heart of her people kept faith; richness
Of her history had not lapsed to oblivion;
And none but the vilest among them would suffer
An enemy's yoke without wincing in shame,
Or bear, without blushing, its naked disgrace.

'We'll not give tribute, let forests be fired first,
Let the last of the Children of Arofan die,
Nor mock our past, nor forswear an old language,
Nor custom as old as our earliest dawn!'

To the bounds of Argoed quickly the word went,
Each of her citizens was constant and sure;

The doom was pronounced, without one to cross it,
The course was ventured, no man flinched from it;
For all his trickery, no foreigner had tribute,
Chattel nor booty, nor man to be beaten;
Nothing was found there, or only a wasteland,
Desolation of ashes, where once were wide woods.

5

Argoed, Argoed of the secret places,
Your hills, your sunken glades, where were they,
Your winding glooms and quiet towns?

Ah, quiet then, till doom was dealt you,
But after it, nothing save a black desert
Of ashes was seen of wide-wooded Argoed.

Argoed, wide-wooded . . . Though you have vanished,
Yet from the unremembering depths, for a moment,
Are you there, unconquerable soul, when we listen—

Listen in silence to the wordless speech
Where the wave of yearning clings to your name,
Argoed, Argoed of the secret places?

JOHN COWPER POWYS
1872–1963

116 *from* The Ridge

I

Aye! What a thing is the passing of Cronos, the angular-minded,
Dragging us all along, leaving us all alone,
Leaving such fields un-furrowed, such corn-shocks unbinded,
Flying sometimes like a bird, sinking sometimes like a stone!
What was that Age of Gold long ago that one of the Muses
Put into Hesiod's head prone on his face with his sheep?
And which of them was it? Aye! But his spirit refuses
Just as of old to say what goddess disturbed his sleep.

JOHN COWPER POWYS

She comes to me too this Muse who found Hesiod sleeping
To me as I climb this hill and leave the wood for the wold,
But like that old farmer-sailor her name I am keeping
Locked in the bin of my heart, shut in the keel of my hold.
As I climb I can talk aloud like the Heedless Blurter of China
Chanting without reserve my De Profundis of truth
Caring not if my voice has the major-tone or the minor,
Or if it murmurs in age what it should have shouted in youth—
Or if its tones resemble the leaves of a garden suburban
That refuses to sigh like a swamp, that refuses to roar like the sea
But insists that a man goes as mad in a bowler as under a turban
And that hearts that can bleed over wine can break over tea.

As I climb I can think aloud without rousing the fury
Of those who wish that all souls but their own were dead;
Don't they know that each man in himself is a judge and a jury,
And we all have webs of spiders under our bed?
I know myself as a toad when they swear I'm a dragon,
I know myself as a midge but they swear I'm a wasp,
I could say such things—but get me a tag to tag on
To prove that I'm a prize slow-worm and not an asp!
But I'm wriggling and shuffling now whatever they call me
Up through the autumn wood to the mountain land;
And though it is easy enough for me to meet what appals me,
I carry a horror within me that few can withstand.
And I find the sheddings of larches when first they start falling
Suit my saurian nature as a drug to my fear;
With the greenness of spruce I can sweetly lotion the mauling
I got when I burst from Bedlam to come up here.
Gold the rent ceiling through which the azure emerges,
A floor of gold is the ground—on gold I am setting my foot.
Yet these are the same larch needles that when the sap rises and surges
Burst like an emerald dew from the tree top down to the root.
And the funguses scarlet-red that had only death-dots on their faces
Lie all spongy and white, wrinkled, dissolving and done.

So I boasted. But hearing these voices and all these mysteries sharing,
I creaked like a crab in a crack, I swished like a snake in the grass,
I gaped like a village-fool or bedlam-idiot staring,
I yawned like a newt in a pond, I brayed like a dazed jack-ass.

153

For the corpse of a man and a fly have the same preposterous issue,
Parasites eating men, parasites eating flies;
And small as *these* creatures are, so sweet is their tissue
To parasites smaller still they're the Milk of Paradise.
Suppose we all uttered together, we men and maggots and midges,
One appalling howl from each body and heart and head,
Would not the scoriac caves and all of the glacial ridges
Echo with: 'Curse it—and die!' Echo with: 'Happy—the dead!'
'And what will you cry?' croaks the mud. 'And what will you wail?'
    scrapes the gravel.
'When the ripples roll on', laughs the sand, 'at Jupiter's nod?'

'You will hear in due course, my friends, when the hour comes to
    unravel
The skein of our quenchless hate for Matter and Life and God!'
Those are the wicked spells wherewith 'nephelegeretay' Zeus
Has, since he conquered Time with bolts more stupid than stone,
Fooled and enslaved and perverted to his own incredibly base use
Everything that had life from a midge to a mastodon.
Matter engenders sex and sex spends its strength in devising
Shrines for the sacred three, Matter and Life and Home;
But a wave, a wave, a wave in the vast dim gulf is arising—
Wait! Only wait! Only wait! It will sweep them away in foam!
Whisper it whisper it whisper it, to each thing that has being!
Whisper it to the bugs, whisper it to the fleas!
Tell it to things so tiny they have no eyesight for seeing
To things that scrabble and scratch, to things that tickle and tease,
The Word has gone forth through Space, yet no man wrought it or
    brought it,
Through Space and the stars in her roof, through Space and the
    seas on her floor,
And all things in fire, earth, air, and all in the seas that have caught it,
'Shake off God's love and God's hate and God's unnatural law!'
Where are the ancient gods? Let them come in their black clouds and
    white clouds!
O how they rise from the depth! O how they dive from the height!
And the dead come gibbering back to enjoy themselves in their night-
    shrouds,
And the prophets dance in their joy and the soothsayers whirl
    through the night!

And what in me says 'I am I', this silly old John as they call me
Edging my way uphill, bracken behind and in front;
I, the brother of fleas and of gnats. What on earth will befall me
When I get to the top of the ridge and have borne the brunt?
A skeleton topped by a skull and arms like a windmill in working
And the soul of a baby louse, and the heart of a hound,
Watching the dead-brown bracken, how some of it shivers in
shirking
The treacherous lash of the wind and some of it soaks on the
ground.
But keeping my eye on the ridge, an eye that can see from its
socket,
For an eye can be rusty and dead like a key in a swinging door,
I tell myself there's a hope—though God and the Universe mock it—
That when I have reached that ridge I shall find my love once more.
For the wretchedest thing alive has its own mysterious 'other',
Its other that answers its howl, its other that answers its groan,
Its other that's nearer to it than brother or father or mother,
Its other that out of a million worlds is for it alone.

John is my name, old John. It's a name not unknown in man's
story,
And yet I'm not Prester John or John who cuddled with God
Or Son-of-the-Piper John who could only play in his glory
'Over the Hills and away', nor am I the royal sod
Who swore we might 'Have the Corpus' of every man he imprisoned,
Nor John of the Cross, nor John of Thelema nor that Jack Straw;
I am the Common John, the John unbedizened,
The John who can eat dry bread and sleep on the floor.
John is my name, old John, and there's one particular reason
Why I should climb up here and aim at that crest.
I'm playing a trick on no one; I'm plotting no treason;
To be at the Death of God is my single quest.

—

II

All of a sudden ice-cold as a polar bear-skin
Grey mist fell upon me shutting me all around;
Without was a world of wonder I had no share in
Inside was the grey cold grass and a whispering sound.

Moss and gravel and naked whistling heather,
Withered bracken, whinberry, foliage wet.
I felt like a beast that had come to the end of its tether,
Like a last red flush in the west when the sun has set.
'Infinite darkness', I thought, 'before of myself I am conscious.
Infinite darkness', I thought, 'after I'm done for and gone!
I am washed from the hands of existence even as Pontius
Washed off the blood of Jesus and hurried on.
There's not a louse in the sacred beard of Moses
But yields to the same annihilation as I.
There's not a worm in the poorest of Sharon's roses
But has its hour like me and like me must die.
I can see the path and I'm still alive and climbing;
Is it nothing to be alive and be able to climb?
The labour of lifting the feet and the labour of rhyming,
Is not their power the art of marching in tune with Time?'

But what are the things on which this rhythmical marcher marches?
Stalks of heather so old that they look like bone;
Leaves of bracken bent into filigree arches,
Beds of emerald moss and pillows of stone,
And little opaque pebbles like eyeless sockets,
And crumbs of gravel the colour of mouldy bread;
And roots of old dead thorns like exploded rockets,
And whinberry leaves that are turning a curious red.
And like cut curls from the beard of an aged Titan
Wisps of lichen under the stalks of ling,
And ferns so green that trampling can only heighten
Their greenness into something beyond the Spring—
But what is this? I climb and in tune with my climbing
I tread the little mosses beneath my feet—
And I rape the virginal words to round off my rhyming . . .

THOMAS JACOB THOMAS (SARNICOL)
1873–1945

Dic Siôn Dafydd   ọ̦

He scorned his land, his tongue denied;
Nor Welsh nor English, lived and died
A bastard mule—he made his own
Each mulish fault, save one alone:
Dick somehow got, that prince of fools,
A vast vile progeny of mules.

EDWARD THOMAS
1878–1917

If I should ever by chance

If I should ever by chance grow rich
I'll buy Codham, Cockridden, and Childerditch,
Roses, Pyrgo, and Lapwater,
And let them all to my elder daughter.
The rent I shall ask of her will be only
Each year's first violets, white and lonely,
The first primroses and orchises—
She must find them before I do, that is.
But if she finds a blossom on furze
Without rent they shall all for ever be hers,
Whenever I am sufficiently rich:
Codham, Cockridden, and Childerditch,
Roses, Pyrgo and Lapwater,—
I shall give them all to my elder daughter.

119 *And you, Helen*

And you, Helen, what should I give you?
So many things I would give you
Had I an infinite great store
Offered me and I stood before
To choose. I would give you youth,
All kinds of loveliness and truth,
A clear eye as good as mine,
Lands, waters, flowers, wine,
As many children as your heart
Might wish for, a far better art
Than mine can be, all you have lost
Upon the travelling waters tossed,
Or given to me. If I could choose
Freely in that great treasure-house
Anything from any shelf,
I would give you back yourself,
And power to discriminate
What you want and want it not too late,
Many fair days free from care
And heart to enjoy both foul and fair,
And myself, too, if I could find
Where it lay hidden and it proved kind.

120 *The New House*

Now first, as I shut the door,
　　I was alone
In the new house; and the wind
　　Began to moan.

Old at once was the house,
　　And I was old;
My ears were teased with the dread
　　Of what was foretold,

Nights of storm, days of mist, without end;
   Sad days when the sun
Shone in vain: old griefs and griefs
   Not yet begun.

All was foretold me; naught
   Could I foresee;
But I learned how the wind would sound
   After these things should be.

121   *The Owl*

Downhill I came, hungry, and yet not starved;
Cold, yet had heat within me that was proof
Against the North wind; tired, yet so that rest
Had seemed the sweetest thing under a roof.

Then at the inn I had food, fire, and rest,
Knowing how hungry, cold, and tired was I.
All of the night was quite barred out except
An owl's cry, a most melancholy cry

Shaken out long and clear upon the hill,
No merry note, nor cause of merriment,
But one telling me plain what I escaped
And others could not, that night, as in I went.

And salted was my food, and my repose,
Salted and sobered, too, by the bird's voice
Speaking for all who lay under the stars,
Soldiers and poor, unable to rejoice.

122   *In Memoriam (Easter, 1915)*

The flowers left thick at nightfall in the wood
This Eastertide call into mind the men,
Now far from home, who, with their sweethearts, should
Have gathered them and will do never again.

123   *Out in the dark*

Out in the dark over the snow
The fallow fawns invisible go
With the fallow doe;
And the winds blow
Fast as the stars are slow.

Stealthily the dark haunts round
And, when the lamp goes, without sound
At a swifter bound
Than the swiftest hound,
Arrives, and all else is drowned;

And star and I and wind and deer,
Are in the dark together,—near,
Yet far,—and fear
Drums on my ear
In that sage company drear.

How weak and little is the light,
All the universe of sight,
Love and delight,
Before the might,
If you love it not, of night.

W. J. GRUFFYDD
1881–1954

124   *This Poor Man*   ọ̦

Because there was disquiet in the wind,
  And sound of ancient tears in beating rain,
And night and day within his soul entuned
  Sad mournful echoes of old cries of pain—

Because the far sea's roar on quiet nights
  Spoke praise of generations dead and gone,
    And the river's voice recites
The storied griefs and passions they had known—
Silent he passed within a haunted pale,
  Till all his comrades fled him one by one,
And he was left in mute mysterious thrall,
  To listen to strange voices all alone.

This man saw beauty where his fellows called
  The wrath of God down on an unclean world;
This man rejected all their paths to heaven
  For echoed strains of fairy pipes half-heard—
The hum of Arawn's bees from out the vineyards,
  Heavy with honeydew from down the vale,
    Nectar in hidden houses stored,
  Caer Siddi's golden ramparts on the hill.
Before he died a seat he had for feasting,
  Ensorcelled heard the choir no man may see,
Rhiannon's birds in pearled embrasures opening
  Upon the old, the unremembering sea.

125   *Gwladys Rhys*   ọ̧

Prayers, Dorcas, Fellowship, and Children's Groups!
And day and night my father's mournful tone
Tiresome as wind, the wind that day and night
Blew shrill through pine twigs round the manse. And
    mother,
Seeking the speech of heaven, knew no speech
But talk of meetings, Fellowship, and Dorcas.
What could I ever do, I, Gwladys Rhys,
The Reverend Thomas Rhys's eldest child—
The Minister of Horeb on the Moor?
What but to yearn, and ever listlessly

124 Arawn] a king of Annwfn, the Celtic Otherworld   Caer Siddi] a
caer or stronghold in the Otherworld   Rhiannon's birds] 'they that
wake the dead and lull the living to sleep' are heard of in the Mabinogion

Cast weary eyes across the down's bare slope,
And rise at mornings to await the nights,
And toss through endless nights longing for morn?
And winter, Oh my God, drawing the blinds
O'er windows at four in the afternoon,
And hear the wind bewailing through the pines,
And listen to my father's talk and mother's!

And then one day, Someone drew nigh the house,
And Something strange I felt within my heart;
The wind bewailed no longer through the pines,
Nor listlessly were weary eyes now cast
Across the down's bare slope. I felt the cool
Touch of a playful beeeze from brighter lands,
I drew the blinds across the window-pane,
Nor made reply to father's weariness,
I heard my mother render long account
Of North Wales Women's Temperance League, and then
Through snow I sallied forth without a word,
Although the wind was sighing through the pines
And it was Fellowship and Dorcas Night.

And therefore, wayfarer, 'tis here I lie
By Horeb Chapel's walls—I, Gwladys Rhys,
Aged thirty years; father and mother pass
To services, and Fellowship, and Groups,
Dorcas, Prayer Meetings, and Committees of
The North Wales Women's Temperance League; yes, here
In dark Oblivion's Vale, because the gust
Of that light playful breeze from brighter lands
Was nothing but the sigh of wind through pines.

126   *In Memoriam*   ℺

When Gwen heard at last
black Death come near,
she remembered the trees of the Gelli
dripping in the rain.

126 the Gelli] the Grove, here a place-name

W. J. GRUFFYDD

Where did all those experiences go
that she knew in days gone by,
and all the generous delight
that surrounded her on every side?

And the fears and the thousand anxieties
which she met on her way,
and many a cold disaster
that had been important to her?

And the comfort of the Promise
to all the host of believers,
when the hour should come to cross
the old black Jordan?

Of all the fulness of life,
tonight nothing will come to her
but a memory of the trees of the Gelli
dripping in the rain.

R. WILLIAMS PARRY
1884–1956

127   *The Fox* $\wr$

Near the mountain's summit, when the bells
of valley churches called all godly men,
and when the bright, still unspent sun of summer
called to the mountain, then—just then—
the silent movement of his thoughtless foot
pathed his rare beauty to our startled eye;
we did not move and did not wish to move,
frozen awhile, like a stone trinity
we stood, as with half-finished, careless stride
sudden he also stopped, the steady light
of the two eyes above the waiting paw
upon us. Then, without haste or fright,
over the ridge his ruddiness moved on,
and like a shooting star had come and gone.

128 *Miraculous Dawn* ⓠ

Strange to step straight into the beautiful dawn
And at once, without crossing Jordan, reach paradise;
To hear the hill-cuckoo call in the trees of the garden,
And see the wood-pigeons glide to the ash-tree boughs;
Strange to see the hedgehog on the peacock's lawn,
And the rabbits nibbling half a field from their tunnels,
The houseless hare at ease in the heart of the down,
The incredible heron displayed in the salty channels.
Stranger still, O sun behind the escarpment,
Should you stay where you are and keep Man in his houses,
Till the green grass came with its crowbars to split the pavement
Before the time-trained smoke came once more from his chimneys,
Saving him from his grief, and earth from his smell and stain
Before harnessing your steeds and riding the skies again.

129 *The Old Boatman of Death's River* ⓠ

Four-score and seven, so the papers say,
The solemn motor-cars that congregated
To speed some dead man just the other day
To where his cemetery plot's located.
Plump, pampered hounds! Flashy the paint on them
At any funeral in any shire,
But in their conduct and their carriage solemn
As if competing in a heavenly choir.
And when flesh wearies on the ferry-road
And the spirit's allotted time runs out,
Is it not quicker to convey a comrade
In these luxurious movers than on foot?
But on the stream, behind dust's curtain fold,
The Boatman takes his time: the boat is old.

130   *'Two Hearts Divided'*   Ọ

Listen, my dearest, once this flesh of mine
Is harvested and trundled through the flames
Of that mill's furnaces, then give my flour
To the wind of heaven, not to parish ground.
But when your own time comes, then head for home
To lie down in the churchyard with your kin,
And from the clearing filled with heather there
May scents of mountain heather cross that spot.
Before that time, your love will be sick with longing
For one who prized it and preserved it fully,
And though you'll have no later sign, my girl,
Of which it is, if I am saved or lost,
Your longing for me will be my salvation,
Your complete forgetting, my complete damnation.

131   *Branwen's Starling*   Ọ

I

O sun, be his protection,
Stand fair, o wind, this day;
O sea, take heed he does not drown
On his unresting way.

The zany of all birds,
Unholy his refrain,
And cached beneath his starling's wing
A sacred screed of pain.

Yesterday by the kitchen fire
Spry to the trough he clung;
Rehearsed and had at last by rote
A plaint in alien tongue.

See how the woman's fingers
With skilful, anxious care,
Stitch to his feather-raiment
That grievous load he'll bear.

Sad, sad, those hands once fine
Are now by torment crossed,
Hang-nailed with cruel toil,
Scarred like the hands of Christ.

Sad, sad, this ill-used queen
Who sends across the sea,
Poor sufferer in her court,
A sister's piteous plea.

II

Today at the opening door
To the sky that plea is given,
The dubious chances of the sea,
The all-or-nothing heaven.

Was it a whitefrost morning?
The gentle evening hour?
Or night, when from the moon's white wheel
A myriad starpoints shower?

No stars, no moon, no sun
Shed lustre on his way;
In the cool sweet daybreak hour
She gives him to the sky.

Before a shaft of smoke
Climbing to heaven's floor
Heralds the brutal hour that brings
The butcher to her door.

Already, like a stain
That stems from pole to pole,
He sees the aery swathe
That ties him to his goal.

And like a sea of glass
The ocean green and long,
Before from his terse-metred brief
Rounds a vast, immortal song.

R. WILLIAMS PARRY

When the uncloistered sun
Gilds mountains' symmetry,
Like distant pyramids they rear
Off deserts of the sea.

Like outcry after silence
The island's giants stand
High-pinnacled against the sky:
And over the water, land.

III

Long, long the time it lasted,
That journey not of earth:
The nothingness of sky above,
The azure void beneath.

Yet reached the land at last,
And circled overhead
Where shoreless billows crawl to seek
Rest in a riverbed.

The rank and file of men,
Their midget throng he scans,
To find one soul apart,
God's image fused with man's.

He found him at Caer Seint.
Pacing the fortress wall
He towered above the island's lords,
God-visaged, giant-tall.

Straight on his shoulder down
Alighted from high air,
A fluttering sprite from heaven above,
Ruffled his feather-gear.

And from his tired wings,
Heavier than tongue can say,
The letter in his sister's hand
Once read brooked no delay.

Caer Seint] Caernarfon, North Wales (Segontium: Caer Seint yn Arfon)

The gallant bird himself
Confirms the script's report,
Bears witness to the woman's tears,
Made scullion in her court.

The fame of his deed will spread
To earth's remotest reach:
His flight from Erin's isle,
And how he mastered speech.

IV

What happened to the brave bird
The legend does not tell:
Whether he pertly winged for home
Or crumpled in a hell

Of deadly grief and pain.
Did Brân come there once more,
Sad sexton of a starling's grave
Four-sided on the shore?

Or did he perch within the ship,
And spry among the host,
Brân's warriors pulling at the oars,
Voyaged to Ireland's coast?

Mocking the songs of the land,
Making a holiday;
A mimic in the sails
Or on the long mast-stay.

Of every bird in turn
A copied melody:
The thrush aboard the ship,
The blackbird in the sea.

And there they laugh and cheer,
The sailors on the sea,
As if no grief were in this world,
Or holy tragedy.

HUW MENAI
1887–1961

from Back in the Return

Where shall the eyes a darkness find
That is a menace to the mind
Save in the coal mine, where one's lamp
Is smothered oft by afterdamp?
Down there is found the deepest gloom,
Where Night is rotting in her tomb:
It is a being, something fraught
With evil, clutching at man's throat.
And O! the stillness underground!
Oppressive silence, ne'er a sound,
Save for a dribble here, and there,
A gas-pop, or a gust of air,
When idle are the wheels, and one
Sits down to listen, all alone;
When one will welcome, with surprise
The unmelodious squeaks of mice;
From Baltic beetles gladly take,
And Jaspers, what small sounds they make—
To face it one must needs be brave,
This silence of an old world's grave!
But when full work is on, the air
Does a more homely garment wear,
When sometimes, floating on the foul,
Comes 'Jesu Lover of my Soul',
Between spat Baccy Juice and smut,
From hewers squatting in the 'cut';
Or, coming from more distant stalls,
The rhythmic tap of mandril falls
Upon the ear till one would swear
The pulse of *Earth* was beating there.

Back in the foul Return
Where bodies of men burn
Out, out before their time,
Where dead is the sublime,

And murdered is the soul
To keep the brute alive;
Where lust is in control,
Still young the sensitive
Must die, still young—
His songs unsung!

The mine is no romantic place—
It stinks of Hell from sump to 'face';
A honeycomb of headings, stalls,
Airways, drifts, and rubbish walls.
Intake fresh, and foul Return,
Which lighted once becomes an urn
For human ashes!

. . . . . .

'A beershop meeting! I've no name;
From out the guts of Chance I came
To shock the goody-goody lot
Who snivel o'er the devil's pot;
Who make from out the devil's wash
An appetizing pulpit hash;
A beershop meeting! I've no name;
A child of sin, a child of shame,
Conceived among the slush and slime
And born to fester into crime
Had I not caught some luck in time
And struck against the sucking in
Of milk that was three parts of gin.
The milk flew up to mother's head,
And, in her tantrums, she fell dead.
And so I was, a babe, set free
To cut my teeth on Charity;
To bite an artificial teat,
To suck my fists, to find my feet
Implanted firmly on the Rates,
The bogey-bo of Christian States;
A nuisance, nameless brat, unwanted!
Yet through it all for life I panted,
For life, for life to tell the Fates
They had no right to burden Rates.

'I grew to corduroy, and clogs;
I grew a skill for cutting logs;
I grew to bite the Labour Master
Who kicked me for not cutting faster,
To butt Tramp Major in the belly
For trying a cure on me with skilly;
I grew to break my share of stones;
I grew a hatred in my bones;
And as one booked to bend my spine
I left the Workhouse for the mine.'

T. H. PARRY-WILLIAMS
1887–1975

133   *A Christmas Carol*   ♀

Close to a quarter of a century since then,
The Christmas morning my father crossed the glen.

A hell of a thing for Death on that holiday
To come by, like Father Christmas on his way,

And take him from us, and with a single stroke
Turn the Feast of Birth to a Feast of Death, as a joke.

We knew Death was all around; but there was no need
For the sneak to show his power, and suddenly

Leap from his carriage, like a monkey-on-a-stick,
Or a circus midget demonstrating a trick,

And this after we had learned all our lives
My Lord Death was the well-bred model of how one behaves.

But possibly, nevertheless, in this matter I
Am taking him the wrong way. Who can say why

The Lord of Terror himself took it into his skull to play
A trick on us on the Son of Man's birthday?

Maybe his Grace, after all, intended no mockery,
But was investing his visit with public dignity.

I beg his pardon for doubting his meaning this way:
I saw him come from the glen with his summons a later day,

One Sunday morning to gather my mother to his breast.—
I've let myself go completely: I take back my words.

134 *These Bones* Ǫ

What shall we be, sweet, you and I,
When the flesh that clothed us is all laid by?

Desire must end when the blood grows chill,
Love and shame and the wayward will.

No joy of touch nor of sight again:
When the nerves have rotted there's no more pain.

No dream can stir, no sweet song rise
In a gaping skull with sightless eyes.

Of all that in you is now my pride
The white teeth only will then abide.

Naught of us when life is done
But bone and bone by speechless bone;

Mute heaps, under the laughing sky,
In fleshless slumber we two shall lie.

Bones only we are—yes, laugh, sweet face,
Till the white teeth flash from their lurking place;

Laugh loud and long; but, the laughter o'er,
Bones only you'll be for evermore,

T. H. PARRY-WILLIAMS

Bones on bones, my beautiful maid,
And kite and raven about your head;

And none to ask of the flying year,
'Where is the flesh that rioted here?'

135   *Llyn y Gadair*   𝒒

The jaunty traveller that comes to peer
Across its shallows to the scene beyond
Would almost not see it. Mountains here
Have far more beauty than this bit of pond
With one man fishing in a lonely boat
Whipping the water, rowing now and then
Like a poor errant wretch, condemned to float
The floods of nightmare never reaching land.

But there's some sorcerer's bedevilling art
That makes me see a heaven in its face,
Though glory in that aspect has no part
Nor on its shore is any excelling grace—
Nothing but peat bog, dead stumps brittle and brown,
Two crags, and a pair of quarries, both closed down.

A. G. PRYS-JONES
1888–

136   *St. Govan*

I

St. Govan, he built him a cell
By the side of the Pembroke sea,
And there, as the crannied seagulls dwell,
In a tiny, secret citadel
He sighed for eternity.

135 Llyn y Gadair] a lake near the poet's birthplace at Rhyd-Ddu, Snowdon

II

St. Govan, he built him a cell
Between the wild sky and the sea,
Where the sunsets redden the rolling swell
And brooding splendour has thrown her spell
On valley and moorland lea.

III

St. Govan still lies in his cell,
But his soul, long since, is free,
And one may wonder—and who can tell—
If good St. Govan likes Heaven as well
As his cell by that sounding sea?

137   *A Day which Endures Not*
                 (after Elidir Sais)

As for me
I have seen Llywelyn
With all the valiant men of Wales around him,
His armies like the hosts of Merfyn;
And have marched with chieftains mustering
On the steep hills and the deep lowlands,
Pillars of war were they all, and mighty.

I have seen brave youth in battle
And heard the high thunder of horsemen:
I have drunk rare wines from chalices,
With rich meats laid on fine linen
In the bountiful palaces of princes.

I have listened to much oratory,
To the jewelled harmonies of bards
Declaiming their lyrics in intricate metres:
I have heard the songs and satires
Of itinerant minstrels,
And shared the merriment of maidens
Tickled by the saucy tales of story-tellers.

A. G. PRYS-JONES

I have had my fill also
Of festivals and ceremonies,
The gleam and glitter of contests
Where strong men rejoiced in their prowess
And the clever in their cunning.

But now all these are gone
Like dreams in the morning:
And thus, each soul must journey forth
At the time of his reckoning
From a day which endures not:
In this the lord of many lands
The poor man's master
Gains no reprieve, no respite:
He passes through the portal with the peasant.

LLEWELYN WYN GRIFFITH
1890–

138   *Silver Jubilee*
1939

Faint now in the evening pallor
answering nothing but old cries,
a troop of men shouldering their way
with a new tune I recognize

as something near to Flanders, but far
from the dragon years we killed
to no purpose, scattered seed
on land none but the devil tilled.

That a poet sings as his heart beats
is no new word, but an ancient tale.
Grey shadows on the pavement
and Europe sick of its own bale.

I have no answer, no rising song
to the young in years who are old
with our arrogance, our failure.
Let it be silence: the world is cold.

139   *from* The Barren Tree

From his own solitude to the world unheeding
the poet offers the silence within the word.
The legions march to another conquest
bannered and sung by the old regime,
the massed cohorts, the main body
at ease and noisy, their arms slung
and the maps folded, the limbers full.
They have forgotten the dark hours
behind the skyline, the thin screen
of solitary men groping, silent,
poised on the sharp edge of danger;
brief signal to the rear, advance,
the search resumed, the column safe.
This is the ease of life, the strong comfort
of the long familiar, no question asked
of first cost, the victory accepted.

The word made spirit by the poet's agony
'mad with much heart' pervades
in cheaper use the common speech,
bright bird of thought wounded and tamed.
So must it be, and a new livery
found for the young perception, a body
shaped afresh by other hands
to walk in glory through the growing dusk.
His dusk another's dawn.
                    The word
made music, counterpoint and chord
new-woven to a pattern free
as the morning air; made image
of the sharp vision, the strict colour,
a line exact to the known shape.

Look back to the past, if need be,
but not with longing. Hope dies,
and with it faith, where comfort lives.
Now in the autumn the barren tree,
the bare standards, clear outline
the sole promise of a new world
stripped of the unrelated, the heart prepared
as the mind for the spare grandeur of form,
disciplined into the quick speech.
                    Truth
crisp as the clean breath of winter
the one reward, the only measure:
still to come the perfected beauty
apt to its time and mood.
                    Spring
and desire let be, age alone
and acceptance now. The large demand
foregone, the distance unexplored.
His feet upon the trodden path
release the eye, inward the search
and in the end the still glory found,
the word made silent.
                    Here begins . . .

WILFRED OWEN
1893–1918

140   *The Send-Off*

Down the close, darkening lanes they sang their way
To the siding-shed,
And lined the train with faces grimly gay.

Their breasts were stuck all white with wreath and spray
As men's are, dead.

Dull porters watched them, and a casual tramp
Stood staring hard,
Sorry to miss them from the upland camp.
Then, unmoved, signals nodded, and a lamp
Winked to the guard.

So secretly, like wrongs hushed-up, they went.
They were not ours:
We never heard to which front these were sent.

Nor there if they yet mock what women meant
Who gave them flowers.

Shall they return to beatings of great bells
In wild train-loads?
A few, a few, too few for drums and yells,
May creep back, silent, to still village wells
Up half-known roads.

141   *The Show*

> We have fallen in the dreams the ever-living
> Breathe on the tarnished mirror of the world,
> And then smooth out with ivory hands and sigh.
>   W. B. YEATS

My soul looked down from a vague height, with Death,
As unremembering how I rose or why,
And saw a sad land, weak with sweats of dearth,
Gray, cratered like the moon with hollow woe,
And pitted with great pocks and scabs of plagues.

Across its beard, that horror of harsh wire,
There moved thin caterpillars, slowly uncoiled.
It seemed they pushed themselves to be as plugs
Of ditches, where they writhed and shrivelled, killed.

By them had slimy paths been trailed and scraped
Round myriad warts that might be little hills.

From gloom's last dregs these long-strung creatures crept,
And vanished out of dawn down hidden holes.

(And smell came up from those foul openings
As out of mouths, or deep wounds deepening.)

On dithering feet upgathered, more and more,
Brown strings, towards strings of gray, with bristling spines,
All migrants from green fields, intent on mire.

Those that were gray, of more abundant spawns,
Ramped on the rest and ate them and were eaten.

I saw their bitten backs curve, loop, and straighten,
I watched those agonies curl, lift, and flatten.
Whereat, in terror what that sight might mean,
I reeled and shivered earthward like a feather.

And Death fell with me, like a deepening moan.
And He, picking a manner of worm, which half had hid
Its bruises in the earth, but crawled no further,
Showed me its feet, the feet of many men,
And the fresh-severed head of it, my head.

142 *Disabled*

He sat in a wheeled chair, waiting for dark,
And shivered in his ghastly suit of grey,
Legless, sewn short at elbow. Through the park
Voices of boys rang saddening like a hymn,
Voices of play and pleasure after day,
Till gathering sleep had mothered them from him.

*   *   *

About this time Town used to swing so gay
When glow-lamps budded in the light blue trees,
And girls glanced lovelier as the air grew dim,—
In the old times, before he threw away his knees.
Now he will never feel again how slim
Girls' waists are, or how warm their subtle hands;
All of them touch him like some queer disease.

*   *   *

There was an artist silly for his face,
For it was younger than his youth, last year.
Now, he is old; his back will never brace;
He's lost his colour very far from here,
Poured it down shell-holes till the veins ran dry,
And half his lifetime lapsed in the hot race,
And leap of purple spurted from his thigh.

       *   *   *

One time he liked a blood-smear down his leg,
After the matches, carried shoulder-high.
It was after football, when he'd drunk a peg,
He thought he'd better join.—He wonders why.
Someone had said he'd look a god in kilts,
That's why; and may be, too, to please his Meg;
Aye, that was it, to please the giddy jilts
He asked to join. He didn't have to beg;
Smiling they wrote his lie; aged nineteen years.
Germans he scarcely thought of; all their guilt,
And Austria's, did not move him. And no fears
Of Fear came yet. He thought of jewelled hilts
For daggers in plaid socks; of smart salutes;
And care of arms; and leave; and pay arrears;
Esprit de corps; and hints for young recruits.
And soon, he was drafted out with drums and cheers.

       *   *   *

Some cheered him home, but not as crowds cheer Goal.
Only a solemn man who brought him fruits
Thanked him; and then inquired about his soul.

       *   *   *

Now, he will spend a few sick years in Institutes,
And do what things the rules consider wise,
And take whatever pity they may dole.
Tonight he noticed how the women's eyes
Passed from him to the strong men that were whole.
How cold and late it is! Why don't they come
And put him into bed? Why don't they come?

Miners

There was a whispering in my hearth,
    A sigh of the coal,
Grown wistful of a former earth
    It might recall.

I listened for a tale of leaves
    And smothered ferns;
Frond-forests; and the low, sly lives
    Before the fauns.

My fire might show steam-phantoms simmer
    From Time's old cauldron,
Before the birds made nests in summer,
    Or men had children.

But the coals were murmuring of their mine,
    And moans down there
Of boys that slept wry sleep, and men
    Writhing for air.

And I saw white bones in the cinder-shard,
    Bones without number;
Many the muscled bodies charred;
    And few remember.

I thought of some who worked dark pits
    Of war, and died
Digging the rock where Death reputes
    Peace lies indeed.

Comforted years will sit soft-chaired
    In rooms of amber;
The years will stretch their hands, well-cheered
    By our lives' ember.

The centuries will burn rich loads
    With which we groaned,
Whose warmth shall lull their dreaming lids
    While songs are crooned.
But they will not dream of us poor lads
    Left in the ground.

The Deluge 1939

I

The tramway climbs from Merthyr to Dowlais,
Slime of a snail on a heap of slag;
Here once was Wales, and now
Derelict cinemas and rain on the barren tips;
The pawnbrokers have closed their doors, the pegging clerks
Are the gentry of this waste;
All flesh had corrupted his way upon the earth.

My life likewise, the seconder of resolutions
Who moves from committee to committee to get the old country
    back on its feet;
Would it not be better to stand on the corner in Tonypandy
And look up the valley and down the valley
On the flotsam of the wreckage of men in the slough of despair,
Men and tips standing, a dump of one purpose with man.

Where there have been eyes there is ash and we don't know that
    we're dead,
Our mothers thoughtlessly buried us by giving us milk of Lethe,
We cannot bleed like the men that have been,
And our hands, they would be like hands if they had thumbs;
Let our feet be shattered by a fall, and all we'll do is grovel to a
    clinic,
And raise our caps to a wooden leg and insurance and a Mond
    pension;
We have neither language nor dialect, we feel no insult,
And the masterpiece that we gave to history is our country's M.P.s.

II

The dregs rose out from the empty docks
Over the dry ropes and the rust of cranes,
Their proletarian flood crept
Greasily civil to the chip shops,
It crawled as blood about the feet of policemen

And spread into a pool of silicon spittle
Through the faceless valleys of the industry of the dole.

Rain poured its assiduous needles
On the soft palms of the old hands of the coalface,
The hail scattered upon the leathern breasts
Of barren mothers and their withered babies,
Cows' milk was turned into umbrella sticks
Where rickets bowed the legs of lasses;
Young lads on the dole were given the pension of old men.

And yet the moon kept her ways
And Apollo washed his hair in the dew
As when the wise men had their respite
Between the hills of the Sabines centuries before;
But Saturn, Jove, and the golden age of the Babe,
In their turn came to an end; the clumsy destruction
Of the ashes of chimneys and the vain birth
Have drowned the stars under the slime of the dole.

III

In the beginning, it wasn't like this we saw things:
We thought that it was only the redeeming ebb and flow, the
   thrifty dislocation
That our masters blessed as part of economic law,
The new scientific order that had cast out natural law
Like Jove usurping Saturn, the summitless progress of being.
And we believed our masters: we put the vestments of priests upon
   them,
Tortoise-shell spectacles and plus-fours to preach,
To preach the sanctity of the surplus of the unemployed and the
   flexible providence of prices;
And one day in seven, not to break a courteous ritual,
We offered an hour to the sweet magic of the old world
And in the Pantheons of the fathers we sang psalms.

Then, on Olympus, in Wall Street, nineteen-twenty-nine,
At their infinitely scientific task of guiding the profits of fate,
The gods decreed, with their feet in the Aubusson carpets,
And their Hebrew snouts in the quarter's statistics,
That the day had come to restrict credit in the universe of gold.

Earth's latest gods did not know
That they had breached the last floodgates of the world;
They did not see the men marching,
The clenched fists and angry arms,
Rank upon rank through the anguish of Vienna,
The deaf fury of the wrangling in Munich,
Nor the dragging feet or the weak twittering of the march
Of the somnambulant unemployed and their stunned agony.

But it had been; the woe of mothers wailing,
The noise of men like the noise of dogs moaning,
And multitudes casting themselves without hope
To the starless ditch and the mute sleep.
The mind of leaders, it lapsed,
There was a sowing of dragons' teeth in Europe,
Bruening went out from their seething passions,
From the sniggering of Basle and its foul usurers,
The husks and shells of that rout of Geneva,
To his long silent fast and exile.
And the frail rabble, the halfpenny demos,
The issue of the dogs and football pools,
It filled its belly with pictures of sluts
And with the rotten husks of radio and newspapers.

But in the region of Ebro the sky grew dark,
Blood turned to wine for our hungry passions,
And paralysis of will froze over the defect
Of the powerless wretches of Basle and Geneva.
We saw we'd been betrayed. The power of our gods
Was the vile illusion of fiends festering our end;
Felling and raping the excellence of reason
And our peerless idol, man without fetters;
The splendid religion of the masters of the planet,
Man's faith in man—that was extinguished:
We the hard-faced great ones—computers
        Of stars and suns above,
        The journey was without gain,
        All ecstasy vain,
Our black refuge is the deluge of despair.

And from over the sea comes the noise of tanks gathering.

145 *Mary Magdalene* ♩

'Touch me not'

About women no one can know. There are some,
Like this one, whose pain is a locked sepulchre;
Their pain is buried in them, there is no fleeing
From it and no casting it off. No ebb
Nor tide of their pain, a dead sea without
Movement upon its depth. Who—is there anyone—
Who will take away the stone from this sepulchre?

See the dust on the path lamely dragging:
No, let her be, Mary moves towards her peace,
Deep calls unto deep, a grave for a grave,
A carcass drawing towards a carcass in that unhappy morning;
Three days was this one in a grave, in a world that died
In the cry in the afternoon. It is finished,
The cry that drew blood from her like the barb of a sword.

It is finished. Finished. Mary fell from the hill
To the emptiness of the last Easter, to the pit of the world
That was no other than a sepulchre, with its breath in a mute grave,
Mary fell into the startling death of perdition,
A world without a living Christ, the horrifying Sabbath of creation,
The abyss of the hundred thousand centuries and their end,
Mary lay down in the grave of the trembling universe.

In the hollow of the night of the senses, in the cauldron of smoke;
The great hair that had wiped his feet turned white,
All the flowers of memory withered except the rain of blood;
Cloud upon cloud upon her, and their foul odour
A cinder in her throat, wasting her sight
Until with their sharp horror God was extinguished,
In the dying together, in the burying together, frowned upon.

See her, Christ's Niobe, drawing with her towards the hill
The rock of her pain from the leaden Easter

Through the dark dawn, through the cold dew, through the heavy
  dust,
To the place where there is a stone that is heavier than her torn
  heart;
Uneasily the awkward feet find their way over thorns
With the annoyance of tears doubling the mist before her,
And her hands reaching out to him in barren grief.

One luxury only under the heavens remains,
One farewell caress, the gentleness of memory, one
Last carnality, sad-consoling, dear,
To weep again over His flesh,
Anoint the feet and wash the harsh wounds,
To kiss the ankles and wipe them once more with her hair,
To touch Thee, Rabboni, O Son of Man.

Let us have pity upon her. He did not pity her.
Beyond pity is that burning, pure love,
That steels the saint through pain on pain,
That pursues the flesh to its stronghold in the soul, and its home
In the heavenly spirit, and its lair in the most holy,
That burns and kills and tears unto the last scrimmage,
Until it bares and embraces its prey with its steel claws.

Little did she know, six days before Easter,
Whilst pouring the wet, precious nard upon him,
That truly 'it was against the day of my burying she kept this';
She did not think, so dear was his praise of her task,
That he would never again touch her with feet or hands;
Thomas could put hand to his thigh; but she, despite her weeping,
Henceforth under the woe of the Bread would come to her the
  broken body.

Behold her in the garden at the first colour of dawn;
She turns her eyes to the cave; runs,
Runs to the remains of her joy. Ah, does she believe,
Does she believe her eyes? That the stone is down,
And the sepulchre empty, the grave bare and silent;
The first lark rising over the bald hill
And the nest of her heart empty, and escheat.

Her moan is as monotonous as a dove's,
Like Orpheus mourning Eurydice
She stands amongst the roses and cries without mourning
'They have taken away my Lord, taken Him away,'
To disciple and angel the same cry
'And I know not where they have laid Him,'
And to the gardener the same frenzy.

Made wild. Broken. She sank within herself in her grief.
The understanding reels and reason's out of joint, until
He comes and snatches her out of the body to crown her—
Quickly like an Alpine eagle falling on its prey—
With the love that moves the stars, the power that is a Word
To raise up and make alive: 'and He said unto her, Mary,
She turned herself and said unto Him, Rabboni.'

146   *To the Good Thief*   ♀

You did not see Him on the mountain of Transfiguration
    Nor walking the sea at night;
You never saw corpses blushing when a bier or sepulchre
    Was struck by his cry.

It was in the rawness of his flesh and his dirt that you saw Him,
    Whipped and under thorns,
And in his nailing like a sack of bones outside the town
    On a pole, like a scarecrow.

You never heard the making of the parables like a Parthenon of
    words,
    Nor his tone when He talked of his Father,
Neither did you hear the secrets of the room above,
    Nor the prayer before Cedron and the treachery.

It was in the racket of a crowd of sadists revelling in pain
    And their screeches, howls, curses and shouts
That you heard the profound cry of the breaking heart of their
    prey:
    'Why hast thou forsaken me?'

You, hanging on his right; on his left, your brother;
    Writhing like skinned frogs,
Flea-bitten petty thieves thrown in as a retinue to his shame,
    Courtiers to a mock king in his pain.

O master of courtesy and manners, who enlightened you
    About your part in this harsh parody?
'Lord, when you come into your kingdom, remember me,'—
    The kingdom that was conquered through death.

Rex Judaeorum; it was you who saw first the vain
    Blasphemy as a living oracle,
You who first believed in the Latin, Hebrew and Greek,
    That the gallows was the throne of God.

O thief who took Paradise from the nails of a gibbet,
    Foremost of the nobilitas of heaven,
Before the hour of death pray that it may be given to us
    To perceive Him and to taste Him.

147   *Ascension Thursday*   ọ̀

What's on this May morning in the hills?
Look at them, at the gold of the broom and laburnum
And the bright surplice on the shoulders of the thorn
And the intent emerald of the grass and the still calves;

See the candlestick of the chestnut tree alight,
The groves kneeling and the mute birch a nun,
The cuckoo's two-notes over the shining hush of the brook
And the form of the mist bending from the censer of the
   meadows:

Come out, you men, from the council houses before
The rabbits scamper, come with the weasel to see
The elevation of the unblemished host
And the Father kissing the Son in the white dew.

148 *The Pine* ♩

The lake of night is still in the valley,
In its windless trough;
Orion and the Dragon sleep on its leaden face,
The moon rises slowly and swims drowsily on her way.

Behold now the hour of her ascension.
Immediately you shine before her with the lance of your leap
From root to tip under her journey
Shooting to the heart of darkness like the Easter Candle under
   its flame:
Hush, the night stands about you in the cool chancel
And the bread of heaven crosses the earth with its blessing.

DAVID JONES
1895–1974

149 *from* In Parenthesis

And to Private Ball it came as if a rigid beam of great weight
flailed about his calves, caught from behind by ballista-baulk
let fly or aft-beam slewed to clout gunnel-walker
below below below.
   When golden vanities make about,
                     you've got no legs to stand on.
   He thought it disproportionate in its violence considering
the fragility of us.
   The warm fluid percolates between his toes and his left boot
fills, as when you tread in a puddle—he crawled away in the
opposite direction.

It's difficult with the weight of the rifle.
Leave it—under the oak.
Leave it for a salvage-bloke
let it lie bruised for a monument

dispense the authenticated fragments to the faithful.
It's the thunder-besom for us
it's the bright bough borne
it's the tensioned yew for a Genoese jammed arbalest and a
scarlet square for a mounted *mareschal*, it's that county-mob
back to back. Majuba mountain and Mons Cherubim and
spreaded mats for Sydney Street East, and come to Bisley
for a Silver Dish. It's R.S.M. O'Grady says, it's the soldier's
best friend if you care for the working parts and let us be 'av-
ing those springs released smartly in Company billets on wet
forenoons and clickerty-click and one up the spout and you
men must really cultivate the habit of treating this weapon with
the very greatest care and there should be a healthy rivalry
among you—it should be a matter of very proper pride and

  Marry it man! Marry it!
Cherish her, she's your very own.

  Coax it man coax it—it's delicately and ingeniously made
—it's an instrument of precision—it costs us tax-payers
money—I want you men to remember that.

  Fondle it like a granny—talk to it—consider it as you would
a friend—and when you ground these arms she's not a rooky's
gas-pipe for greenhorns to tarnish.

  You've known her hot and cold.
You would choose her from among many.
You know her by her bias, and by her exact error at 300, and
by the deep scar at the small, by the fair flaw in the grain,
above the lower sling-swivel—
but leave it under the oak.

Slung so, it swings its full weight. With you going blindly on
all paws, it slews its whole length, to hang at your bowed neck
like the Mariner's white oblation.

  You drag past the four bright stones at the turn of Wood
Support.

It is not to be broken on the brown stone under the gracious
tree.

  It is not to be hidden under your failing body.

  Slung so, it troubles your painful crawling like a fugitive's
irons.

The trees are very high in the wan signal-beam, for whose slow gyration their wounded boughs seem as malignant limbs, manœuvring for advantage.

The trees of the wood beware each other
and under each a man sitting;
their seemly faces as carved in a sardonyx stone; as undiademed princes turn their gracious profiles in a hidden seal, so did these appear, under the changing light.

For that waning you would believe this flaxen head had for its broken pedestal these bent Silurian shoulders.

For the pale flares extinction you don't know if under his close lids, his eye-balls watch you. You would say by the turn of steel at his wide brow he is not of our men where he leans with his open fist in Dai's bosom against the White Stone.

Hung so about, you make between these your close escape.

The secret princes between the leaning trees have diadems given them.

Life the leveller hugs her impudent equality—she may proceed at once to less discriminating zones.

The Queen of the Woods has cut bright boughs of various flowering.

These knew her influential eyes. Her awarding hands can pluck for each their fragile prize.

She speaks to them according to precedence. She knows what's due to this elect society. She can choose twelve gentle-men. She knows who is most lord between the high trees and on the open down.

Some she gives white berries
some she gives brown
Emil has a curious crown it's
made of golden saxifrage.
Fatty wears sweet-briar,
he will reign with her for a thousand years.
For Balder she reaches high to fetch his.
Ulrich smiles for his myrtle wand.
That swine Lillywhite has daisies to his chain—you'd hardly credit it.

She plaits torques of equal splendour for Mr. Jenkins and Billy Crower.

Hansel with Gronwy share dog-violets for a palm, where they lie in serious embrace beneath the twisted tripod.

Siôn gets St. John's Wort—that's fair enough.

Dai Great-coat, she can't find him anywhere—she calls both high and low, she had a very special one for him.

Among this July noblesse she is mindful of December wood —when the trees of the forest beat against each other because of him.

She carries to Aneirin-in-the-nullah a rowan sprig, for the glory of Guenedota. You couldn't hear what she said to him, because she was careful for the Disciplines of the Wars.

At the gate of the wood you try a last adjustment, but slung so, it's an impediment, it's of detriment to your hopes, you had best be rid of it—the sagging webbing and all and what's left of your two fifty—but it were wise to hold on to your mask.

You're clumsy in your feebleness, you implicate your tin-hat rim with the slack sling of it.

Let it lie for the dews to rust it, or ought you to decently cover the working parts.

Its dark barrel, where you leave it under the oak, reflects the solemn star that rises urgently from Cliff Trench.

It's a beautiful doll for us
it's the Last Reputable Arm.

But leave it—under the oak.

Leave it for a Cook's tourist to the Devastated Areas and crawl as far as you can and wait for the bearers.

Mrs. Willy Hartington has learned to draw sheets and so has Miss Melpomené; and on the south lawns,
men walk in red white and blue
under the cedars
and by every green tree
and beside comfortable waters.

But why dont the bastards come—
Bearers!—stret-cher bear-errs!

or do they divide the spoils at the Aid-Post.
  But how many men do you suppose could bear away a third
of us:
drag just a little further—he yet may counter-attack.

Lie still under the oak
next to the Jerry
and Sergeant Jerry Coke.
  The feet of the reserves going up tread level with your fore-
head; and no word for you; they whisper one with another;
pass on, inward;
these latest succours:
green Kimmerii to bear up the war.

Oeth and Anoeth's hosts they were
who in that night grew
younger men
younger striplings.

The geste says this and the man who was on the field . . . and
who wrote the book . . . the man who does not know this
has not understood anything

150   *from* The Sleeping Lord

            Tawny-black sky-scurries
                            low over
            Ysgyryd hill
            and over the level-topped heights
                            of Mynydd Pen-y-fal
                            cold is wind
                            grey is rain, but
                            BRIGHT IS CANDELA
            where this lord is in slumber.

            Are his wounded ankles
                            lapped with the ferric waters
            that all through the night
                            hear the song

from the night-dark seams
                    where the narrow-skulled *caethion*
labour the changing shifts
                    for the cosmocrats of alien lips
in all the fair lands
                    of the dark measures under
(from about Afon Lwyd
                    in the confines of green Siluria
westward to where the naiad of the *fons*-head
                    pours out the Lesser Gwendraeth
high in the uplands
                    above Ystrad Tywi
and indeed further
                    west & south of Merlin's Caer
even in the lost cantrevs
                    of spell-held Demetia
where was Gorsedd Arberth, where the *palas* was
                    where the prince who hunted
met the Prince of Hunters
                    in his woof of grey
and gleam-pale dogs
                    not kennelled on earth-floor
lit the dim chase).

Is the Usk a drain for his gleaming tears
who weeps for the land
                    who dreams his bitter dream
for the folk of the land
does Tawe clog for his sorrows
do the parallel dark-seam drainers
                    mingle his anguish-stream
with the scored valleys' tilted refuse.
Does his freight of woe
                    flood South by East
on Sirhywi and Ebwy
                    is it southly bourn
on double Rhondda's fall to Taff?

caethion] slaves   Afon Lwyd, Lesser Gwendraeth, Usk, Tawe, Sirhywi,
Ebwy, Rhondda Fawr, Rhondda Fach, Taff] South Wales river names

DAVID JONES

Do the stripped boughs grapple
above the troubled streams
                    when he dream-fights
his nine-day's fight
                    which he fought alone
with the hog in the Irish wilderness
                    when the eighteen twilights
                    and the ten midnights
and the equal light of the nine mid-mornings
were equally lit
                    with the light of the saviour's fury
and the dark fires of the hog's eye
which encounter availed him nothing.

                         Is his royal anger ferriaged
where black-rimed Rhymni
                    soils her Marcher-banks
                    Do the bells of St. Mellon's
toll his dolour
                    are his sighs canalled
where the mountain-ash
                    droops her bright head
for the black pall of Merthyr?

Do Afan and Nedd west it away
does grimed Ogwr toss on a fouled ripple
his broken-heart flow
                    out to widening Hafren
                    and does she, the Confluence Queen
queenly bear on her spume-frilled frock
a maimed king's sleep bane?
                    Do the long white hands
would you think, of the Brides of the Déssi
                    unloose galloons
to let the black tress-stray
                    web the pluvial Westerlies
does the vestal flame in virid-hilled Kildare
                    renew from secret embers

Rhymni, Afan, Nedd]   South Wales river names   Hafren] Severn:
Sabrina

195

DAVID JONES

the undying fire
                    that sinks on the Hill Capitoline
   Does the wake-dole mingle the cormorant scream
does man-*sídhe* to fay-queen bemoan
the passage of a king's griefs, westing far
                    out to moon-swayed Oceanus
   Does the blind & unchoosing creature of sea know the
marking and indelible balm from flotsamed sewage and the
seeped valley-waste?
   Does the tide-beasts' maw
                    drain down the princely tears
with the mullocked slag-wash
                    of Special Areas?
Can the tumbling and gregarious porpoises
does the aloof and infrequent seal
                    that suns his puckered back
                    and barks from Pirus' rock
tell the dole-tally of a drowned *taeog* from a
Gwledig's golden collar, refracted in Giltar shoal?

   Or, is the dying gull
                    on her sea-hearse
that drifts the oily bourne
                    to tomb at turn of tide
her own stricken cantor?
Or is it for the royal tokens
                    that with her drift
that the jagg'd and jutting *morben* echoes
and the deep hollows of *yr ogof* echo
and the hollow eddies echo:
                    Dirige, dirige
and out, far, far beyond
on thalassic Brendan's heaving trackway
to unknown *insulae*
                    where they sing
their west In Paradisums
                    and the corposants toss

taeog] serf   Gwledig] the title of a ruler or sovereign   *morben*]
promontory   *yr ogof*] the cave

196

for the dying flax-flame
> and West-world glory
in transit is.

But yet he sleeps:
> when he shifts a little in his fitful
slumber does a covering stone dislodge
> and roll to Reynoldstone?
When he fretfully turns
> crying out in a great voice
> in his fierce sleep-anger
does the habergeon'd sentinel
> alert himself sudden
from his middle-watch doze
> in the crenelled traverse-bay
of the outer bailey wall
> of the *castell* these Eingl-Ffrancwyr
call in their lingua La Haie Taillée
that the Saeson other ranks
> call The Hay
(which place is in the tongue of the men of the land,
Y Gelli Gandryll, or, for short, Y Gelli)
does he cock his weather-ear, enquiringly
lest what's on the west wind
> from over beyond the rising contours
may signify that in the broken
> *tir y blaenau*
these broken dregs of Troea
> yet again muster?
Does he nudge his drowsing mate?
> Do the pair of them
say to each other: 'Twere not other
than wind-cry, for sure—yet
> best to warn the serjeant below.
He'll maybe
> warn the Captain of the Watch
or some such
> and he, as like as not

Saeson] Saxons, Englishmen   *tir y blaenau*] 'region of (river) sources',
i.e. Uplands

may think best to rouse the Castellan
           —that'll please him
in his newly glazed, arras-hung chamber
           with his Dean-coal fire
nicely blazing
snug with his dowsabel
           in the inner keep
Wont improve his temper, neither, come the morrow
with this borough and hereabouts alerted
           and all for but a wind-bluster.
Still, you never know, so
           best stand on Standing Orders
and report to them as has the serjeancy
the ordering and mandate, for
you never know, mate:
           wind-stir may be, most like to be
as we between us do agree
           or—stir of gramarye
or whatsomever of ferly—who should say?
           or solid substantiality?
you never know *what* may be
           —not hereabouts.
No wiseman's son *born* do know
           not in these whoreson March-lands
of this Welshry.

Yet he sleeps on
           very deep is his slumber:
how long has he been the sleeping lord?
are the clammy ferns
           his rustling vallance
does the buried rowan
           ward him from evil, or
does he ward the tanglewood
           and the denizens of the wood
are the stunted oaks his gnarled guard
           or are their knarred limbs
strong with his sap?
Do the small black horses
           grass on the hunch of his shoulders?

Are the hills his couch
                    or is he the couchant hills?
Are the slumbering valleys
                    him in slumber
                    are the still undulations
the still limbs of him sleeping?
Is the configuration of the land
                    the furrowed body of the lord
are the scarred ridges
                    his dented greaves
do the trickling gullies
                    yet drain his hog-wounds?
Does the land wait the sleeping lord
                    or is the wasted land
that very lord who sleeps?

D. GWENALLT JONES (GWENALLT)
1899–1968

151   *Rhydcymerau*   ♀

Near Rhydcymerau,
On the land of Esgeir-ceir and the fields of Tir-bach,
They have planted the saplings
                    to be trees of the third war.

I call to mind my grandmother at Esgeir-ceir
As she sat, pleating her apron, by the fireside,
The skin yellow and dry on her face
                    like a manuscript of Peniarth,
And the Welsh on her old lips the Welsh of Pantycelyn.
A bit of the Puritan Wales she was of last century.
Although I never saw him, my grandfather
Was a 'character'—a brisk and twinkling little creature,
Fond of his pint;
He'd just strayed in from the eighteenth century.
They reared nine children,

D. GWENALLT JONES (GWENALLT)

Poets, deacons, and Sunday School teachers,
And each, locally, a man of authority.

My Uncle Dafydd used to farm Tir-bach,
And was, besides, a poet, the countryside's rhymester;
His song to the little cockerel was famous in those parts:
>   '*The little cock goes scratching*
>   *In the garden here and there.*'
It was to him I went for the summer holidays
To watch the sheep and fashion lines of cynghanedd,
Englynion, and eight-line stanzas
            of eight-seven measure.
He brought up eight children,
The eldest son a minister with the Calvinistic Methodists,
And he too wrote verses.
In our family we'd a real nestful of poets.

And by this time there's nothing there but trees.
Impertinent roots suck dry the old soil:
Trees where neighbourhood was,
And a forest that once was farmland.
Where was verse-writing and scripture
            is the South's bastardized English.
The fox barks where once cried lambs and children,
And there, in the dark midst,
Is the den of the English minotaur;
And on the trees, as if on crosses,
The bones of poets, deacons, ministers, and teachers of
            Sunday School
Bleach in the sun,
And the rain washes them, and the winds lick them dry.

152 *The Earth* ℔

How intimate was the earth in days gone by,
As intimate as a neighbour, and fluent in the Welsh dialects;
We kept her in good shape, and we brought forth her colours,
The colours of wheat, barley and oats;

D. GWENALLT JONES (GWENALLT)

We put a wave in her hair with the ploughshare,
And combed its sheen with the clanking harrows:
To the romantic ears of city poets
The bubbling brook was a distant yearning,
And in lonely mountain retreats
They built hospices fit for angels between two worlds.

The earth has been converted into a vast laboratory,
The cowshed into a factory where cogged cattle chew the cud;
No longer do the haughty bulls come
To mount cows on heat in the farmyard;
Their time-honoured dung-heaps have disappeared,
An alien chemistry is making the soil barren.

The earth no longer speaks man's homely language:
Her speech has a machine's syntax; the grammar of x, y, z:
The neighbour has become a distant monster;
A monster whose hydrogenous jaws
Are about to swallow the husbandry and civilization of man.

Pylons where once were angels
And the concrete damming the brook.

153   *Cymru*   ọ̀

The dust of all the saints of the ages
And the martyrs lies in your bosom;
It was you who gave them breath,
And you who took it from them.

The angels would be walking here,
Their footprints on your roadways,
And the Holy Spirit nested
Dovelike in your branches.

Poets heard on wind and breeze
His cry of sacrifice, His gasp of pain,
And in the middle of your forests
The Tree of the Cross was seen.

153 Cymru] Wales

D. GWENALLT JONES (GWENALLT)

His resurrection was your springtide,
Your summer was His green salvation,
And in the winter of your mountains
He raised tabernacles of grace.

The dew and rain of Providence He shed
On your cornfields and your oats,
And His glory was on the trappings
And the bridles of your chargers.

Your boats and your sailing-ships
Glided over the seaways,
With merchandise of Calvary
Stowed beneath their deckboards.

God chose you for his handmaiden,
And called on you for witness;
And He inscribed His Covenant
On your doors and your doorposts.

Your saints are a noble fellowship,
They love you, and you love them,
And you gather them under your wing
Like chicks in under the hen.

19th–20th centuries

Twelve Englynion

154   *Merioneth*   ♀

Living paradise of flowers, land of honey, land of violets and blossoms,
land rich in crops, land of nut-bushes, and dear land of the hills.

JOHN MACHRETH REES (MACHRETH), *fl.* 1900

155   *Heather Flowers*   ♀

Gaily they grow, the quiet throng, fair gems of the realm of sun and
wind, the hanging bells of the high crags, flowers of the rocks, like
cups of honey.   ELISEUS WILLIAMS (EIFION WYN), 1867–1926

156   *The Pole Star*   ♀

A lamp are you, above all stars of night, to guide sailors in the dusk;
lovely is your colour, sweet maid, standing in the doorway of the Pole.
                    COSLETT COSLETT (CARNELIAN), 1834–1910

157   *Nightfall*   ♀

Silence brought by the dark night: Eryri's
    Mountains veiled by mist:
    The sun in the bed of brine,
    The moon silvering the water.
        WALTER DAVIES (GWALLTER MECHAIN), 1761–1849

158   *Eaves*   ♀

Giving, while the rain lasts, soft noises
    Like a thousand being milked;
    When the roof's thick with ice,
    Under it, strange teats appear.
                    ELLIS JONES, 20th century

157 Eryri] Snowdonia

159   *Old Age*   ̧

'Old age never comes alone'—it brings sighs
    With it, and complaining,
    And now a long lack of sleep,
    And, soon enough, long slumber.
                    JOHN MORRIS-JONES, 1864–1929

160   *The Beloved*   ̧

A fair cheek under a merry blue eye, two brows
    Under a lattice of yellow curls:
    For sure the sons of heaven were called
    To splinter the gold for her hair.
                    DAVID ROBERTS (DEWI HAVHESP), 1831–1884

161   *An Old Woman*   ̧

Scant and straggling her yellow hair, from her lip
    The bees' honey has fled;
    Withered and poor is the white skin,
    Briars instead of roses.
                    D. GWENALLT JONES (GWENALLT), 1899–1968

162   *On a Woman*   ̧

Stay! Beneath your feet is a wonder of women,
    Diligent, ardent in affection.
    You too, reader, on this spot
    Lay you love's roses.
                    ROBERT WILLIAMS (TREBOR MAI), 1830–1877

163   *Life's Morning*   ǭ

Life's morning—O, how quickly—fleets
    Hope on its adventure:
  It would sing less if it saw the pain
  Of the flowers beneath the scythe.

               HOWELL ELVET LEWIS (ELFED), 1860–1953

164   *The Hour of Sleep*   ǭ

The hour of sleep has come silently, the hour of forgetfulness,
    Over the ranks of being,
  A drowsy hour on the heavy shore
  Of the sea men call mortality.

             ROBERT ELLIS (CYNDDELW), 1812–1875

165   *On a Soldier killed in the Great War*   ǭ

He gave his strength and his loveliness for his country,
    For peaceful hearths:
  Mourn for him, all ye his companions!
  A shapely lad is quiet dust.

               R. WILLIAMS PARRY, 1884–1956

RICHARD HUGHES
1900–1976

166   *Gipsy-Night*

To Pamela Bianco, 1919

When the feet of the rain tread a dance on the roofs,
And the wind slides through the rocks and the trees,
And Dobbin has stabled his hoofs
In the warm bracken-litter, noisy about his knees;

And when there is no moon, and the sodden clouds slip over;
Whenever there is no moon, and the rain drips cold,
And folk with a shilling of money are bedded in houses,
And pools of water glitter on Farmer's mould;
   Then pity Sally's girls, with the rain in their blouses:
   Martha and Johnnie, who have no money:
   The small naked puppies who whimper against the bitches,
   The small sopping children who creep to the ditches.

But when the moon is run like a red fox
Cover to cover behind the skies;
And the breezes crack in the trees on the rocks,
Or stoop to flutter about the eyes
Of one who dreams in the scent of pines
At ease:
   Then would you not go foot it with Sarah's girls
   In and out the trees?
   Or listen across the fire
   To old Tinker-Johnnie, and Martha his Rawnee,
   In jagged Wales, or in orchard Worcestershire?

167   *Winter*

   Snow wind-whipt to ice
     Under a hard sun:
   Stream-runnels curdled hoar
     Crackle, cannot run.

   Robin stark dead on twig,
     Song stiffened in it:
   Fluffed feathers may not warm
     Bone-thin linnet.

   Big-eyed rabbit, lost,
     Scrabbles the snow,
   Searching for long-dead grass
     With frost-bit toe:

RICHARD HUGHES

Mad-tired on the road
    Old Kelly goes:
Through crookt fingers snuffs the air
    Knife-cold in his nose.

Hunger-weak, snow-dazzled,
    Old Thomas Kelly
Thrusts his bit hands, for warmth,
    'Twixt waistcoat and belly.

J. KITCHENER DAVIES
1902-1952

168 *from* The Sound of the Wind that is Blowing ♩

Today,
there came a breeze thin as the needle of a syringe,
cold, like ether-meth on the skin,
to whistle the other side of the hedge from me.
For a moment, I felt a numbness in my ego,
like the numbness of frost on the fingers of a child
climbing the stiles of Y Dildre and Y Derlwyn to school;
only for a moment, and then the blood flowed again,
causing a burning pain such as follows numbness on fingers,
or ether-meth on the skin after the first shiver.
    It did not come through the hedge
though I could recognize its sound blowing,
and feel on my face
the foul breath of graves.
But the hedge is thick-trunked, and high,
and its shelter firm so that nothing comes through it,
—nothing at all but the sound of the wind that is blowing.

—

Ha!
You are the one who always boasted

Y Dildre, Y Derlwyn] the Little (or Leafy?) Homestead, the Oak Grove

you had no fear of dying,
but were afraid of having to suffer pain.
You've never had a chance
to fear either dying or suffering pain
—never once, because of the hedge's shelter around you.
    Yes, yes, like everyone in your time,
you've seen people in pain—other people—
without the wind that is blowing getting to you deeper than the skin,
with nothing at all occurring within what you are.
    To you, something for them, the others,
is suffering and death,
every testing of faith, indeed,
just like acting in a play.
    Remember coming back in Tre-wern's trap
from mother's funeral? You got to sit on the front seat with Ifan
and everyone felt sorry for you—a hero, so little, so noble.
Not everyone gets a chance to lose his mother at six,
and learn to act so early.

⚊

The land of Y Llain was on the high marsh
on the border between Caron-is-Clawdd and Padarn Odwyn
slanting from Cae Top down to Y Waun,
and beyond Cae Top was a glade of dark trees—
pines and tall larches—to break the cold wind,
the wind from the north.
And there were the small four-sided fields
like a checkerboard, or a patchwork quilt,
and around each of the fields, a hedge.

    My father planted the hedges farthest from the house,—
the hedges of Cae Top and Cae Brwyn,—
myself a youngster at his heels
putting the plants in his hand:
three hawthorns and a beech-tree,
three hawthorns and a beech-tree in turn;
his feet measuring the distance between them along the top of the ditch,
squeezing them solidly into the loose earth-and-chalk.

Y Llain] the Strip   Cae Top, Y Waun] Top Field, the Moor
Field   Cae Brwyn] Field of the Rushes

J. KITCHENER DAVIES

Then the patterned wiring outside them—
the square posts of peeled oak-wood
sunk deep in the living earth—
and I getting to turn the wiring-engine on the post
while he did the stapling,
the hammer ringing in my ears with the pounding.
And I daring on the sly
to send a telegram back over the taut wires
to the other children at the far end of the ditch,
the note of music raising its pitch
with each turn I gave the old wiring-engine's handle.

 My grandfather, said my father, had planted the Middle Fields—Cae
   Cwteri, Cae Polion, Cae Troi—
but generations we knew nothing at all about,
except for the mark of their handiwork on Cae Lloi and Cae Moch,
had planted the tall strong stout-trunked trees round the house,
and set sweet-plums here and there in the hedges.

 And there we children would be
safe in a fold in the ditch under the hedges,
the dried leaves a coverlet to keep us warm
(like the babes in the story hidden with leaves by the birds).
The breeze that trickled through the trunks of the hedges
was not enough to ruffle the wren's and the robin's feathers:
but above the hedges and the trees, above the house,
aloft in the firmament, the wind was
tumbling the clouds, tickling them till their white laughter
was unruly hysteria like children on a kitchen floor,
till the excess of play turns suddenly strange
and the laughter's whiteness scowls, and darkens,
and the tears burst forth, and the clouds escape
in a race from the wind, from the tickling and the tumbling,
escaping headlong from the wind's provocation—
the pursuing wind outside me,
and I fast in the fold in the ditch beneath the leaves
listening to its sound, outside,
with nothing at all occurring within what I am
because of the care and craft of generations of my fathers

Cae Cwteri, Cae Polion, Cae Troi] Ditch Field, Post Field, Turning Field
Cae Lloi, Cae Moch] Field of the Calves, Field of the Pigs

planting their hedges prudently to shelter me in my day,—
nothing—despite my wishing and wishing.

—

You went down to Tonypandy for the Strike and the General Strike,
for the jazz carnival, and the football of strikers and police,
to the soup-kitchens and the cobbling,
the jumble-sales for sore-ridden Lazarus,
helping to sweep the spare crumbs from the boards for the dogs
     under the tables,
pouring alms like rubble on the tips
or sowing basic slag on allotment gardens of ashes
to cheat the arid earth into synthetic fertility.
   Then the hedges had fallen and the gaps were gaping
and the narrow streets were like funnels for the whirlwind's
pouring, blast upon blast,
to whip the corners and raise the house-tops,
whirling wretches like empty chip-bags
from wall to post, from gutter to gutter;
the cloudbursts and the hailstones choking every grating
splitting the pavements and flooding through the houses,
and clanging like a death-rattle in the windowless cellars;
and famine like a stiff brush sweeping through the homes
from front to back and over the steep garden-steps,
down the back-lane to the river's floods,—
the wrack and black water pouring from the cwm,
to be battered and spewed to the level land's hollow banks,
rubbish abandoned to rot.
   And there you were like Canute on the shore,
or like Atlas in a coal pit
with your shoulder under the rocks holding back a fall,
or with your arms outstretched between the crag and the sea
shouting 'Hey! Hey!'
in the path of the lunatic Gadarene swine.

   Remember,
there was no need for you, more than the rest of your fellows,
to scream your guts out on a soap-box
on the street-corners and the town squares;
no call for you to march in the ranks of the jobless,

your dragon-rampant hobnobbing with the hammer-and-sickle;
there was no need for you
to dare the packed Empire and the Hippodrome on Sunday evening,
—you a dandy bantam on the dung-heap of the spurred cocks
of the Federation and the Exchange—
but you ventured,
and ventured in elections for the town Council and the County
and Parliament all in good time
against Goliath in a day that knows no miracle.
   Yes, I confess that I tried to hurl myself
into the whirlwind's teeth to be raised on its wings
and be blown by its thrust where it willed
as a hero to save my land.
Since it not only blows where it will, the tempest,
but blows what it will before it where it will;
'Who at its birth knows its growth,' I said.

—

O shut your mouth with your lying self-pity
and your false unctuous boasting.
You know it was a giddy game with squirrels
to slip from bough to bough;
and a more reckless game to hover in the wind
like a paper kite, a string tying you safe to the ground,
where the crowd gathered to marvel at your feats
on the pantomime trapeze and your clowning in the circus.
Not riding the whirlwind, but hanging to the mane
of a little roundabout horse, that was your valour,
a child's wooden-horse in a nursery,
and the sound of the wind no more to you than the crackle of recorded
      music from vanity fair's screeching machine.

—

May God who is slow to anger forgive my presumption,
pulpiteering, singing hymns and praying to Him,
who wore about Him the breeze of the day,
to come to tickle my ribs to wake me from my dozing.
I asked for the wind that was probing the skeletons
to breathe into my dry bones the breath of life.
I pleaded with the tempest to winnow with the whirlwind
my desert's draff, and drench with its rains

211

my wasteland's parched ground till it bloomed as a garden.
I appealed with fervour without considering—
without considering (O terror) He could take me at my word,
He could take me at my word and answer my prayer.
And answer my prayer.

 Listener to prayers, be merciful,
and turn a deaf ear from hearing my false petition,
from having to create a saint from my fickle earth.

 Steadfast One, with never a shadow of change,
do not smother me with single-minded devotion,
but let me gather honey with dilettante piety,
from flower to flower in Your garden while the weather is fair.

 Supreme Doctor,
who carve with Your scalpel between the bone and the marrow,
hold Your hand from the treatment that would carve me
free from my fellows and my neighbourhood,
wholly apart from my household and family.

 Pilgrim of the wilderness,
do not set my steps on the martyrs' wandering path
and the loneliness of the soul's pilgrimage.

 O Father of Mercies, be merciful,
leave me my comrades' company, and my acquaintances' trust,
and the strength that is mine in my wife and children.

 Familiar of grief, do not grieve me
by baring the soft soul, leaving it skinned
of the protective shell that has been settling for half a century
as a layer of sloth over the spirit's daring,
so that no grain of sand might disturb the core of my ego.

 I am too old and too weak and too happy in my world,
too comfortable, too self-satisfied,
to be shaken into the unknown in the teeth of Your whirlwind.
Let me lurk in the shelter of my hedges, and the folds in my ditch.

 King of kings, legions of angels flying at Your summons,
volunteers glorying in Your livery—Your crown of thorns and Your
  five wounds with which I have wounded You—
stop pressing me and conscripting me to the hosts that are Yours
on the Sea of Glass in the Far Country.

 Atonement who purchased freedom,
leave me in the cocktail parlour to shake them and share them
with the trivial customs of my civility

and the manners in fashion among my people.
Do not tangle me in my prayers like Amlyn in his vow,
do not kill me at the altar by whose horns I have blasphemed,—
but let me, I pray, despite each wound, however hideous,
fail to be a saint.
   '*Quo vadis, quo vadis*,' where are you going?
Stop pursuing me to Rome, to a cross, my head towards the ground.
   O Saviour of the lost,
save me, save me, save me,
from Your baptism that washes the Old Man so clean:
keep me, keep me, keep me,
from the inevitable martyrdom of Your elect.
Save and keep me
from the wind that is blowing where it will.
So be it, Amen,
   and Amen.

GWILYM R. JONES

1903–

169   *Psalm to the Creatures*   Ọ

Let us celebrate the single-cloaked beings
Content in their coats of fur and feathers,
And the swimmers who wish no other garb than their skins.

Let us sing
The ants who do not reckon their hours of diligence
On their hillock-years
Because a forest of heather-bells
Sweetens their labour;
The common newt is wiser than men,
And the woolly-bear who zig-zags on cabbage wine.

---

168 Amlyn] *Amlyn ac Amig* is the Welsh version of the famous medieval metrical romance of destructive vows and tangled sacrifices, *Amis and Amiloun*

Let us envy
The cormorant who bathes in the precious colours
Of sunset on the sea;
The salmon, sunny his bliss,
Who knows how to breed young without charity;
The moon-drunk owl
Proud because night is the other side of day,
And the squirrel who slinks to Annwfn
To doze away the long barren season.

Let us weave praise
For the birds of legends,
Noah's dove and Branwen's starling
Who carried the mail across the waters,
And Rhiannon's birds
Who gave merry nights to the dead
And caused bones to dance.

And let us not forget
The hopping gander
Who gave a few quills to Bishop Morgan,
Giving the haven of its wings to the Welsh language,
And the mother-hens who provided
Welsh beds with their warmth.

EUROS BOWEN

1904–

170   *Winged in Gold*   ǫ

The bird swerved dapple-white in the blue sky, paused, and then
swam into the commotion of rays between the sun and the lake.

The sleek wings vibrating in the still air stirred a venture in the

169 Annwfn] the Celtic Otherworld   Branwen's starling] see no. 131
and note   Rhiannon's birds] see no. 124   Bishop Morgan] of
Llandaff and later St. Asaph's, translated the Bible into Welsh, 1588

heart, and yielding to the brightness, every fear fled with the wonder of the flight.

But the bird began to falter in the flame, and then slipped and fell into the fire on the water below, and all the feathers were burned in the intense ferment.

Blinded by the light, the soul followed the thrill, the sparkle drawing it into the embracing brightness, until all the senses fell into the shimmering fire.

The imagination, as it watched, weakened with discontent the mind adding faults to regrets at the sight of body and wings perishing like dross in the embers.

Then with a sudden turn, out of the scattered ashes the bird rose high, all winged in purified gold.

171   *Nettles in May*   ǫ

Do nettles mar the month of May,
When crooks of fern are swans' heads?
A breeze haunts the walls of burial grounds,
And the last of the churchyard's daffodils hang
Like the scent of bluebells
Bent on following the wind:
Long-necked briers in possession
Swim
Over crested rhododendrons,
And the hawthorn's green blood
Is sadness of the colour of a slow ache,
The sadness of long evenings.
Does thunder, trailing its substance over mountain,
Destroy early summer,
And the day heavy now on the lake's bed?
No, not so.
There's a flash over the astonished earth,
Like stinging a tired hand,
It needles the swollen cloud,
Injecting the shanks of grass—pain's restitution.

172   *Blackthorn*   ọ

The bush, a gathering smoke
on blackthorn. Yesterday a sharp wind
blew over its cold impoverished branches,
and like solitariness
turning into a slow thaw when the sun warms,
it just melted today
on the sun's return into a mass of white.
By the time of the evening blaze
all its feathered branches were scorched
with the heat from the fire,
like the solitariness
we ourselves know in the world
as a burning bush,
burned, but not consumed.

GWYN WILLIAMS
1904–

173   *from* Aspects of Now

Today has it all, sunshine,
snow to the north, the lake
frozen over, the Sunday leisure
of friends, a silence like

a seizing up of the megamachine,
a forgetting of towns.
Broken pieces of ice skipped
over ice sing no tunes

but hit one high sweet note
each time they touch the ice,
hold the note to its twittering death
halfway over the lake. Wild geese

are frozen in attitudes, improbably
secure from the fowler. Nothing forages.
Five of us and a happy dog
alone now on the crisp ridges.

The barrowed dead live for us,
we banish fear of raucous change
to this lake, this moorland, this
Wales, dismiss the sly danger

with laughter, love, attention
to now, as given us by all
our senses, the sight, the sound,
the feel, the taste, the ice-sweet smell

of a cerulean winter's day
on water, skin and grass
now we are together and absolute
in this moment of grace.

WALDO WILLIAMS
1904–1972

174   *A Summer Cloud*   ♀

'Durham', 'Devonia', 'Allendale',—their houses, those,
And every name is the same name,
The name of slow time's ancient place and fountainhead
In the cave that is brighter than the sky
And the house that is out in all weathers.

A fistful of larks flung here and there
To summon the day's companions,
In their midst was a noble blood-line's honour.
Hail the great far-faring steed with his crescent of hair
And his lovely gait a lordly cywydd's glory,
To us as well it seemed he showed his shoes.

WALDO WILLIAMS

And look, up from the river,
Meek dignity, milch dignity, like the night,
Bending the rushes with her udder,
And bearing the heavens on her horns.
And in our midst, lords of words, were some greater
Than history's kings and queens.
Secureness, in all weathers, was the weather,
Loving-kindness was the house.

Once a mighty giant's spirit descended
Through the summer sun, at the hour you could not surmise,
Striking the crew of climbers from their ropes of song,
Not mist at play, nor night at play,
A damp, grey stillness,
The one that awaits us,
See, it came, without coming.
It closed the mountains each side of the pass,
And after, after
The mountains like years moved farther away
In a world too silent for living.
The rushes grew like trees and perished
In a world too enormous for being.
No over there. Only me is here.
Me
with no father or mother or sisters or brother,
And the beginning and the end closing about me.

Who am I? Who am I?
A stretch of my arms and then, between their two stumps
The dread of thinking about myself,
And the question that is the ground of all questions:
Who is this?
The sound of water. I wade it for an answer.
Nothing but the cold current.

Through the ditch homewards if it is homewards.
I hefted the gate-post, still doubtful,
And O, before I reached the back-door,
The sound of building a new earth, new heaven,
Were my mother's clogs on the kitchen floor.

218

In Two Fields ϙ

Where did it roll in from, that sea of light
Whose floor was on Weun Parc y Blawd and Parc y Blawd?
After I had quested long in the dark land
Where did it come from, that which had always existed?
Or who, who was the archer, the sudden revealer?
The sea's unroller was the field's life-giving hunter.
From on high, above bright-billed curlews, the wary swerving of
    lapwings,
He brought me the great stillness.

He stirred my soul where nothing stirred
Save the sun's thought spinning the haze into verse,
The ripe gorse clicking in the hedgerows,
The host of rushes dreaming the blue sky.
Who is it calls when the imagination wakens,
'Rise, walk, dance, look on creation!'?
Who is it hides in the midst of the words?
—These things on Weun Parc y Blawd and Parc y Blawd.

And when the huge and fugitive pilgrim clouds
Were red with the sunset of November's tempest,
Down in the ash and the sycamore parting the fields
The song of the wind was deep as deep silence.
Who is there, amidst that extravagant splendour?
Who stands there, containing it all?
Each witness's witness, each memory's memory, life of each life.
The tranquil calmer of the turmoil of self.

Till the whole world came sometimes into the stillness,
And on the two fields his people walking;
And through them, among them, there spread all around them
The spirit rising out of concealment and making all one;

Weun Parc y Blawd and Parc y Blawd] two flowery moorland fields with
rush-grown areas near the poet's childhood home in Pembrokeshire. 'It was
in a gap between these two fields, about forty years ago, I suddenly and
vividly realized in a very definite personal experience, that people are above
all else brothers to one another'

As it was for us few, when wielding our pitchforks
Or culling reluctant thatch from the heavy rushland.
How close we grew one to the other!
The silent hunter was drawing his net about us.

O through the ages of blood on the straw and through the light the
    lamenting,
What whistling was that which only the heart might hear? O who was
    he,
Foiler of every presumption, runner on every man's trail,
And, ho there! escaper from armies,
Whistling in recognition, recognition that asks recognition?
Glorious the soaring and fusion of hearts after their cruel freezing:
Fountains were there, breaking out heavenwards,
And falling back, their tears like the leaves of a tree.

Upon these things the day broods under sun, under cloud,
And night through the cells of her many-branched brain:
How still they are, and she with her untroubled breathing
Over Weun Parc y Blawd and Parc y Blawd,
And their hold on the object, the fields full of people.
Surely the moment will come! And what hour shall it be
When the outlaw comes, and the hunter; the claimant comes to the
    gap in the hedge;
The Exiled King comes, and the rushes are parted before him.

176 *Daffodil* ǫ̇

Gay blade on the gentle hedgerow,
Sleek green glaive out of the ground,
Countryside's sword defying the cold wind,
For spectrum and song's sake stabbing the breeze.
Many quick piercers are here pleached together,
Quest of a host, who's first to hoist colour
Through slender throat of the sere sheath
Towards six-petal frill: It's a torque,
Countryside's blazon, fanfare of trumpet,
Golden in battle's forefront.

WALDO WILLIAMS

Dai Dilly, bareheaded boy,
Takes for a cap a fine colour.
After the training, the straining at leash,
March picks him to play in the goalmouth of joy.
Long his stay in the cold wind,
Strong his play with wind-giants,
Sturdy, he'll laugh off their hard body-tackles.
Be merry, young fellow, fine-fettled,—
A captain would like in a cuptie
Ten champions like this on the field.

Lead out to the field, Lady of March,
Be gallant of challenge, March-maiden who's golden.
Only the little white snowdrop precedes you,
Nor ever a purer or fairer dare show.
Bring in your train, Lady, I pray you,
The multiple foison of seasonal gardens,
Even to Michaelmas, month most quiescent,
With its eventide pearl and its summerlost daisy,
The desolate copse and the cornfield deserted:
Lady of March, lead out to the field.

IDRIS DAVIES

1905–1953

177   *Do you remember 1926?*

Do you remember 1926? That summer of soups and speeches,
The sunlight on the idle wheels and the deserted crossings,
And the laughter and the cursing in the moonlit streets?
Do you remember 1926? The slogans and the penny concerts,
The jazz-bands and the moorland picnics,
And the slanderous tongues of famous cities?
Do you remember 1926? The great dream and the swift disaster,
The fanatic and the traitor, and more than all,
The bravery of the simple, faithful folk?
'Ay, ay, we remember 1926,' said Dai and Shinkin,
As they stood on the kerb in Charing Cross Road,
'And we shall remember 1926 until our blood is dry.'

178   *Consider famous men, Dai bach*

Consider famous men, Dai bach, consider famous men,
All their slogans, all their deeds,
And follow the funerals to the grave.
Consider the charlatans, the shepherds of the sheep!
Consider the grease upon the tongue, the hunger of the purse!
Consider the fury of the easy words,
The vulgarity behind the brass,
The dirty hands that shook the air, that stained the sky!
Yet some there were who lived for you,
Who lay to die remembering you.

Mabon was your champion once upon a time
And his portrait's on the milk-jug yet.
The world has bred no champions for a long time now,
Except the boxing, tennis, golf, and Fascist kind,
And the kind that democracy breeds and feeds for Harringay,
And perhaps the world has grown too bitter or too wise
To breed a prophet or a poet ever again.

179   *Mrs. Evans fach, you want butter again*

Mrs. Evans fach, you want butter again.
How will you pay for it now, little woman
With your husband out on strike, and full
Of the fiery language? Ay, I know him,
His head is full of fire and brimstone
And a lot of palaver about communism,
And me, little Dan the Grocer
Depending so much on private enterprise.

What, depending on the miners and their
Money too? O yes, in a way, Mrs. Evans,
Yes, in a way I do, mind you.
Come tomorrow, little woman, and I'll tell you then

178 bach] little (fem. *fach*): a term of endearment, commiseration, or entreaty

What I have decided overnight.
Go home now and tell that rash red husband of yours
That your grocer cannot afford to go on strike
Or what would happen to the butter from Carmarthen?
Good day for now, Mrs. Evans fach.

GLYN JONES
1905–

180   *Esyllt*

As he climbs down our hill, my kestrel rises,
Steering in silence up from five empty fields,
A smooth sun brushed brown across his shoulders,
Floating in wide circles, his warm wings stiff.
Their shadows cut; in new soft orange hunting boots
My lover crashes through the snapping bracken.

The still gorse-hissing hill burns, brags gold broom's
Outcropping quartz; each touched bush spills dew.
Strangely last moment's parting was never sad,
But unreal like my promised years; less felt
Than this intense and silver snail calligraphy
Scrawled here in the sun across these stones.

Why have I often wanted to cry out
More against his going when he has left my flesh
Only for the night? When he has gone out
Hot from my mother's kitchen, and my combs
Were on the table under the lamp, and the wind
Was banging the doors of the shed in the yard.

181   *Again*

Lamplight from our kitchen window-pane
Shines out on the leaves of the little apple-tree
Dripping in the rain.

Inside the warm room, those two women together
Cleaning the brass candlesticks in silence
Are my daughter and my mother.

She has become a woman to me, my daughter,
Her dress heavy with her breasts, her arms heavy;
She is desired now, she is a lover.

But what will have come to her, and been hers,
Her crooked hands idle on the table
And her feet slow on the stairs?

Her granny, tired out, her mouth dropped open,
Sits with her eyes shut, facing the lamplight.
She has seen so much happen.

Shall my daughter too run through the streets to the pit-head,
And stand cold among the women crowding the gateway,
And see the young men brought up dead?

182   *Profile of Rose*

Hair-bowed Rose, deep in lush grass of the river
Bank, watched through the crystal unflawed block of
Afternoon, broad waters of her tenth birthday
Under sunglare, bottomless ebony
Sheeted with green and shine, and elms black
Along the far brink, and the gold field
Beyond, a shallow dishful of buttercup
Liquor. The painted tin toy, Rose's first

Dragonfly, blue, brilliant, then, oh, glassy,
Rinked glittering above the lit blades.
   In his ironmonger's villa her
   Camphor-coated father, her silk-sashed frock,
   Her bed- and heaped tableful of presents.
Motherless Rose hugged her kissing Jinny.
Not destined for philosophy or verse
She cried a child's laugh at the river bend
When, on the shining flats of lawn-like water,
Flocks of full-grown swans, thirty or forty,
Floated their perfection into what was
Already perfect.

                        In boarding school, where
Philosophy, in the brochure, was not
In any schoolroom, Rose, in love with
Interchangeable goodness, beauty, truth,
Loved also spiteful, ill-favoured and lying
Angela, who loved nobody.
                              In the
Abandoned boathouse, gloomy by the lake,
Motherless Rose, with swerve-necked orphan Angela,
Found sanctuary for gush and cake, where the girls'
Foundling swan, beguiled by Jinny's sponge, floated
And, webbed, walked the floorboards.
                                   After a summer
Quarrel, innocent repentant Rose,
Sobbing, creaked open the boathouse door,
Shooting into the gloom sunlight, a stream
Of bullets sprayed around the walls, and saw,
Hanging heavily from low boathouse rafters,
The head battered, the great bulk of bright-plumaged
Body turning, leaden in sudden gold
Nettings of watery sunlight, on a neck
Stretched rigid and blood-sodden from the knotted
Rudder-ropes, their swan! Dead, dead, dead! Putty-
Coloured Angela, eating, watched it revolve,
The bleeding snapped-off oar-stump beneath her foot.

The two eyes of the ironmonger's head,
And Jinny's, Rose, disgraced swan-slayer, was returned
Villa-ward, where, from her delirious bed,
She screamed, unremitting, for the truth, the truth.

Rose, her dress, amber and bee-barred, pelted
With sunlight and perfume, went on long, slim
And hairless legs to the river, to tan-skinned Charles.
Charles's surface was very beautiful.

The doting ironmonger's agony
Over, he died rich.
                  All Rose thought black blazed
Holy and unearthly. The swans gathered
Swaggering, the paddle of a webbed foot flamed,
Fidgetting the water, a black elbow,
Wrinkled as a dowager's, broke the surface.
Charles, lying, leaned over, grazing upon her
Golden, cheek-brusher lashes, each one curved
In the long shape of the beautiful
Avocet's slim bill; eyes lobelia-gay
Blue; straight, immature, early-catkin-
Yellow hair. 'The flesh in agony, the hurt
Heart desolate with disbelief, will the arms
And plaid of your tenderness be warm
Always about me?' Lightly the daisies
Pelted her lids. Charles's words were broken
For her like the living bread of truth.
'Always, always. My Rose. They will, they will.'

Shuffling old woman, loutish, her sick, fringe-string
Hair lank, her hat knitted, her black cardigan
A mass of darns, smiled, with her sewing mouser
On the shanty sill, at the rain, sinking
Round as onion-rings in the marsh, and death.

At night, the great birds thronged the darkness, crashing
Through high marsh mist, blinded, wings torn off
On wires, bleeding, stunned, and Rose watched the wide

Flock, defiled in marsh slime, drown.

       Beauty was

Beauty, truth was Angela's untruth; was
Lying Charles the flying hero, dead Jinny's
Whiskey-pipe in a good overcoat, her
Father's Charlie, fit only for the kitchen
Fire-back, Rose's Charles the cheat, Charles brutal,
Charles adulterous, Charles and beggary;
Truth was age and abandonment, the starry
Firmament above and the malignant
Growth within, and death; the writhing head,
Deadlier than lies, whose tranquil stare is stone.

On wide muds under rain, the wings severed,
Lay the plunging swans. Night—and the shining marsh
Held in its upward glare the moon, and milky
Majestic thunder, the rhythmic boom of
Throbbing voyagers broke out, the ruthless night
Swans' moon-blanched arrogance, that shook the marsh
And the heart of Rose shaken with laughter.

VERNON WATKINS
1906–1967

183   *The Collier*

When I was born on Amman hill
A dark bird crossed the sun.
Sharp on the floor the shadow fell;
I was the youngest son.

And when I went to the County School
I worked in a shaft of light.
In the wood of the desk I cut my name:
Dai for Dynamite.

The tall black hills my brothers stood;
Their lessons all were done.
From the door of the school when I ran out
They frowned to watch me run.

The slow grey bells they rang a chime
Surly with grief or age.
Clever or clumsy, lad or lout,
All would look for a wage.

I learnt the valley flowers' names
And the rough bark knew my knees.
I brought home trout from the river
And spotted eggs from the trees.

A coloured coat I was given to wear
Where the lights of the rough land shone.
Still jealous of my favour
The tall black hills looked on.

They dipped my coat in the blood of a kid
And they cast me down a pit,
And although I crossed with strangers
There was no way up from it.

Soon as I went from the County School
I worked in a shaft. Said Jim,
'You will get your chain of gold, my lad,
But not for a likely time.'

And one said, 'Jack was not raised up
When the wind blew out the light
Though he interpreted their dreams
And guessed their fears by night.'

And Tom, he shivered his leper's lamp
For the stain that round him grew;
And I heard mouths pray in the after-damp
When the picks would not break through.

They changed words there in darkness
And still through my head they run,
And white on my limbs is the linen sheet
And gold on my neck the sun.

184 *Returning to Goleufryn*

Returning to my grandfather's house, after this exile
From the coracle-river, long left with a coin to be good,
Returning with husks of those venturing ears for food
To lovely Carmarthen, I touch and remember the turnstile
Of this death-bound river. Fresh grass. Here I find that crown
In the shadow of dripping river-wood; then look up to the burning
    mile
Of windows. It is Goleufryn, the house on the hill;
And picking a child's path in a turn of the Towy I meet the prodigal
    town.

Sing, little house, clap hands: shut, like a book of the Psalms,
On the leaves and pressed flowers of a journey. All is sunny
In the garden behind you. The soil is alive with blind-petalled
    blooms
Plundered by bees. Gooseberries and currants are gay
With tranquil, unsettled light. Breathless light begging alms
Of the breathing grasses bent over the river of tombs
Flashes. A salmon has swallowed the tribute-money
Of the path. On the farther bank I see ragged urchins play

With thread and pin. O lead me that I may drown
In those earlier cobbles, reflected; a street that is strewn with palms,
Rustling with blouses and velvet. Yet I alone
By the light in the sunflower deepening, here stand, my eyes cast
    down
To the footprint of accusations, and hear the faint, leavening
Music of first Welsh words; that gust of plumes
'They shall mount up like eagles', dark-throated assumes,
Cold-sunned, low thunder and gentleness of the authentic Throne.

Yet now I am lost, lost in the water-wound looms
Where brief, square windows break on a garden's decay.
Gold butter is shining, the tablecloth speckled with crumbs.
The kettle throbs. In the calendar harvest is shown,

Goleufryn] Clear Hill or Hill of Light

Standing in sheaves. Which way would I do you wrong?
Low, crumbling doorway of the infirm to the mansions of evening,
And poor, shrunken furrow where the potatoes are sown,
I shall not unnumber one soul I have stood with and known
To regain your stars struck by horses, your sons of God breaking
    in song.

185   *The Mare*

The mare lies down in the grass where the nest of the skylark is
    hidden.
Her eyes drink the delicate horizon moving behind the song.
Deep sink the skies, a well of voices. Her sleep is the vessel of Summer.
That climbing music requires the hidden music at rest.

Her body is utterly given to the light, surrendered in perfect abandon
To the heaven above her shadow, still as her first-born day.
Softly the wind runs over her. Circling the meadow, her hooves
Rest in a race of daisies, halted where butterflies stand.

Do not pass her too close. It is easy to break the circle
And lose that indolent fullness rounded under the ray
Falling on light-eared grasses your footstep must not yet wake.
It is easy to darken the sun of her unborn foal at play.

186   *Ode to Swansea*

      Bright town, tossed by waves of time to a hill,
      Leaning Ark of the world, dense-windowed, perched
      High on the slope of morning,
      Taking fire from the kindling East:

      Look where merchants, traders, and builders move
      Through your streets, while above your chandlers' walls
      Herring gulls wheel, and pigeons,
      Mocking man and the wheelwright's art.

Prouder cities rise through the haze of time,
Yet, unenvious, all men have found is here.
Here is the loitering marvel
Feeding artists with all they know.

There, where sunlight catches a passing sail,
Stretch your shell-brittle sands where children play,
Shielded from hammering dockyards
Launching strange, equatorial ships.

Would they know you, could the returning ships
Find the pictured bay of the port they left
Changed by a murmuration,
Stained by ores in a nighthawk's wing?

Yes. Through changes your myth seems anchored here.
Staked in mud, the forsaken oyster beds
Loom; and the Mumbles lighthouse
Turns through gales like a seabird's egg.

Lundy sets the course of the painted ships.
Fishers dropping nets off the Gower coast
Watch them, where shag and cormorant
Perch like shades on the limestone rocks.

You I know, yet who from a different land
Truly finds the town of a native child
Nurtured under a rainbow,
Pitched at last on Mount Pleasant hill?

Stone-runged streets ascending to that crow's nest
Swinging East and West over Swansea Bay
Guard in their walls Cwmdonkin's
Gates of light for a bell to close.

Praise, but do not disturb, heaven's dreaming man
Not awakened yet from his sleep of wine.
Pray, while the starry midnight
Broods on Singleton's elms and swans.

GWYN JONES

1907–

The Blue Day Journey

Tumbled out of heaven
On a day the sky was rising,
Air's blue blazon with white cirrus scrolled;
Saw Wales the welcome, well-combed, comely,
Her vanquished hills wore crowns of beaten gold.
To lap her seas, smell grass, hear missel song,
Dropped through the cloud
White wool that rolled
Upwards in veils some seven yet homely.
High-air-bewethered thought it time I landed,
But journey now began I found,
Not ended.

Left clouds. Saw birds.
Half bird myself inclined
My eyebrow-feathers whistling in the wind;
Fell through the birds, clove first a pelt of kestrels,
Tell-tail jesters with a tally of larks;
Then kites and curlews stringing off the highland,
Buzzards that mew like cats that mew like hawks;
And grave-hued corvée-ravens of this Island
Sweeping through wind-flues in tall chimney rocks.
There were Branwen starlings now grown wastrels,
Stonechats, whinchats, chiff-chaffs, choughs,
And bushy bully finches;
All birds that dally high in hollow sky,
And gallows-bird that lynches
Frayed tremulants who pipe but once then die,
O soft red feathered darlings!

Left birds. Saw trees.
Sprawled on to trees, still falling, foliage-lifted,
Wrapt in warm firs, and spruce, oak-apple-happy,
From ash to ashes drifted,

Now ivy blue, now holly buried red
In beechen greenleaved books the rooks had sifted.
Green smoke blew off the sycamore.
Half tree myself I said,
Bough-legged, wych-haired, bay-crowned my birdlimed head.

Left trees. Saw flowers.
Floated on flowers, rose, stalled and rose again,
White chasubles, red chalices below me,
Girl-merry named and bright-veined Mary blossoms
(By their day's eyes they know me),
Such dandy lions' teeth, Welsh butter bowls,
And goldspoked whirwheels burnishing a frieze
Of gold-dust pollen on the golden bees.
Swung low on blue bell chime and clang
To levels where sun hammers rang
On grass that sang like glass.
Heard drone, saw dragon fly and hover,
Spelled myself deep in clover,
Then under flowers saw sea.

Spilled sideways into sea,
Off cliff past pebble belt where high tide spreethed
And gulls' white wingspread baffled my wet eyes;
Felt springe of ocean seize me
— Half fish myself I found.
Dabhanded, codpieced, gilled, I floundered round
Where rainbow-scaled cool tippling mackerel pass
The brightfire smolten bass.
There were seven pound sea-trout gravel-bed bound,
And swordblade salmon blue for redds.
Behind them rolled the porpoise shoal,
And eels
And cassocked seals,
Round priests who shrive with blubbered eye
Taut penitents that swirl and dive and then deep-riven lie
— Far better fish than I,
Who burst to surface, crawling shorewards
Under a brawling sky. .

At foam's edge sat and pondered:
Half man I thought at least.
Heard echo cry
Half fish half bird half tree half flower half beast,
And which half best I wondered.

Familiarly
Saw naked self,
Dog-otter-toed, fin-fingered primal elf
Of genial slime and time.
Saw with blue Merlin eyes
Red fox at heart, black rabbit in the thighs,
And rosewreath asshead braying after myrtle
Till all my halves for shame turn tail or turtle.
Suddenly
Long-spined the rose spins feathers in my brain
Sting me and wing me,
Wound me to man again,
From man to god.
— And now the sea I leave,
Spell myself out of flowers,
Cleave trees,
Till hawk bemews me, addled as an egg
By upward soar to floor with blues deep felted.
Rolled on through clouds white, veiled and seven,
Winged, maned, and songscaled,
Tumbled into heaven.

MARGIAD EVANS

1909–1958

188   *Snowdrops*

When night-time bars me in
And I am sitting sewing,
My fancy takes the whim
To think of snowdrops growing.

They sprinkle grudging places
With slender drops of white,
And hang their orphan faces
In narrow hoods of light.

So frail I must recall
The shoulder of the cloud,
The scratching of the squall,
The rain, the frost, the flood.

Child kindness of the year,
Young promise of beguilement
More tender and more dear
Than old fulfilment,

How strange it is to see
And hard to understand
Your silver shine! Like charity
In winter's stubborn hand.

189   *Rain*

The poet felt the rain
Falling on his hair
Like a dreamer's light
Given everywhere;

Falling from the cloud,
Falling from the moon,
From the shells of spheres
Hidden in the noon.

Underneath a leaf
A silent bird, aloof,
Listened to the rain
On his trembling roof.

190 *Resurrection*

My candle burns up lank and fair,
The gale is on the pane,
The dead leaves on the whirlwind's branch
Are risen trees again.

And can I sleep tonight, my heart,
With candle and with storm?
And dare I sleep, my heart, my heart,
And see my dreams alone?

For when in my resurgent hands
I take the mirror weedy with brown hair:
Rustling the dark wind through the glass—
Oh, who is there?

TOM EARLEY

1911–

191 *Rebel's Progress*

When idle in a poor Welsh mining valley,
Dissatisfied with two pounds five a week,
I got invited to a marxist rally
And found to my amazement I could speak.

I soon could spout about the proletariat,
The bourgeoisie and strikes and lockouts too,
Could run an AGM or commissariat
As well as boss-class secretaries do.

At first I joined Aneurin Bevan's party
But soon got disillusioned with all that.
Joined Harry Pollitt and became a commy.
They turned down all my pacifism flat.

TOM EARLEY

The hungry thirties found me hunger marching
To squat with Hannington inside the Ritz.
Then PPU. For just this I'd been searching
Before the war and long before the blitz.

I liked the people in the Peace Pledge meeting
But found that they were holier than me,
So marched with Collins and quite soon was greeting
My former comrades in the CND.

To sit with Russell next became my hobby,
Vanessa Redgrave's fame I hoped to share,
Got thrown around in Whitehall by a bobby
And then a broken arm in Grosvenor Square.

So now I'll leave the politics to others
And not be an outsider any more.
I'll go back to the valley, to my mother's,
And never set my foot outside the door.

Except to go to chapel on Bryn Sion
And maybe join the Cwmbach male voice choir,
I'll sit at home and watch the television
And talk about the rugby by the fire.

HENRY TREECE
1912–1966

192   *Conquerors*

By sundown we came to a hidden village
Where all the air was still
And no sound met our tired ears, save
For the sorry drip of rain from blackened trees
And the melancholy song of swinging gates.
Then through a broken pane some of us saw
A dead bird in a rusting cage, still

Pressing his thin tattered breast against the bars,
His beak wide open. And
As we hurried through the weed-grown street,
A gaunt dog started up from some dark place
And shambled off on legs as thin as sticks
Into the wood, to die at least in peace.
No one had told us victory was like this;
Not one amongst us would have eaten bread
Before he'd filled the mouth of the grey child
That sprawled, stiff as a stone, before the shattered door.
There was not one who did not think of home.

BRENDA CHAMBERLAIN

1912–1971

193   *Talysarn*

Bone-aged is my white horse;
Blunted is the share;
Broken the man who through sad land
Broods on the plough.

Bone-bright was my gelding once;
Burnished was the blade;
Beautiful the youth who in green Spring
Broke earth with song.

194   *Islandman*

Full of years and seasoned like a salt timber
The island fisherman has come to terms with death.
His crabbed fingers are coldly afire with phosphorus
From the night-sea he fishes for bright-armoured herring.

193 Talysarn] Road's End

Lifting his lobster pots at sunrise,
He is not surprised when drowned sailors
Wearing ropes of pearl round green throats,
Nod their heads at him from underwater forests.

His black-browed wife who sits at home
Before the red hearth, does not guess
That only a fishscale breastplate protects him
When he sets out across ranges of winter sea.

195   *Dead Ponies*

There is death enough in Europe without these
Dead ponies on the mountain.
They are the underlining, the emphasis of death.
It is not wonderful that when they live
Their eyes are shadowed under mats of hair.
Despair and famine do not gripe so hard
When the bound earth and sky are kept remote
Behind clogged hairs.

The snows engulfed them, pressed their withered haunches flat,
Filled up their nostrils, burdened the cage of their ribs.
The snow retreated. Their bodies stink to heaven,
Potently crying out to raven hawk and dog;
Come! Pick us clean; cleanse our fine bones of blood.

They were never lovely save as foals,
Before their necks grew long, uncrested;
But the wildness of the mountain was in their stepping,
The pride of Spring burnt in their haunches,
They were tawny as the rushes of the marsh.

The prey-birds have had their fill, and preen their feathers:
Soft entrails have gone to make the hawk arrogant.

ALUN LLYWELYN-WILLIAMS
1913–

196   *When I was Young*   ♩

All day and every day the sea shone, steeped in its blueness;
the sun foresaw no storms of tomorrow, wept no yesterday's guilt;
I walked the quay in the white morning, questioning masts,
prying and spying under the swoop of raucous gulls
till there was my *Gwennan Gorn*, my spray whelp, my sea-spearer.

I would lie in the boat's prow and trail my hands in the water;
nearing the unbearable purity of the island lighthouse,
where the fish swayed and sped under the soundless rock;
how gaily the sail leapt to the blue heavens,
how prettily then it sank to the depth of my daring sinews!

The green land hung like a dream between the eyelids,
the furrows of the sea never counted the youthful hours of my course;
harsh, on returning, it was to tread the unheaving earth,
to traverse the heavy clay,
and to hear, now from its cell, the mortal knell of the flesh.

A return without returning: those suns wore
to their late long setting; but the darkling light over the bay
stays on, as though some miracle had snatched to that virginal tower
the warming eye of the world:
and, just as before time's watchmen besieged me, it shines
still on a voyage unfinished.

197   *In Berlin, August 1945: Lehrte Bahnhof*   ♩

Heledd and Inge, when the torches are red—
Inge, or Heledd, which one? deceiving us are the years—
see us meeting, at some interweaving of the swift threads,
the far travellers by chance beneath the clock.
By chance, I wonder? From this station, there is
no journey's beginning, nor end, unless one find

in its shattered platforms an end of all journeying further.
Purchase your poor ticket for wherever you wish;
long, long the waiting this crowd will have,
long its patience and without fuss,
since the blind bullet that hurled my stunned carcass
to fester on the rust of the rails
ricochetted as well, shattered the convex glass, ripped the fingers away
that pointed the coming and going
of the harsh wheels' dignified bustle.

The whirlwind went by—
and from the cleft in the wall, from the crack in the pavement,
the water pours without singing the song of the brook.
The night drips around us.
You forgotten travellers, since you are so still,
I gather together my terror, and lay it a while
here at the foot of existence, lifting it from the damp floor,
and share your waiting for the station master.
Let the stillness flow between us; let us watch once more,
after the profitless centuries,
the lava trickling slowly along the road,
the spreading of sand over the graves of kings,
and praise this hearth's purity under the grey lichen's blight.
(That was many a day past, the memory's not at all clear
whether our fate has been the same every time;
but before the bridges blew up, you too were in flight.)

Sharp is the breeze; Heledd, do not shiver, do not weep;
take courage, hidden on the handy bed of the rubble,
as a gift for savouring the cigarette, for sucking the chocolate,
you can reach out your love to the lonely conqueror.
The night drips without mercy.
When will he come, when, when, the blue official,
his uniform spruce, his aloof good taste,
to sound his horn and start the crowd once more?
A gross, pompous city this has always been,
and fit to be ruined;
and have you heard, Heledd,—no, wounded Inge,—
the greedy eagle's fierce laughter,
have you seen, in his half-closed eyes,
the predestined image of all our frail cities?

198 *Yesterday's Illusion* or *Remembering the Thirties* ♀

> Part of the regret is for adolescence in a period when enemies
> seemed conveniently well defined . . .   RICHARD HOGGART

In those painful days, we knew
who the enemy was: the sleek, corpulent capitalist,
the lunatic politician, and the guilty scientist:
it was easy to recognize the authors of our cancer and our disease.

On the edge of the city, the furrows of the unfinished street
fell into the rubble of the night, and the lovers
disappeared there two by two, like anxious missionaries
into the barbarians' cauldron, into the ashes of the world.

In fear we awaited the apocalyptic judgement,
in fear—and in joy. For this were we born,
to confidence in the destruction of false idols; we were privileged
in our anger, and in our pity for the poor and lonely.

We did not see, at that time,
the Black Sow lurking in the fierce bonfire,
nor the devil craving for the pigs' souls.

199   *Pont y Caniedydd*   ♀

I

There are two bends in the road, and an unexpected dip
going down to the brook;
and there is the bridge, linking the two banks,
and the stream is the sweet-sounding boundary, before one climbs
through the birches and hazels towards the mountain gate
and the long slope that predicts the pass.

Here is the bridge.
'Have I been here before, have I . . .?'

199 Pont y Caniedydd] the Bridge of the Singer, or Poet

we ask, each in his turn.
We are fearful, a bit,
Fearing an empty past, or a past grown strange
perhaps, here constantly close;
after leaving the snug city
and its cosseting walls,
the voices in the street,
the tribal comforts,
the music on tap
and the flash on the screen,
the appointment by phone,—
the pitiless grinding
of the gravel unmans one.

This is the road of the infrequent farmer,
the rare shepherd, the hiker in summer,
and the inaccessible climber on the trail of his sickly dream.
Overhead, the winged pilot, the shining quester,
smiling at the incredible map of the old slow world,
and its rusty fields and squat churches:
and he goes back briskly to history's highway, its bustling dwelling
where our own busy age is bound with steel thin as nylon.
We are fearful of all yesterdays but our own brief yesterday.

Have we been here before, I wonder, here
where the old hunchback stood,
one whose language is strange to his children
and his words' secret the width of Breconshire
as unclear as an imprecise wave-length?
He has not traced his blood-line, and wise, he says,
is one who knows his own perplexing yesterday.
'Here was a village once, many a day gone by,—
I remember my father telling me how his grandad would
wind back the houses: the tavern where the rough tump stands,
the church yonder, where the grasping yew grows today,
and the image of roadside cottages.'
But if the tale is true,
the domestic rose does not grow now,
and there is no trace of its soft perfume;
it faded, like the cry of the town beneath the lake;

ALUN LLYWELYN-WILLIAMS

it prospered before the remembrance that we now live at its heart
was born, and we are not in the least
indebted to its colour or its pain.
And today, the ruins are spreading, and the bracken
presses below.
Old man, where is the secret of your white boyhood?

We have learned all the stories:
Saturday afternoons, we have gone on pilgrimage
many times to the sacred places,
to the ancient nobleman's tower, to the zealous
prophet's college, to the grave of the bard.
These were the fountains of promise,
powerhouses of energy, like youth's spendthrift summers;
they proved futile, reservoirs of useless yearning,
and we were left fondling in astonishment
the back galleries' worthless old relics;
now, the track comes to an end, disappears without warning
in the ford's darkness, or the moor's emptiness,
or the tangle of streets destroyed by the bomb.

In a separate, untrodden section
of the ancient house, we go through to the empty room
where the grains of the air sleep as mutely
as the unruffled dust: the curtains were lowered
when the messenger came unexpectedly by
reporting the death of the first-born; a severe
fright to the family, the day the ice-age
flowed their way, freezing
all the furniture precisely as it was.
The private pictures remain on the wall,
the candlesticks upon the mantelpiece,
and the signature in the book in the lost language.
And we, the trespassers from the age of doubt,
forerunners of the pilot's final devastation,
the small remnant tormented between two
cultures, we enjoy the distant scent

the tower . . . the college . . . the grave] the ruins of the ancient castle at
Tretower; the home of the evangelist Howel Harris at Trefeca; the burial
place of Henry Vaughan at Llansantffraid; all in Breconshire

of withered flowers, and half-sense their meaning.
To the unpedigreed stranger, no homeland is here,
nor the nearest yesterday, nor his dwelling-place;
but the names surrender to him, the names
that grew from the red earth, and created
the guardian ridges—Tor y Foel,
and Craig Cwm Cynwyn and Cefn Llwch: these bottle
their ancient secret in their spoken sound.

II

One must cross; some kind of echo is here,
some harmony older than time,
in the sound of the brook, in the leap of the wind
across the chimney of the Fan; here is the sonata
we heard cleansing fear in the sober chamber
the night before going to the wars;
here is an undertone of the blessed ring
of pure eternal light a poet of yesterday
saw shining overhead.
But one must cross the sweet-sounding boundary and start for the
   pass.
Over there across the ridges is the town,
our comfortable city, where the cinema-cathedrals
sprout like contented weeds from lower-class houses;
around the angry arteries
that pour their endless flood past the empty chapel,
the petrol pumps glitter;
and there, by night, when the stars are banished,
the lonely faces rush fretfully here and there
on their inexpressible quest.
After the return, all this will be strange,
a new city, and one with a new note.

What we have received, that we hand over,
willing or unwilling;
what has been is what we know—in a tale

Tor y Foel] the Belly of the Bald Hill, a prominent feature of the landscape
from Henry Vaughan's home, where he saw eternity like a great ring of pure
and endless light   Cefn Llwch] the Ridge of the Lake

that was painfully learned;
what is we imagine: a mystery;
and what will come, we do not know, nor what sort of race
will inherit the city,
what architecture it will use to rebuild,
what language employ for its poems,
what belief God will set as a snare for its scientists,
what power enlighten it.

Our distant descendants will have their museums;
they will be born, like us, to the day and the night,
to the restless pendulum's sway, and the spasms
of being born and dying and their interminable riddle.
When the examiner comes by, we are mute,
yesterday or tomorrow can give him no answer;
we cling to oblivion, to recalling the fame
of all the town's transient civilizations.

But between the two banks, here at the chosen juncture,
this hidden fold in time, the ceaseless song
flows to those who hear it like life-giving blood;
day speaks to night, and water to fire,—
in you, lonely pilgrim, is found
today's fulfillment and its redeeming sorrow.

R. S. THOMAS

1913–

200   *A Peasant*

Iago Prytherch his name, though, be it allowed,
Just an ordinary man of the bald Welsh hills,
Who pens a few sheep in a gap of cloud.
Docking mangels, chipping the green skin
From the yellow bones with a half-witted grin
Of satisfaction, or churning the crude earth
To a stiff sea of clods that glint in the wind—

246

So are his days spent, his spittled mirth
Rarer than the sun that cracks the cheeks
Of the gaunt sky perhaps once in a week.
And then at night see him fixed in his chair
Motionless, except when he leans to gob in the fire.
There is something frightening in the vacancy of his mind.
His clothes, sour with years of sweat
And animal contact, shock the refined,
But affected, sense with their stark naturalness.
Yet this is your prototype, who, season by season
Against siege of rain and wind's attrition,
Preserves his stock, an impregnable fortress
Not to be stormed even in death's confusion.
Remember him, then, for he, too, is a winner of wars,
Enduring like a tree under the curious stars.

201   *The Hill Farmer Speaks*

I am the farmer, stripped of love
And thought and grace by the land's hardness;
But what I am saying over the fields'
Desolate acres, rough with dew,
Is, Listen, listen, I am a man like you.

The wind goes over the hill pastures
Year after year, and the ewes starve,
Milkless, for want of the new grass.
And I starve, too, for something the spring
Can never foster in veins run dry.

The pig is a friend, the cattle's breath
Mingles with mine in the still lanes;
I wear it willingly like a cloak
To shelter me from your curious gaze.

The hens go in and out at the door
From sun to shadow, as stray thoughts pass
Over the floor of my wide skull.
The dirt is under my cracked nails;

The tale of my life is smirched with dung;
The phlegm rattles. But what I am saying
Over the grasses rough with dew
Is, Listen, listen, I am a man like you.

202   *Welsh History*

We were a people taut for war; the hills
Were no harder, the thin grass
Clothed them more warmly than the coarse
Shirts our small bones.
We fought, and were always in retreat,
Like snow thawing upon the slopes
Of Mynydd Mawr; and yet the stranger
Never found our ultimate stand
In the thick woods, declaiming verse
To the sharp prompting of the harp.

Our kings died, or they were slain
By the old treachery at the ford.
Our bards perished, driven from the halls
Of nobles by the thorn and bramble.

We were a people bred on legends,
Warming our hands at the red past.
The great were ashamed of our loose rags
Clinging stubbornly to the proud tree
Of blood and birth, our lean bellies
And mud houses were a proof
Of our ineptitude for life.

We were a people wasting ourselves
In fruitless battles for our masters,
In lands to which we had no claim,
With men for whom we felt no hatred.

We were a people, and are so yet.
When we have finished quarrelling for crumbs
Under the table, or gnawing the bones
Of a dead culture, we will arise,
Armed, but not in the old way.

R. S. THOMAS

A Blackbird Singing

It seems wrong that out of this bird,
Black, bold, a suggestion of dark
Places about it, there yet should come
Such rich music, as though the notes'
Ore were changed to a rare metal
At one touch of that bright bill.

You have heard it often, alone at your desk
In a green April, your mind drawn
Away from its work by sweet disturbance
Of the mild evening outside your room.

A slow singer, but loading each phrase
With history's overtones, love, joy
And grief learned by his dark tribe
In other orchards and passed on
Instinctively as they are now,
But fresh always with new tears.

The Moor

It was like a church to me.
I entered it on soft foot,
Breath held like a cap in the hand.
It was quiet.
What God was there made himself felt,
Not listened to, in clean colours
That brought a moistening of the eye,
In movement of the wind over grass.

There were no prayers said. But stillness
Of the heart's passions—that was praise
Enough; and the mind's cession
Of its kingdom. I walked on,
Simple and poor, while the air crumbled
And broke on me generously as bread.

DYLAN THOMAS
1914-1953

205   *The force that through the green fuse drives*
       the flower

The force that through the green fuse drives the flower
Drives my green age; that blasts the roots of trees
Is my destroyer.
And I am dumb to tell the crooked rose
My youth is bent by the same wintry fever.

The force that drives the water through the rocks
Drives my red blood; that dries the mouthing streams
Turns mine to wax.
And I am dumb to mouth unto my veins
How at the mountain spring the same mouth sucks.

The hand that whirls the water in the pool
Stirs the quicksand; that ropes the blowing wind
Hauls my shroud sail.
And I am dumb to tell the hanging man
How of my clay is made the hangman's lime.

The lips of time leech to the fountain head;
Love drips and gathers, but the fallen blood
Shall calm her sores.
And I am dumb to tell a weather's wind
How time has ticked a heaven round the stars.

And I am dumb to tell the lover's tomb
How at my sheet goes the same crooked worm.

206   *Especially when the October wind*

Especially when the October wind
With frosty fingers punishes my hair,
Caught by the crabbing sun I walk on fire
And cast a shadow crab upon the land,
By the sea's side, hearing the noise of birds,
Hearing the raven cough in winter sticks,
My busy heart who shudders as she talks
Sheds the syllabic blood and drains her words.

Shut, too, in a tower of words, I mark
On the horizon walking like the trees
The wordy shapes of women, and the rows
Of the star-gestured children in the park.
Some let me make you of the vowelled beeches,
Some of the oaken voices, from the roots
Of many a thorny shire tell you notes,
Some let me make you of the water's speeches.

Behind a pot of ferns the wagging clock
Tells me the hour's word, the neural meaning
Flies on the shafted disk, declaims the morning
And tells the windy weather in the cock.
Some let me make you of the meadow's signs;
The signal grass that tells me all I know
Breaks with the wormy winter through the eye.
Some let me tell you of the raven's sins.

Especially when the October wind
(Some let me make you of autumnal spells,
The spider-tongued, and the loud hill of Wales)
With fists of turnips punishes the land,
Some let me make you of the heartless words.
The heart is drained that, spelling in the scurry
Of chemic blood, warned of the coming fury.
By the sea's side hear the dark-vowelled birds.

207 *After the funeral*

(In memory of Ann Jones)

After the funeral, mule praises, brays,
Windshake of sailshaped ears, muffle-toed tap
Tap happily of one peg in the thick
Grave's foot, blinds down the lids, the teeth in black,
The spittled eyes, the salt ponds in the sleeves,
Morning smack of the spade that wakes up sleep,
Shakes a desolate boy who slits his throat
In the dark of the coffin and sheds dry leaves,
That breaks one bone to light with a judgement clout,
After the feast of tear-stuffed time and thistles
In a room with a stuffed fox and a stale fern,
I stand, for this memorial's sake, alone
In the snivelling hours with dead, humped Ann
Whose hooded, fountain heart once fell in puddles
Round the parched worlds of Wales and drowned each sun
(Though this for her is a monstrous image blindly
Magnified out of praise; her death was a still drop;
She would not have me sinking in the holy
Flood of her heart's fame; she would lie dumb and deep
And need no druid of her broken body).
But I, Ann's bard on a raised hearth, call all
The seas to service that her wood-tongued virtue
Babble like a bellbuoy over the hymning heads,
Bow down the walls of the ferned and foxy woods,
That her love sing and swing through a brown chapel,
Bless her bent spirit with four, crossing birds.
Her flesh was meek as milk, but this skyward statue
With the wild breast and blessed and giant skull
Is carved from her in a room with a wet window
In a fiercely mourning house in a crooked year.
I know her scrubbed and sour humble hands
Lie with religion in their cramp, her threadbare
Whisper in a damp word, her wits drilled hollow,
Her fist of a face died clenched on a round pain;
And sculptured Ann is seventy years of stone.

These cloud-sopped, marble hands, this monumental
Argument of the hewn voice, gesture and psalm,
Storm me forever over her grave until
The stuffed lung of the fox twitch and cry Love
And the strutting fern lay seeds on the black sill.

208   *A Refusal to Mourn the Death, by Fire,*
              of a Child in London

Never until the mankind making
Bird beast and flower
Fathering and all humbling darkness
Tells with silence the last light breaking
And the still hour
Is come of the sea tumbling in harness

And I must enter again the round
Zion of the water bead
And the synagogue of the ear of corn
Shall I let pray the shadow of a sound
Or sow my salt seed
In the least valley of sackcloth to mourn

The majesty and burning of the child's death.
I shall not murder
The mankind of her going with a grave truth
Nor blaspheme down the stations of the breath
With any further
Elegy of innocence and youth.

Deep with the first dead lies London's daughter,
Robed in the long friends,
The grains beyond age, the dark veins of her mother,
Secret by the unmourning water
Of the riding Thames.
After the first death, there is no other.

209 *Fern Hill*

Now as I was young and easy under the apple boughs
About the lilting house and happy as the grass was green,
          The night above the dingle starry,
               Time let me hail and climb
          Golden in the heydays of his eyes,
And honoured among wagons I was prince of the apple towns
And once below a time I lordly had the trees and leaves
               Trail with daisies and barley
          Down the rivers of the windfall light.

And as I was green and carefree, famous among the barns
About the happy yard and singing as the farm was home,
          In the sun that is young once only,
               Time let me play and be
          Golden in the mercy of his means,
And green and golden I was huntsman and herdsman, the calves
Sang to my horn, the foxes on the hills barked clear and cold,
               And the sabbath rang slowly
          In the pebbles of the holy streams.

All the sun long it was running, it was lovely, the hay
Fields high as the house, the tunes from the chimneys, it was air
          And playing, lovely and watery
               And fire green as grass.
          And nightly under the simple stars
As I rode to sleep the owls were bearing the farm away,
All the moon long I heard, blessed among stables, the night-jars
               Flying with the ricks, and the horses
          Flashing into the dark.

And then to awake, and the farm, like a wanderer white
With the dew, come back, the cock on his shoulder: it was all
          Shining, it was Adam and maiden,
               The sky gathered again
          And the sun grew round that very day.

So it must have been after the birth of the simple light
In the first, spinning place, the spellbound horses walking warm
    Out of the whinnying green stable
      On to the fields of praise.

And honoured among foxes and pheasants by the gay house
Under the new made clouds and happy as the heart was long,
    In the sun born over and over,
      I ran my heedless ways,
    My wishes raced through the house high hay
And nothing I cared, at my sky blue trades, that time allows
In all his tuneful turning so few and such morning songs
    Before the children green and golden
      Follow him out of grace,

Nothing I cared, in the lamb white days, that time would take me
Up to the swallow thronged loft by the shadow of my hand,
    In the moon that is always rising,
      Nor that riding to sleep
    I should hear him fly with the high fields
And wake to the farm forever fled from the childless land.
Oh as I was young and easy in the mercy of his means,
      Time held me green and dying
    Though I sang in my chains like the sea.

ALUN LEWIS

1915–1944

210   *All day it has rained*

All day it has rained, and we on the edge of the moors
Have sprawled in our bell-tents, moody and dull as boors,
Groundsheets and blankets spread on the muddy ground,
And from the first grey wakening we have found
No refuge from the skirmishing fine rain
And the wind that made the canvas heave and flap
And the taut wet guy-ropes ravel out and snap.

All day the rain has glided, wave and mist and dream,
Drenching the gorse and heather, a gossamer stream
Too light to stir the acorns that suddenly
Snatched from their cups by the wild south-westerly
Pattered against the tent and our upturned dreaming faces.
And we stretched out, unbuttoning our braces,
Smoking a Woodbine, darning dirty socks,
Reading the Sunday papers—I saw a fox
And mentioned it in the note I scribbled home;—
And we talked of girls, and dropping bombs on Rome,
And thought of the quiet dead and the loud celebrities
Exhorting us to slaughter, and the herded refugees;
—Yet thought softly, morosely of them, and as indifferently
As of ourselves or those whom we
For years have loved, and will again
Tomorrow maybe love; but now it is the rain
Possesses us entirely, the twilight and the rain.

And I can remember nothing dearer or more to my heart
Than the children I watched in the woods on Saturday
Shaking down burning chestnuts for the schoolyard's merry play,
Or the shaggy patient dog who followed me
By Sheet and Steep and up the wooded scree
To the Shoulder o' Mutton where Edward Thomas brooded long
On death and beauty—till a bullet stopped his song.

211   *The Mahratta Ghats*

The valleys crack and burn, the exhausted plains
Sink their black teeth into the horny veins
Straggling the hills' red thighs, the bleating goats
—Dry bents and bitter thistles in their throats—
Thread the loose rocks by immemorial tracks.
Dark peasants drag the sun upon their backs.

High on the ghat the new turned soil is red,
The sun has ground it to the finest red,
It lies like gold within each horny hand.
Siva has spilt his seed upon this land.

Will she who burns and withers on the plain
Leave, ere too late, her scraggy herds of pain,
The cow-dung fire and the trembling beasts,
The little wicked gods, the grinning priests,
And climb, before a thousand years have fled,
High as the eagle to her mountain bed
Whose soil is fine as flour and blood-red?
But no! She cannot move. Each arid patch
Owns the lean folk who plough and scythe and thatch
Its grudging yield and scratch its stubborn stones.
The small gods suck the marrow from their bones.

Who is it climbs the summit of the road?
Only the beggar bumming his dark load.
Who was it cried to see the falling star?
Only the landless soldier lost in war.

And did a thousand years go by in vain?
And does another thousand start again?

212   *In Hospital: Poona*

Last night I did not fight for sleep
But lay awake from midnight while the world
Turned its slow features to the moving deep
Of darkness, till I knew that you were furled,

Beloved, in the same dark watch as I.
And sixty degrees of longitude beside
Vanished as though a swan in ecstacy
Had spanned the distance from your sleeping side.

And like to swan or moon the whole of Wales
Glided within the parish of my care:
I saw the green tide leap on Cardigan,
Your red yacht riding like a legend there,
And the great mountains, Dafydd and Llewelyn,
Plynlimmon, Cader Idris and Eryri
Threshing the darkness back from head and fin,
And also the small nameless mining valley

Whose slopes are scratched with streets and sprawling graves
Dark in the lap of firwoods and great boulders
Where you lay waiting, listening to the waves—
My hot hands touched your white despondent shoulders

—And then ten thousand miles of daylight grew
Between us, and I heard the wild daws crake
In India's starving throat; whereat I knew
That Time upon the heart can break
But love survives the venom of the snake.

213   *The Jungle*

I

In mole-blue indolence the sun
Plays idly on the stagnant pool
In whose grey bed black swollen leaf
Holds Autumn rotting like an unfrocked priest.
The crocodile slides from the ochre sand
And drives the great translucent fish
Under the boughs across the running gravel.
Windfalls of brittle mast crunch as we come
To quench more than our thirst—our selves—
Beneath this bamboo bridge, this mantled pool
Where sleep exudes a sinister content
As though all strength of mind and limb must pass
And all fidelities and doubts dissolve,
The weighted world a bubble in each head,
The warm pacts of the flesh betrayed
By the nonchalance of a laugh,
The green indifference of this sleep.

II

Wandering and fortuitous the paths
We followed to this rendezvous today
Out of the mines and offices and dives,
The sidestreets of anxiety and want,

Huge cities known and distant as the stars,
Wheeling beyond our destiny and hope.
We did not notice how the accent changed
As shadows ride from precipice to plain
Closing the parks and cordoning the roads,
Clouding the humming cultures of the West—
The weekly bribe we paid the man in black,
The day shift sinking from the sun,
The blinding arc of rivets blown through steel,
The patient queues, headlines and slogans flung
Across a frightened continent, the town
Sullen and out of work, the little home
Semi-detached, suburban, transient
As fever or the anger of the old,
The best ones on some specious pretext gone.

But we who dream beside this jungle pool
Prefer the instinctive rightness of the poised
Pied kingfisher deep darting for a fish
To all the banal rectitude of states,
The dew-bright diamonds on a viper's back
To the slow poison of a meaning lost
And the vituperations of the just.

III

The banyan's branching clerestories close
The noon's harsh splendour to a head of light.
The black spot in the focus grows and grows:
The vagueness of the child, the lover's deep
And inarticulate bewilderment,
The willingness to please that made a wound,
The kneeling darkness and the hungry prayer;
Cargoes of anguish in the holds of joy,
The smooth deceitful stranger in the heart,
The tangled wrack of motives drifting down
An oceanic tide of Wrong.
And though the state has enemies we know
The greater enmity within ourselves.

Some things we cleaned like knives in earth,
Kept from the dew and rust of Time
Instinctive truths and elemental love,
Knowing the force that brings the teal and quail
From Turkestan across the Himalayan snows
To Kashmir and the South alone can guide
That winging wildness home again.

Oh you who want us for ourselves,
Whose love can start the snow-rush in the woods
And melt the glacier in the dark coulisse,
Forgive this strange inconstancy of soul,
The face distorted in a jungle pool
That drowns its image in a mort of leaves.

IV

Grey monkeys gibber, ignorant and wise.
We are the ghosts, and they the denizens;
We are like them anonymous, unknown,
Avoiding what is human, near,
Skirting the villages, the paddy fields
Where boys sit timelessly to scare the crows
On bamboo platforms raised above their lives.

A trackless wilderness divides
Joy from its cause, the motive from the act:
The killing arm uncurls, strokes the soft moss;
The distant world is an obituary,
We do not hear the tappings of its dread.
The act sustains; there is no consequence.
Only aloneness, swinging slowly
Down the cold orbit of an older world
Than any they predicted in the schools,
Stirs the cold forest with a starry wind,
And sudden as the flashing of a sword
The dream exalts the bowed and golden head
And time is swept with a great turbulence,
The old temptation to remould the world.

The bamboos creak like an uneasy house;
The night is shrill with crickets, cold with space.
And if the mute pads on the sand should lift
Annihilating paws and strike us down
Then would some unimportant death resound
With the imprisoned music of the soul?
And we become the world we could not change?
Or does the will's long struggle end
With the last kindness of a foe or friend?

ROLAND MATHIAS

1915–

214 *Craswall*

With a long stirrup under fern
From a small blast of oaks and thorn
The shepherd scours the circling hill
And the sharp dingle creeping to the well.

A trickle from the canting neck
A pony coughing in the track
Are all the stranger hears, and steep
Among the fern the threading of the sheep.

This is the boundary: different burrs
Stick, stones make darker scars
On the road down: nightingales
Struggle with thorn-trees for the gate of Wales.

215 *Departure in Middle Age*

The hedges are dazed as cock-crow, heaps of leaves
Brushed back to them like a child's hair
After a sweat, and clouds as recently bundled

Out of the hollows whimper a little in the conifers higher up.
I am the one without tears, cold
And strange to myself as a stepfather encountered
For the first time in the passage from the front door.

But I cannot go back, plump up the pillow and shape
My sickness like courage. I have spent the night in a shiver:
Usk water passing now was a chatter under the Fan
When the first cold came on. They are all dead, all,
Or scattered, father, mother, my pinafore friends,
And the playground's echoes have not waited for my return.
Exile is the parcel I carry, and you know this,
Clouds, when you drop your pretences and the hills clear.

RHYDWEN WILLIAMS
1916–

216   *The Baboon*   ♀

He sat in his cell staring,
lonely as an astronaut in space,
continents from his world,
and the faces around as empty as stars to him.

Without pain, without need—only the damned lice in his armpit—
picking his food off the floor among his own excrement,
and wondering for ages at his fingers and his navel and his organs
as though the glory of every species—
our anatomy and our doings and the last bit of flesh—
belonged to no one but him.

I looked at him. His head—
a pot half-made on the potter's wheel,
and the clay weeping in two funny eyes
for fingers from somewhere to perfect his mouth and his ears.

RHYDWEN WILLIAMS

A smell passed by his nose,
a smell from the straw and the dung,
and awoke him to his own haunches,
and sent him like a rocket with his backside on fire
into the spiteful orbit of sex.
And when I saw his face afterwards—O laughable sadness—
I saw that whole nervous apparatus
that has travelled over the ancient maps of art and song
become one hopeless knot,
alive for damn-all
except the final vast achievement
of picking his nose.

EMYR HUMPHREYS
1919–

217   *From Father to Son*

There is no limit to the number of times
Your father can come to life, and he is as tender as ever he was
And as poor, his overcoat buttoned to the throat,
His face blue from the wind that always blows in the outer darkness
He comes towards you, hesitant,
Unwilling to intrude and yet driven at the point of love
To this encounter.

You may think
That love is all that is left of him, but when he comes
He comes with all his winters and all his wounds.
He stands shivering in the empty street,
Cold and worn like a tramp at the end of a journey
And yet a shape of unquestioning love that you
Uneasy and hesitant of the cold touch of death
Must embrace.

Then, before you can touch him
He is gone, leaving on your fingers
A little more of his weariness
A little more of his love.

218   *An Apple Tree and a Pig*

Oian a parchellan, ni hawdd cysgaf
Rhag godwrdd y galar y sydd arnof.

1   All men wait for battle and when it comes
Pass along the sword's edge their resilient thumbs.

Men clasp in faithless arms their sobbing wives
Tasting even in the salt kiss the bliss pricking points of knives.

Men clip on armour and see in their children's eyes
Their swollen images, their godlike size.

Men assemble together, create a new sea
That floods into battle. Men become free

Of the dull bonds of life, become locked in a fight
In love in league with Death, lost in icy delight.

2   In such a frenzy I slaughtered my sister's son.
My sword cut open his face and I screamed as though I had won

Glory to nurse in the night, until I turned and saw
The flesh of Gwenddolau, the young king who loved me, raw

And Rhydderch's sword dull with Gwenddolau's blood
And his great mouth trumpeting joy. Ah then I understood

That rooted and nourished in my own affectionate heart
Was the spitting devil tearing our world apart.

3   When I fled to the wood, alone I lay under a tree
Still hearing the clash of our swords, still dumb in my agony.

So much despair had crowded into my heart
My tongue was cold, speech a forgotten art.

As I lay in the wood I suffered the germ of peace
To penetrate my veins like a lethal disease.

Oian a parchellan] Hail, little pig, sleep comes not lightly / For the surging
of the sorrow that is upon me (trans. H. I. B.)

4   I have lost all desire to communicate with men.
My sighs do not disturb the building wren.

An apple tree and a pig: these are my friends
With whom I share my wisdom that no longer pretends

To be wise, since nothing my wisdom brings
Can restore the lost kingdom or challenge the armour of kings.

I have eaten the apple of knowledge and all I know
Is that love must fail and lust must overthrow

And in the nights of winter when the ice-winds howl
A pity and a terror fasten themselves on my soul

And I cry upon death to wrap his white redress
Without mercy about the stillness of the merciless
And remedy my madness with long silence.

T. H. JONES
1921–1965

219   *Difference*

Under God's violent unsleeping eye
My fathers laboured for three hundred years
On the same farm, in the expected legend.
Their hymns were anodynes against defeat,
But sin, the original and withering worm,
Was always with them, whether they excelled
In prayers, made songs on winter nights,
Or slobbered in temptation, women, drink.

I inherit their long arms and mountain face,
The withering worm sleeps too within my blood
But I know loneliness, unwatched by God.

The Welshman in Exile Speaks

(for Brin)

Being a boy from the hills, brought up
Believing that fornication is a sin,
Adultery abomination, what should I do
But fornicate until I'm caught, and then
Commit adultery in my dreams. *My* dreams
—You have to plough the furrows I have ploughed,
Or pick the stones off the bitter fields
Before they're fit for ploughing, all day, all day,
Or lift potatoes until your back is breaking,
And then go home to the grudged candlelight
And the green bacon—you want your childhood
Spent like that—and with the compensations:
An old man's voice like something out of Daniel
Making the Belshazzars of the tractors tremble,
Hills, like Mam's breasts, homely and tremendous,
Schooled wildness of sheepdogs, ponies stubborn
As myself, and each winter's killing snow.
And the capel, God in a little *bwthyn*
Once whitewashed—but God in the voices
Of the mean, the crippled, the green bacon eaters,
The lead me beside still waters buggers, the wild boys,
The sin-eaters, and the godly daughters,
All of them suddenly in unison
In the ugliest building I have ever seen
—Pisgah I shall never see again—
All suddenly bursting—not bursting,
All suddenly startled into song, to praise
The god of fornication and the world we lived in.

Boyo, if you come from a country like that
You can talk to me of sin and related matters.

bwthyn] cottage, cot

LESLIE NORRIS
1921–

Water

On hot summer mornings my aunt set glasses
On a low wall outside the farmhouse,
With some jugs of cold water.
I would sit in the dark hall, or
    Behind the dairy window,
Waiting for children to come from the town.

They came in small groups, serious, steady,
And I could see them, black in the heat,
Long before they turned in at our gate
To march up the soft, dirt road.
    They would stand by the wall,
Drinking water with an engrossed thirst. The dog

Did not bother them, knowing them responsible
Travellers. They held in quiet hands their bags
Of jam sandviches, and bottles of yellow fizz.
Sometimes they waved a gratitude to the house,
    But they never looked at us,
Their eyes were full of the mountain, lifting

Their measuring faces above our long hedge.
When they had gone I would climb the wall,
Looking for them among the thin sheep runs.
Their heads were a resolute darkness among ferns,
    They climbed with unsteady certainty.
I wondered what it was they knew the mountain had.

They would pass the last house, Lambert's, where
A violent gander, too old by many a Christmas,
Blared evil warning from his bitten moor,
Then it was open world, too high and clear
    For clouds even, where over heather
The free hare cleanly ran, and the summer sheep.

I knew this; and I knew all summer long
Those visionary gangs passed through our lanes,
Coming down at evening, their arms full
Of cowslips, moon daisies, whinberries, nuts,
     All fruits of the sliding seasons,
And the enormous experience of the mountain

That I who loved it did not understand.
In the summer, dust filled our winter ruts
With a level softness, and children walked
At evening through golden curtains scuffed
     From the road by their trailing feet.
They would drink tiredly at our wall, talking

Softly, leaning, their sleepy faces warm for home.
We would see them murmur slowly through our stiff
Gate, their shy heads gilded by the last sun.
One by one we would gather up the used jugs,
     The glasses. We would pour away
A little water. It would lie on the thick dust, gleaming.

222   *Elegy for Lyn James*

I saw your manager fight. He was
Useful, but his brother had the class.
In shabby halls in Wales, or in tents
On slum ground, I saw your like
Go cuffed and bleeding from a few
Crude rounds to set the mob aloud
Before the big men came, who had the class.

Even they did not all escape. Tim
Sheehan, whose young heart burst
In a dirty room above a fish shop;
Jerry O'Neill bobbing his old age
Through a confusion of scattered
Fists all down the High Street; brisk
Billy Rose, blind; all these I knew.

And Jock McAvoy, swinging his right
From a wheel-chair. Your murderers hide
Fatly behind the black lines of the
Regulations, your futile hands are closed
In a gloveless death. In rotting lanes
Behind silent billiard halls, I hear
Your shuffling ghost, who never had the class.

DANNIE ABSE

1923–

223   *Epithalamion*

Singing, today I married my white girl
beautiful in a barley field.
Green on thy finger a grass blade curled,
so with this ring I thee wed, I thee wed,
and send our love to the loveless world
of all the living and all the dead.

Now, no more than vulnerable human,
we, more than one, less than two,
are nearly ourselves in a barley field—
and only love is the rent that's due
though the bailiffs of time return anew
to all the living but not the dead.

Shipwrecked, the sun sinks down harbours
of a sky, unloads its liquid cargoes
of marigolds, and I and my white girl
lie still in the barley—who else wishes
to speak, what more can be said
by all the living against all the dead?

Come then all you wedding guests:
green ghost of trees, gold of barley,
you blackbird priests in the field,
you wind that shakes the pansy head
fluttering on a stalk like a butterfly;
come the living and come the dead.

Listen flowers, birds, winds, worlds,
tell all today that I married
more than a white girl in the barley—
for today I took to my human bed
flower and bird and wind and world,
and all the living and all the dead.

JOHN ORMOND

1923–

224   *At his Father's Grave*

Here lies a shoe-maker whose knife and hammer
Fell idle at the height of summer,
Who was not missed so much as when the rain
Of winter brought him back to mind again.

He was no preacher but his working text
Was *See all dry this winter and the next*.
Stand still. Remember his two hands, his laugh,
His craftsmanship. They are his epitaph.

225   *Lament for a Leg*

*Near the yew tree under which the body of Dafydd ap Gwilym is buried
in Strata Florida, Cardiganshire, there stands a stone with the following
inscription: 'The left leg and part of the thigh of Henry Hughes, Cooper,
was cut off and interr'd here, June 18, 1756.' Later the rest of Henry
Hughes set off across the Atlantic in search of better fortune.*

A short service, to be sure,
With scarcely half a hymn they held,
Over my lost limb, suitable curtailment.
Out-of-tune notes a crow cawed
By the yew tree, and me,
My stump still tourniquéd,

JOHN ORMOND

Awkward on my new crutch,
Being snatched towards the snack
Of a funeral feast they made.
With seldom a dry eye, for laughter,
They jostled me over the ale
I'd cut the casks for, and the mead.
'Catch me falling under a coach',
Every voice jested, save mine,
Henry Hughes, cooper. A tasteless caper!
Soon with my only, my best, foot forward
I fled, quiet, to far America:

Where, with my two tried hands, I plied
My trade and, true, in time made good
Though grieving for Pontrhydfendigaid.
Sometimes, all at once, in my tall cups,
I'd cry in *hiraeth* for my remembered thigh
Left by the grand yew in Ystrad Fflur's
Bare ground, near the good bard.
Strangers, astonished at my high
Beer-flush, would stare, not guessing,
Above the bar-board, that I, of the starry eye,
Had one foot in the grave; thinking me,
No doubt, a drunken dolt in whom a whim
Warmed to madness, not knowing a tease
Of a Welsh worm was tickling my distant toes.

'So I bequeath my leg', I'd say and sigh,
Baffling them, 'my unexiled part, to Dafydd
The pure poet who, whole, lies near and far
From me, still pining for Morfudd's heart',
Giving him, generous to a fault
With what was no more mine to give,
Out of that curt plot, my quarter grave,
Good help, I hope. What will the great God say
At Dafydd's wild-kicking-climbing extra leg,
Jammed hard in heaven's white doorway
(I'll limp unnimble round the narrow back)
Come the quick trumpet of the Judgement Day?

226 *Ancient Monuments*

for Alexander Thom

They bide their time off serpentine
Green lanes, in fields, with railings
Round them and black cows; tall, pocked
And pitted stones, grey, ochre-patched
With moss, lodgings for lost spirits.

Sometimes you have to ask their
Whereabouts. A bent figure, in a hamlet
Of three houses and a barn, will point
Towards the moor. You find them there,
Aloof lean markers, erect in mud.

Long Meg, Five Kings, Nine Maidens,
Twelve Apostles: with such familiar names
We make them part of ordinary lives.
On callow pasture-land
The Shearers and The Hurlers stand.

Sometimes they keep their privacy
In public places: nameless, slender slabs
Disguised as gate-posts in a hedge; and some,
For centuries on duty as scratching-posts,
Are screened by ponies on blank uplands.

Search out the farthest ones, slog on
Through bog, bracken, bramble: arrive
At short granite footings in a plan
Vaguely elliptical, alignments sunk
In turf strewn with sheep's droppings;

And wonder whether it was this shrunk place
The guide-book meant, or whether
Over the next ridge the real chamber,
Accurate by the stars, begins its secret
At once to those who find it.

Turn and look back. You'll see horizons
Much like the ones that they saw,
The tomb-builders, millenniums ago;
The channel scutched by rain, the same old
Sediment of dusk, winter returning.

Dolerite, porphyry, gabbro fired
At the earth's young heart: how those men
Handled them. Set on back-breaking
Geometry, the symmetries of solstice,
What they awaited we, too, still await.

Looking for something else, I came once
To a cromlech in a field of barley.
Whoever framed that field had true
Priorities. He sowed good grain
To the tomb's doorstep. No path

Led to the ancient death. The capstone,
Set like a cauldron on three legs,
Was marooned by the swimming crop.
A gust and the cromlech floated,
Motionless at time's moorings.

Hissing dry sibilance, chafing
Loquacious thrust of seed
This way and that, in time and out
Of it, would have capsized
The tomb. It stayed becalmed.

The bearded foam, rummaged
By wind from the westerly sea-track,
Broke short not over it. Skirted
By squalls of that year's harvest,
That tomb belonged in that field.

The racing barley, erratically-bleached
Bronze, cross-hatched with gold
And yellow, did not stop short its tide
In deference. It was the barley's
World. Some monuments move.

1926–

227   *The Dance*   ọ̣

I saw two hares in the corn
sparring and chasing:
four tall ears to-ing and fro-ing,
two shapely bodies coupling
and parting, clasping
and tossing
like two full ears of the corn
a-sway in the wind's dance.
The gnarled feet and strong stalks
had roots like claws in the earth.

This was the primal dance,
copulation of grain and ground,
the chord between summons and blood.
Around and above them
the corn-waves washed
till bright foam stood
on the high nostrils,
and somewhere, somewhere,
the seed was gambled on the womb's fruition.
This was the primal dance.

Through the wide-eyed ancient stars
I see the two hares eternal
on fields of yesterday and yesteryear,
leaping and loping
under the reaper's moon of September
and the majestic madness of March—
their chase
today-and-forever's,
in lair and bed among the blood-brothers,
and in nooks of the barley.

And they bear
within each velvet paw,

sustain
within each wild eye-flicker,
being—
just being:
light, nimble, and crazy,
aery as birdsong
or well-spring's bubbling,
or their own primal dance on the meadow.

T. GLYNNE DAVIES
1926–

228 *Old Man in a Moon Loft* ☿

Someone is locking out the stars and the yellow flowers,
Murdering the mildewed toads in the grass,
Whisking the bearded barley into oblivion.

The old man in his cradle blubbering,
The gorse-fires spluttering their death
On the mountains of his mind.

On them he is still a red-kneed boy
Long loitering in the pudding fields:
Big brown eyes watching the lark
Climbing the hurdy-gurdy stairs to the sun.

But someone's locking out the stars, the dungheaps and the barley
   husks,
Hobnailing the lapwing nests in the furrow.

Old man in an antiseptic ward,
Old man with the pan of life boiled dry,
His sixty years goose-pimpled in his mind
As he still clutches the warm, sleek neck of the midged mare
On the misty bog-graveyard:
Only that steel-cold long manicured fingers
Are squeezing his little red hand,
Tearing his soul by the bones from his old skin body.

Who is locking out the stars and the yellow flowers,
Pounding the eternal stones of the spring-water,
Burning the seed in the soil?

The old man in his moon loft
Sees the gorse fires spluttering their death
On the mountains of his mind.

What do they know about the red-round apple boy
Still loitering in the pudding fields?
They are lost in their clouds of hard concrete,
They who are trying to reassemble the jumble of wires
Under that white hair crop,

They who squeak with their stethoscopes
Over the over-polished wood floors,
Ploughing the marl of his mind
With a rat-tat-tat of bullet pills.

The old man tense in the moon loft
Sees the gorse fires whimpering to death
On the dead mountains of his mind.

229   *Sentences while Remembering Hiraethog*   ọ̀

It was a summer evening
they were all there
oh I remember them I tell you

old people that are this scorching hour
no more than tattered lips in the wind
and the others
the red-ripe hearts
with their laughter in fragments amongst the reeds
and their hair unkempt

where are the buttermilk voices that used to flow
through the kitchen and the dairy and the cowshed

229 Hiraethog] Mynydd Hiraethog, an upland region including the Denbigh
Moors in north-eastern Wales

and the laughter in fragments among the reeds

where are the round eyes
that disappeared in a cloud of laughter

I prayed that I might be one of the colts
on the Oerfa mountain for ever
it would be damned cold in winter of course
said Jo laughingly
odd that his voice that minute was like a bell

It was a summer evening
they were all there
the wind idly meandered through the corn

oh I remember them I tell you.

230 *Caernarfon, 2 July 1969* ♀

Castle to castle—
Is there peace?

Those who came for a song
In Lloyd George's parlour
And for a hooray on the field have gone.

The cheer and the boo have gone,
And the proper hats of all the Prince's aunts,
Everyone who said 'lovely', 'love', and 'thanks'.
The velvet cushions have gone:
Five guineas' worth of memories.

The policemen have gone,
And Scotland Yard's fill of suspicious names
And pictures and fingerprints.
The cameras and the microphones have gone,
And the cavalry and battalion of dragons
And the clamour about American tourists
And the cost of the plainclothesmen's Bed and Breakfast
And all the rush for the special stamps
Gone.

On the quay, the soldier has gone
In a fiery chariot like some chapter from the Old Testament,
And the cry of Llywelyn has gone
And of Owain Glyndŵr and status and 1282.

The sober dignified benches
Have become a hundred thousand planks,
What they were before yesterday and long days before.

Another Prince has started on his journey:

Castle to castle:
Is there peace?

BOBI JONES
1929–

231   *Portrait of an Engine Driver*   ♭

Smoke contending with smoke which will be maddest;
Light chewing chunks in the cloud and then belching;
Blasphemous grunting in a garden of grease.
See the driver crouched singing in the steel ball
'And the lightning fading in the blood,'
Touching the plates and the gear, like a blackbird
Rubbing its herbal scent into every spot,
And his carnal filth on the wheels, his strength's stamp
With the furnace's mirth warm on the instruments.
Wil is the name,
Son of Ed Williams the Cwm and brother of Elen.
He orders the uproar's work in his own wilful way
And plants his green personality in the oil,

230 Llywelyn] lord of North Wales, killed by the English in the wars of independence, 1282. See no. 22 and note to that poem   Owain Glyndŵr] Shakespeare's Owen Glendower. He had himself proclaimed Prince of Wales in 1400, fought an unsuccessful war against the English, and disappeared in 1412 without a known grave or recorded bardic elegy

He who is utterly splendid to five children;
He plumbs his blood's clicking for the piston's vein
And tapeworms his terms through the metal.
Through the nights of their fellowship
And their diligent void
The machine has become a beautiful hill-breast home,
A sanctuary, since here he thought of God best,
God on the axle, and God in the crunching,
And gloried in them as his forebears did in a horse
Till he felt the newly-washed coal a petal in his nostrils,
And the iron cogs played at fondling his hard hands,
His happiness under his armpits.
(Yesterday my love came to buy a ready-made frock
And wore it and made it part of her own enchantment.)
Christmas today, the warmth of home on his cheek,
His children's sweat in place of the piston's laughter,
But at the same God's strong feet he cradles himself
Like a comely village in a mountain niche.

232   *Spring at Nant Dywelan*   ♀

I entered it before I understood it,
Knew it before I knew about it. Like smoke
The light ingathered round me
Head over heels through the leaves and the birds and the pasture
Like an unblemished lamb
In the primal freedom we sprang from
And O, I too leapt on the scent
Of vigour astir in the grass,
Of life and liveliness in the new-born brook.

The year has known conversion.
It has; energy is everywhere. It splits the world.
It is the boundless Mystery that comforts being.
Down on the bank of the river the toads
And the water-vole bestir themselves
Beyond good and evil—off I go!—
Spreading their tender feet on the carcass of winter.

Winter has gone to its fathers.
It was sharp; alive. And look at them here:
Life has triumphed over life, and death death
On this everlasting meadow that is
A Cross for the year.
Spring came through the mouth of the morning
Its tongue clamouring hotly on the petals of sunrise
Like the boots of a soldier coming home.

Mournful and joyful is movement.
I saw white tips slyly poking
Like children's eyes from their hideouts.
I saw the tremor of wind caressing a primrose
As soft as a prayer, and as seemly.
I saw the full-breasted rushing waterfall
Leaping through to the meaning of being
With no object, self-impelled, subjective,
The complete thing, the concourse, the concord.

Meaning will rest in the breeze now, and be tested.
And down by the river are three daffodils,
Golden, golden, enclosing the sunshine in their hearts,
And the old look of mischief on them like schoolgirls
In a corner, sharing a secret.

233   *Portrait of a Nun*   ǫ

Your legs would be pretty, if you had legs,
When you rise at my bedside each day like a cold morning
To bandage and tend to my arms—if I had arms.
(In religion and war, the first casualty's caution.)
No legs—no arms—a fair warning, we two, against life:
And you, in black and white, a proclamation you are,
A proclamation of breezy death; your breast's cross his windmill.

You didn't want to be a mother—O! no:
You serve Mary in soldiers
And hear her song in curses.

Instead of babies' white-skinned purity you took
Our soul's muck to your bosom, our flesh's sewers.
Look at Huw in the corner bed, there's a baby for you,
Whining about the enemy stealing his nose.
Harri is another, calling 'Mommy' every night
And screaming his head off when the doctor comes to examine him.
Yes. You took a queer family into your hands
And you'll never have a proper family to fondle.
But you will go to your Lover; and He will not doubt your past.
He will not be concerned about the sweetness of your body
Or the chasteness of the company you kept,
And you will ever be a shining wife in the bed of His care.

234   *Portrait of a Pregnant Woman*   ọ̌

Today she parades her shape like swellings of song,
The wings that free her, her throne, her tower.
She bursts the land with her being, her brand, her blossom,
Her passion's lofty monument, her belly's dance.

The trickling that was a stream to her hope breaks through its banks,
Swirling in floods. Come, everyone, out of the way.
Where's the great mountain that will not be drowned?
What terror! Look at this. There is nothing loftier.

Along the length and breadth of our fields the world makes its way.
O everyone, run to the side. She is spacious as time.
Watch out for your toes. She carries the stresses
Of the season's muse, her mite of a chick's hidden thumping.

And upon her face is the smile of the Almighty.
Who? Has anyone seen this fulfilling before?
On her tomorrow's sunny roof her rapture warbles:
It chirps, a live coal, in the twigs of her breast.

Cautious her step lest she trample the eggs of Creation,
Light her heart lest she weigh down the little one.
She walks, like Peter on water, doubtfully joyful,
Till she beaches her glory's pyramid in a dry Canaan.

GLORIA EVANS DAVIES
1932–

235   *Her Name like the Hours*

Blodwen,
Her name like the hours,
Wales
All done by mirrors of lakes, waterfalls and rivers,
Children's first boat a coracle on the Teifi,
Signposts the only spoken Welsh.

In the first days of Primary
She traced her name in a box of sand,
Her hand a balancing gull to the tide's pull.

The sea turns to pearl in the shell of time.

GWYN THOMAS
1936–

236   *Little Death*   ♀

Somewhere in his body a blood-clot is moving
Like a naked sword through his veins:
Death is within him, in his arms or his feet.

A delicate red drop is inching its way
Through the map of his bloodstream,
Drawing him from us, drawing him away.

In the carnal complex that we call living,
In the moist commotion breathing under the skin,
In the tough white strings and the twisted pipes,
Out of reach of the steel knife—little death.

GWYN THOMAS

In Revelations death is a fearsome horseman,
It is pallid bones and black hollows.
In the *danse macabre* it is a naked skull,
White, and with famished bones.
And here the fat-bellied drop, the rosy-cheeked speck
Lurks in a man's jellies and his body's ravenous paths
Striking fear in us now
                    in its own way.

237   *Microscope*   ǫ

Through lenses the world opens,
Disclosing movement, restless and ravening;
A look at the other side of stillness.

Strangeness.

The small things amplify their being,
And armour is bred of brittleness;
Fierceness is born of frailty,
And the weak organs grow strong.

The caterpillar is metamorphosed to a hustle of shields
And its belly becomes like an army, living by moving.
It obliterates the leaves with the machines of its head.

The grasshopper develops complexity—
Legs' links, links legs,
Links legs, leg's links,
    Agonized iron.

An insect leaps into largeness.
Its countless eyes a latticework.
Its body turns metal, black, in layers.
    Glass and steel.

The other side of stillness:
Hardness.
The world, beneath its surface:
Harshness.

Horses

Suddenly there were forms there:
Heads bright of eye
Leapt out of the alien dark,
Out of the night into the headlights' gleam.

The twentieth century braked
And in the tousled manes before us
Pieces out of the past were
Gazing at us brightly.

Neighing and snorting nostrils,
Legs teeming with terror;
Scattering then. After the hooves
Stopped threshing the darkness: stillness.

After the nerves of seeing
Stopped twitching with the imprint of the flurry
Of the forms that came before our faces
Like a fist, the light was full of quietness.

Shifting into gear and moving
On a road that wound along the face of the world
In a wide night where time was untied
And let loose in a fearful roaming.

NOTES AND REFERENCES

Standard works of information are *A History of Welsh Literature* (Oxford, 1955), translated from Thomas Parry's *Hanes Llenyddiaeth Gymraeg hyd 1900* by Sir Harold Idris Bell, with an Appendix by the translator on Welsh literature in the twentieth century; and *The Dictionary of Welsh Biography* (London, 1959). The chief sources of translations drawn on for this volume are H. I. Bell, *The Development of Welsh Poetry* (1936); *A History of Welsh Literature* (as above); Joseph P. Clancy, *Medieval Welsh Lyrics* (1965), *The Earliest Welsh Poetry* (1970), and *Twentieth Century Welsh Verse* (forthcoming); Anthony Conran, *The Penguin Book of Welsh Verse* (1967); Kenneth H. Jackson, *A Celtic Miscellany* (1951); Gwyn Williams, *Presenting Welsh Poetry* (1959) and *Welsh Poems* (1973).

1. The poem records a victory of the North British led by Urien king of Rheged and his son Owain over the Angles of Deira and Bernicia. Owain son of Urien would in time be transmuted into a knight of King Arthur and a main personage of Mabinogion romance. Of the poet Taliesin we know next to nothing, and the Middle Ages knew little more. For them he was not only the celebrant of the hero-kings of the North, but like a lesser and later Virgil was viewed as a legend, a vaticinator, a shape-changer, a mnemonic, and therefore an utterer of gnomic profundities—qualities prominent in no. 14 and to be presumed in no. 24. Of the miscellany of poems known as the Book of Taliesin barely a dozen are the work of the 'historical' Taliesin.

3. *The Gododdin* is a poem, or assemblage, consisting of roughly a hundred stanzas preserved in the so-called Book of Aneirin. The manuscript contains two versions of the poem: Version A (88 stanzas) written in the orthography of the thirteenth century; Version B (42 stanzas) in the orthography of the ninth or tenth. The poem is attributed to the sixth-century poet Aneirin, but the date or dates of its composition and the history of its transmission from the oral to the written stage remain the subject of debate. It tells in its own order and fashion how Mynyddog Mwynfawr, a king of the North British people known as the Gododdin, drew together an élite of Celtic fighting men from the length and breadth of Britain, and feasted them for a year at his royal court in Edinburgh. Then they rode south on a warlike mission fraught with destiny for the British and English kingdoms of the North. At Catterick in northern Yorkshire the Three Hundred encountered the hosts of England —more particularly the men of Deira and Bernicia. Despite or perhaps because of their valour, in a battle from which none held back, they were

destroyed save for one man—or maybe three, or even four, since factua
consistency is not essential to heroic utterance. It was thus that like other
famed war bands of the Celtic and Germanic heroic age they paid for their
mead with their lives and, so dying, earned immortal fame. The battle was
fought *c.* A.D. 600.

The twelve stanzas printed here are representative of most or all aspects
of *The Gododdin.* They have been placed in a more or less consecutive
order to assist the reader. The roman numerals indicate their order in Ifor
Williams, *Canu Aneirin* (Cardiff, 1961).

4. This charming little song of a mother to her child, which surely has
nothing to do with Aneirin or his works, somehow found refuge among the
martial agonies and splendours of the *Gododdin* manuscript, where it is stanza
87 of the A version. The meaning of line 3 (*chwid, chwid, chwidogaith*) is
unclear. It may consist of such nonsense words as are not uncommon in
nursery rhymes; it may have a specific meaning now lost; or it may represent
a mother whistling to her child as part of a hunting song. Giff and Gaff are
the names of dogs.

6–7. Wales has few saga narratives to show from early times, not because
none were composed, but because they were not preserved. But it is likely
that several sets of early Welsh poems in the form of dialogue or monologue,
of a pronouncedly dramatic and emotional nature, were part of a body of
saga whose more direct narrative was conducted in prose. Two such sagas,
telling of events and personages of the sixth and seventh centuries respec-
tively, were known in Powys (north-eastern Wales) in the mid-ninth century.
The first related to Llywarch Hen (the Old) and is the classic Welsh portrayal
of the 'Angry Old Man'; the second to Heledd, the Proud Maiden. Our
knowledge of both sagas is unsure, in that we must reconstruct the content
of the vanished prose from the preserved verses; but their common theme is
private and tribal disaster, where the facts of history are interpreted as the
workings of fate and the nemesis of human pride.

Llywarch was a warrior of North Britain in the sixth century, who bore
the severed head of his lord King Urien of Rheged from the battlefield, that
it might be buried not humiliated, and eventually found refuge south in
Wales, in Powys. Here again he fought against the English invader, and his
twenty-four sons, impelled by their own ready valour and their father's bitter
tongue, fought too. One after the other they perished in their father's pride.

> If you survive, I shall see you again;
> If you are killed, I shall weep for you.
> Bring no shame on me, a warrior!

And now he has grown old, and his poet gives him one more opportunity to
reveal himself to the in-every-sense bitter end: angry, baffled, useless to man,

woman, or beast, a prey to pain, remorse, lacerated vanity, and a desperate loneliness. His king, his fellow-countrymen, his patria, his sons are all in ruins. Where has it all gone? And where is longed-for Death?

The poems of the saga of Heledd were composed for the mouth of the saga's heroine. She has seen all her brothers killed in an unavailing defence of the townships of Powys against the English invader; and she has reason to blame their destruction on herself. 'By my accursèd tongue they are slain!' Heledd's laments are at once heart-rending and fiercely controlled, and many of the *englynion* on the hall of Cynddylan, the Eagle of Pengwern (and that other corpse-despoiler, the Eagle of Eli), the chapels of Bassa and the White Town, have the inevitability of great poetry.

> Stafell Gynddylan ys tywyll heno,
>   Heb dân, heb wely;
>   Wylaf wers, tawaf wedy.

> The hall of Cynddylan, it is dark tonight,
>   Without fire, without bed;
>   I shall weep awhile, then be silent.

We leave the bereft Princess of Powys in her thin cloak, driving her solitary cow over the mountain pasture. In the soil that moulded her brothers they now moulder. 'Ah God, I go on living!'

The translation of stanzas from *Hateful Old Age* first appeared in 'The Angry Old Men', *Scandinavian Studies* (Seattle, Wash.: 1965).

8. Seventy-three of these proud-titled 'Stanzas of the Graves' (*Englynion y Beddau*) or 'The Graves of the Warriors of the Island of Britain' (*Beddau Milwyr Ynys Prydain*) are preserved in the Black Book of Carmarthen, most of them in a hand of the second quarter of the thirteenth century. They come from the ninth or tenth century, and the graves remarked on are those of heroes of Welsh saga, legend, and folktale, many known, some unknown. But even of the unknown we may believe the old proverb: *Tyst yw'r chwedl i'r englyn*, 'The story bears witness to the *englyn*'. Among the personages of the stanzas here translated are Owain son of Urien, Cynddylan, Bedwyr (Bedivere), Gwalchmai (Hawk of May, Gawain), March (Mark), and Arthur himself. The line referring to Arthur's grave is one of the most legend-inducing in early European poetry: *Anoeth bid bet y Arthur*: a thing hard to find, a portent and secret, the world's wonder, the burial place of Arthur, the vanished king and Sleeping Lord (no. 150) who will yet return to his people.

9. Geraint like Owain would become an important figure of native Arthurian romance. The poem's reference to Arthur, 'strife's commander', is notably pre-romance, though not as early as that in *The Gododdin* to a warrior who 'though he was not Arthur' brought black crows (i.e. for carrion) to a fort's

rampart, which is thought to be the first known literary reference to the folk hero and later king and emperor. For another decisive stage in the growth of the Arthurian legend see no. 8 above and note.

10. These are the opening stanzas of a puzzling but dramatic poem whose subjects are winter and warfare, with some curious reflections on cowardice.

14. The translation first appeared in Sir Ifor Williams's *Lectures on Early Welsh Poetry* (Dublin, 1944). It is here reprinted from his *The Poems of Taliesin*, English version by J. E. Caerwyn Williams (Dublin, 1968).

16-17. 'Tall Hywel, hawk of war' was the natural son of Owain Gwynedd, lord of Gwynedd in North Wales and the main prop of Welsh national fortunes in the twelfth century. Owain died in 1170, and in the struggle that followed Hywel was killed by his half-brothers Dafydd and Rhodri. Nos. 16 and 17 are sometimes printed as one poem, but appear likelier to be two. The first belongs to the genre known to contemporary poets as *Gorhoffedd*, meaning Boast, Vaunt, Exultant Utterance, Celebration, and what was boasted about or celebrated was the poet's valour in war, the beauty of his beloved homeland, and his delight in and success with his countrywomen. The second has nothing to tell of warfare or Gwynedd but celebrates eight lady-killings from Chester to the coast of South Wales.

22. Llywelyn ap Gruffudd, lord of North Wales, was killed in a minor and almost accidental clash with the English at Builth in 1282. His head was struck off and exhibited on a stake in London. His death was disastrous for Welsh hopes of national independence and called forth many elegies, of which this apocalyptic outburst is the most remarkable. Its last section plays forcibly on the two meanings of *pen*, 'chief or chieftain' and 'head'. I reproduce the last eighteen lines of the Welsh poem, which will illustrate to a close-scanning English reader its rhetorical effects and sound patterns (for example, there is only one rhyme used throughout the entire poem); and the problems attendant on the translation of Court Poetry:

> Pen pan las, ni bu gas gymraw;
> Pen pan las, oedd lesach peidiaw.
> Pen milwr, pen moliant rhag llaw,
> Pen dragon, pen draig oedd arnaw.
> Pen Llywelyn deg, dygn o fraw—i'r byd
>   Bod pawl haearn trwyddaw.
> Pen f'arglwydd, poen dygngwydd a'm daw;
> Pen f'enaid heb fanag arnaw.
> Pen a fu berchen ar barch naw—canwlad,
>   A naw canwledd iddaw.

Pen tëyrn, hëyrn heaid o'i law,
Pen tëyrnwalch balch, bwlch ei ddeifnaw.
Pen tëyrnaidd flaidd flaengar ganthaw.
Pen tëyrnedd nef, Ei nawdd arnaw.
Gwyndëyrn orthyrn wrthaw,—gwendorf gorf,
Gorfynt hynt hyd Lydaw.
Gwir freiniawl frenin Aberffraw,
Gwenwlad nef boed addef iddaw.

24. The poetic device of the *llatai*, or love messenger, was not unknown to earlier poets, but Dafydd ap Gwilym made it very much his own by right of poetic conquest. He established it as a *cywydd*-kind which outlasted the Poets of the Nobility. The *llatai-cywydd* is normally much less concerned with the lady in the case, or the poet's devotion, than with the creature entrusted with the delivery of his message. Practically anything with the power of locomotion could be a *llatai*; bird, fish, animal, sun, wind or wave. To use crude categories, what resulted was a prescribed nature poem set in the context of a not very personal love poem. It allowed the poet to describe by comparison and analogy (*dyfalu*) an affectionately regarded and closely observed creature or natural phenomenon, as here and in no. 52 the seagull, and in no. 27 the wind; it challenged him to a set-piece; it demanded that he show, and show off, his poetical skills. The results at their best are dazzlingly fine.

25. In Rolfe Humphries, *Nine Thorny Thickets* (Kent, Ohio, 1969), this poem is entitled 'In Morvith's Arms, the First Time'. In his lines about 'Arthur's loveliest' the translator has introduced the early Welsh triad which enumerates 'The Three Splendid Ladies of Arthur's Court'.

26. No lover in any language, and certainly no poet, has confessed to missing the mark more often than Dafydd ap Gwilym. Uncooperative husbands, quick-triggered alarms, crones and walls, strong locks, floods and fogs and bogs and dogs are for ever interposing themselves between him and golden-haired Morfudd, black-browed Dyddgu, or Gwen the infinitely fair. But a great trier, even in church.

30. The translation of 'Lament for Lleucu Llwyd' has been revised by Professor Clancy for this volume.

34. M. C. Llewelyn's translation of 'The Saxons of Flint' is taken from Charles Wilkins, *The History of the Literature of Wales from the Year 1300 to the Year 1650* (Cardiff, 1884).

37. The unheroic self-mockery of this poem, unthinkable in the poetry of the Cynfeirdd and Gogynfeirdd, had been heard as early as Dafydd ap Gwilym, who when informed by a dark-browed maid that no coward should ever possess her, replied (I paraphrase): 'Better for a girl a fearless lover than a fearful fighter. Better for a man one girl in his arms than two kingdoms in war's balance.' Other times, other manners. At the turn of the last century young girls in the South Wales valleys were encouraged to sound forth the battle-cry: 'Lips that touch liquor shall never touch mine!' But children continued to be born.

41-2. Gwerfyl Mechain was a poetess, and so a *rara avis* of the Welsh fifteenth century. No. 41 is the opening of a *cywydd* which she hopes will prompt the gift of a harp from a local notable. With this harp she will fault-lessly entertain the men who come to her hostelry with silver (the price of a dinner is twopence). No. 42 is composed of two *englynion*. What we know of her life would hardly fill a wren's egg. She has been credited with a number of avidly sexual poems, but this is to add the unknowable to the unknown.

45. The Tristan–Iseult story is preserved in Welsh in a series of twenty-five early *englynion* embedded in a brief connecting narrative of later prose. The *englyn* quoted is the triumphant climax of the story.

49. The poem *Against Women*, of which these stanzas are but a part, be-longing as it does to a well-known European satirical genre, and written in a kind of skeltonics, provoked as such poems often do a *Defence of Women* from the traditionalist William Cynwal later in the century. Cynwal clashed likewise with the metrical innovator Archdeacon Edmwnd Prys (no. 53); he died during their prolonged exchange of *cywyddau*, and the Archdeacon had the last word with an elegy.

51. From *Poems from the Welsh*, translated by H. I. Bell and C. C. Bell (Carnarvon, 1913). The translator of 'Mary's Dream' writes: 'The version of the charm from which this rendering is made was taken down from an old man at Aber. The charm, in various forms, has been recorded in many parts of Wales, and some Irish versions of it are given by Douglas Hyde in his *Religious Songs of Connacht*. I am told that it is known also in Brittany.' I have assumed that the verse is much older than the time of its recording.

54. Thomas Prys, gentleman, of Plas Iolyn, Denbighshire, was reputed to be one of 'the two filthy Welshmen who first smoked publicly in the streets'. He was also a soldier, sailor, pirate, and poet, and up to his eyes in everything. The phrases printed in italics appear in English in the original, though with a Welsh spelling, which the translator has here anglicized.

56-67. Nos. 56, 58, 66, and 67 of these folk verses are from *The Welsh Review*, III, iv (1944); 57, 59–63 are here published for the first time. No. 64

is from *The Poetical Works of Richard Llwyd, the Bard of Snowdon* (London, n.d. [1837?]); no. 65 first appeared in R. S. Thomas, *The Stones of the Field* (Carmarthen, 1946), and subsequently in *Song at the Year's Turning* (1955).

68. This is one of the verse tributes prefatory to the First Folio edition of Shakespeare's plays, 1623.

69. The English and Latin poems of Lord Herbert of Cherbury were edited by G. C. M. Smith, 1923.

72. This is a very 'Welsh' poem of Herbert's, entirely given up to *dyfalu*, the almost riddling description of an object by a series of comparisons and analogues arising out of the poet's pleasure in his skills as well as his desire (as here) to convey the otherwise indescribable. Cf. nos. 27, 31, 39, 40, 52, and some stanzas of Vaughan's 'The Night' (no. 80).

74. From the tenth edition of *Epistolae Ho-Elianae*, 1737 (first edition 1645 and 1647; standard edition by Joseph Jacobs, 2 vols., 1892).

76. From *Flamma Sine Fumo*, 1662, edited by Paul C. Davies (Cardiff, 1968).

78. From *Anthroposophia Theomagica*, 1650. In A. E. Waite, *The Works of Thomas Vaughan* (*Eugenius Philalethes*), 1919, reprinted 1968, the last line shows an amendment (not followed here) to: 'Or eccentricity'.

79–82. Instead of a fifth poem by the Silurist, the reader may welcome this letter written by him to his kinsman John Aubrey, 9 October 1694, concerning the bards and druids of antiquity, the puzzling nature of the *Awen* or poetic furor, and the green-garlanded young man with a hawk on his fist who made not just another poet out of a shepherd lad but the most famous Bard in all the Country in his time:

> Honoured Cousin:—I received yours and should have gladly served you, had it been in my power. But all my search and consultations with those few that I could suspect to have any knowledge of Antiquity came to nothing, for the ancient Bards, though by the testimony of their enemies the Romans a very learned society, yet (like the Druids) they communicated nothing of their knowledge, but by way of tradition; which I suppose to be the reason that we have no account left us, nor any sort of remains, or other monuments of their learning, or way of living.
>
> As to the later Bards, who were no such men, but had a society and some rules and orders among themselves, and several sorts of measures and a kind of lyric poetry, which are all set down exactly in the learned John David Rhees, or Rhesus his Welsh or British grammar, you shall have

there, in the later end of his book, a most curious account of them. This vein of poetry they call Awen, which in their language signifies as much as Raptus, or a poetic furor; and in truth as many of them as I have conversed with are, as I may say, gifted or inspired with it. I was told by a very sober and knowing person (now dead) that in his time there was a young lad fatherless and motherless, and so very poor that he was forced to beg; but at last was taken up by a rich man that kept a great stock of sheep upon the mountains not far from the place where I now dwell, who clothed him and sent him into the mountains to keep his sheep. There in summer time, following the sheep and looking to their lambs, he fell into a deep sleep, in which he dreamed that he saw a beautiful young man with a garland of green leaves upon his head and a hawk upon his fist, with a quiver full of arrows at his back, coming towards him (whistling several measures or tunes all the way) and at last let the hawk fly at him, which he dreamed got into his mouth and inward parts, and suddenly awaked in a great fear and consternation, but possessed with such a vein, or gift of poetry, that he left the sheep and went about the Country, making songs upon all occasions, and came to be the most famous Bard in all the Country in his time.

> MS. Aubrey 13, fol. 340. Reproduced in *The Works of Henry Vaughan*, ed. L. C. Martin (Oxford, 1914), p. 675.

85. From *Miscellaneous Poems* (1726). Dyer was a Carmarthenshire man.

87. From MS. Cwrtmawr 20 in the National Library of Wales.

88. From *The Works of . . . Sir Chas. Hanbury Williams: With Notes by Horace Walpole*, 3 vols. (1822).

90–2. William Williams, more often known by the name of his birthplace, Pantycelyn, was the most notable Welsh hymn-writer of the eighteenth century, and in the finest of his voluminous and uneven work provides the best contribution made by Methodism to Welsh literature. Far removed from the bardic tradition and the strict metres, untrammelled by *cynghanedd* and the demands of a formally 'correct' syntax and vocabulary, often appearing to flout beauty of phrase and melody in favour of colloquial ease and immediate intelligibility, he frequently pays the penalty of being a law unto himself. But he offered his eighteenth-century reader and the singer of his 800 hymns a new experience of God. When Meilyr and Cynddelw and their like addressed the Almighty they knew their place in His household, their rights as well as their duties; they had a hierarchical relationship to heaven's Lord, and their poems were governed by protocol. Not so Williams Pantycelyn, whose relationship with God was intensely and at times agonizingly

personal. For him the experience and enjoyment of God were the inspira-
tion of song, and absolute committal in joy and sorrow. Comparatively little
of his work has been translated by others than himself. I have judged it
proper to include 'Guide me, O thou great Jehovah' (in large measure his own
version of '*Arglwydd, arwain trwy'r anialwch*', 1771–2) partly for this reason,
but even more because it has soared on wide wings through two hundred
years of Welsh chapel-going, and though Jehovah and Jesus and Jordan
should now join the defeated mythologies, seems destined by virtue of its
twentieth-century alliance with John Hughes's marvellously congruent
hymn tune 'Cwm Rhondda' to live on as a battle hymn while Wales stays on
the winning side and rugby balls stay oval.

The idyll of 'The Marriage in Eden' is here translated for the first time
from Pantycelyn's long religious poem *Golwg ar Deyrnas Crist* (1756).

93. No copy is known to exist of the first edition of *Chepstow: A Poem*, 1784.
There was a second edition in 1786.

94–6. The bracketed lines at the head and tail of the passage from *Jubilate
Agno* are from the same poem. We may hope that Smart, Lewis Morris's
'young Cymro at Cambridge', knew the value set on earlier Jeoffrys by the
medieval Welsh laws:

> . . . Whoever kills the cat that guards the king's barn, or steals it, its
> head is to be set down on a clean level floor, and its tail is to be held up,
> and then wheaten grains are to be poured around it until they cover the tip
> of its tail. Any other cat is worth four legal pence . . . In law, essential
> qualifications of a cat are that it should be perfect of ear and eye and tail
> and teeth and claws, not singed by the fire; and that it should kill mice
> and not eat its kittens, and should not be caterwauling every full moon . . .

The original manuscript of *Jubilate Agno* is in the Houghton Library of
Harvard University. For *A Song to David*, 1763, see Smart's *Collected Poems*,
edited by N. Callan, 2 vols. (1949).

97–8. Goronwy Owen was the best Welsh poet of his time, and one of the
best of the entire modern period. An unstable man, the son of a labourer
and grandson of a tinker, he achieved a good education and in time a prob-
lem with strong drink. He became a clergyman, and one of his curacies was
at Northolt in Middlesex. In 1755 he was elected secretary of the recently
founded Cymmrodorion Society, which later helped him emigrate to
America, where he became master of a school attached to William and Mary
College, in Virginia, in 1758. In 1760 he was dismissed for bad conduct, and
once more became a clergyman. He died in Virginia in 1769.

Goronwy was at once an earnest student of eighteenth-century English
critical theory and poetry and a devoted admirer of the golden age of Welsh

poetry. On both counts he was a powerful exponent of clarity, precision, and decorum of language, together with good sense and significant meaning. As always in Wales, the poet must speak usefully and unambiguously to men. He excelled at the *cywydd* which he often (as in no. 97) invested with Horatian elegance and dignity. Even so he hankered after the great Christian heroic poem which had already proved such a weighty will-o'-the-wisp in England. His views, honourable in themselves, passionately held, and eloquently pleaded, were to have considerable influence, and did much to establish the norms of worthy abstraction, reworked history, and self-satisfied morality which dominated and then dogged the Eisteddfod till well into the next century.

The translation of 'The Invitation' is from *George Borrow. Welsh Poems and Ballads*, with an Introduction by Ernest Rhys (1915).

99. Evan Evans was the foremost Welsh scholar of his day. Educated by the classicist Edward Richard at Ystrad Meurig, and thereafter at Merton College, Oxford, he was a poet in Welsh, English, and Latin, and the author of a famous pioneering history of Welsh poetry from the age of Taliesin (with pioneering translations), *Some Specimens of the Poetry of the Ancient Welsh Bards*, 1764. He was known to Thomas Gray, to whom he communicated some renderings of Welsh verse, and was the valued correspondent on matters Celtic and medieval of Bishop Percy. His approach to the study and understanding of early manuscripts was exemplary; his verdict on the claims to antiquity of Macpherson's *Ossian* was a model of method and truth; but 'as prudence is not always the companion of a great genius' (*Gentleman's Magazine*, 2.10.1788), his life was not without vicissitude and misfortune, including not only the empty pocket and the oft-filled glass but a brief enlistment in the 34th Regiment of Foot, from which, 'being disordered in his mind, and finding him to be the Rev. Mr. Evans', he was after four days' service discharged. His stanzas (*englynion*) on the hall of Ifor Hael, probably composed about 1780 when he was a curate at Basaleg in Monmouthshire, are at once reminiscent of early Welsh elegy and redolent of the romantic melancholy which he and so many of his contemporaries in Wales admired in the poetry of Gray and Goldsmith.

100. Evan Lloyd was David Garrick's 'A man of genius, and a Welch man'. 'Helen Like the Rose' is from *The Powers of the Pen*, 2nd edition (1768).

102. Iolo Morganwg (Edward Williams) was a stonemason, antiquary, poet, lover of his native Glamorgan (whence his bardic title), and friend of mankind. A compulsive romantic, he dreamt of the primitive purity of the ancient druidic system, and woke not to forget but to evangelize. In that system 'bardism', he felt, had its place, and the evidence that was unfortunately lacking he unfortunately supplied. He manufactured triads, proverbs, a system of ancient metres, and a chronicle; invented poets and wrote

their poems; and acting on a hint in the Welsh laws he devised 'The Gorsedd of the Bards of the Island of Britain', its provenance, procedures, and colourful ceremonial. The National Eisteddfod still shows a bold set of Iolo's prints; and as a poet it now begins to look as though the only pockets he ever picked were his own. It is hard to deny him the title of genius.

104. From A. H. Miles, *The Poets and Poetry of the Century*, 10 vols. (London, 1891–7). Emily Jane Pfeiffer, *née* Davies, is included, with a short piece about her by A. H. Japp, in volume VII.

116. First published in *A Review of English Literature*, IV, i, Jan. 1963.

125. This and no. 13 above ('On Christians, Mercy Will Fall') are from D. M. and E. M. Lloyd, *A Book of Wales* (1953).

131. The starting-point of the poem is the Mabinogion story of 'Branwen daughter of Llŷr', which tells how the king of Ireland came to Wales with thirteen ships to ask for the hand of Branwen, sister of Brân the Blest, king over this Island. Her half-brother, furious that his consent too had not been asked, insulted the Irishmen unforgivably. Soon, back in Ireland, Branwen was driven from the king's chamber and forced to cook in the kitchen, where every day the butcher gave her a box on the ear. 'Not less than three years they continued thus. And meantime she reared a starling on the end of her kneading-trough and taught it words and instructed the bird what manner of man her brother was. And she brought a letter of the woes and the dishonour that were upon her. And the letter was fastened under the root of the bird's wings and sent towards Wales. And the bird came to this Island. The place where it found Brân was at Caer Seint in Arfon, at an assembly of his one day. And it alighted on his shoulder and ruffled its feathers so that the letter was seen and it was known that the bird had been reared among dwellings.' Brân mustered his fighting men, crossed the Irish Sea, and rescued his sister after so mortal a fray that only seven men returned to Wales and only five pregnant women remained alive of the people of Ireland. Branwen died as she reached Wales. '"Alas, Son of God," said she, "woe is me that ever I was born; two good islands have been laid waste because of me." And she heaved a great sigh, and with that broke her heart. And a four-sided grave was made for her, and she was buried there on the bank of the Alaw.' (Both quotations from *The Mabinogion*, translated by Gwyn Jones and Thomas Jones, Everyman, 1974.)

Williams Parry's poem operates at several levels. There is that of the original story, with a transfer of interest from human beings to starling, the all-important messenger. What happened to it after its fleeting appearance in the story of Branwen? Did it die of exhaustion after its journey? Was it buried like Branwen in a four-sided grave on the bank of the Alaw? Did it return with the avengers to Ireland? Second, what is the religious, the Christian, significance of the poem? A creature who is heaven-sent bears a holy epistle of pain from one whose hands are scarred like Christ's to a god in the shape of man. Is the message of heaven not one of comfort and joy only but also of suffering and grief? Then, third, the starling is the buffoon of the birds of the world. The sailors who cross to Ireland are un-moved by the holy epistle of pain; they laugh as though the world holds no grief or divine tragedy. And the starling, his message delivered, laughs too and mocks and mimics the rest of the creation. Is the starling the poet, every poet, with his message of unholy mirth and divine tragedy? Is he the poet Williams Parry? The poem offers a simple story and a profound enigma.

143. In line 8 I have preferred 'fauns' to 'fawns'; in line 23, 'Many the muscled bodies charred' and line 34, 'Left', I have retained the original readings of the B.M. fair copy.

149–50. The passage from *In Parenthesis* is the conclusion of the poem, whose seven parts bear on their title-pages mottoes from *The Gododdin* (no. 3). The main title-page bears as motto a line from the stanza about Isaac of the South: *Seinnyessit e gledyf ym penn mameu*: 'His sword rang in the heads of mothers'. See page 5.

'The Sleeping Lord' is David Jones's reworking of the legend, folktale, myth, of the hero who is also the saviour who will be woken or resurrected or otherwise restored to his people in the hour of their deepest need. The protagonists here are Arthur and Twrch Trwyth, the Great Boar who must be hunted to his death by the Hero and his Helpers. In the Mabinogion story of 'Culhwch and Olwen' Twrch Trwyth rampages on a swathe of death and destruction across South Wales till the huntsmen and their horses and dogs drive him headlong into Severn (Hafren) and away out into the western sea. The poem is also a lament for the wrecked splendours of the Celtic past and the pollution and alienation from its maternal culture of industrialized South Wales today.

The poet's notes to no. 149 have been omitted, and the notes to no. 150 have been edited.

154–65. The *englyn* is a strictly regulated, four-lined, thirty-syllabled, *cynghanedd*-patterned, rhymed verse form so native to the Welsh tongue (many *englynion* are said with a proper poetic licence to be born rather than written), and so alien to English, that it has defied all attempts at translation and transition over the centuries. But it cannot be ignored in a volume pro-fessing to present Welsh poetry; and half a loaf, or even the tithe of a loaf, is better than no bread. The *englyn* can be used magnificently for every poetic purpose comprised within a loose definition of epigram: amatory, satiric, elegiac, exhortatory, descriptive, reflective, religious, cautionary, and comic.

Here are the texts of two *englynion*, the first composed in the fifteenth century by Llawdden (no. 43), the second by R. Williams Parry (no. 165) half a millennium later:

(1)   Y gleisiad, difrad yw ef,—o'i ddichwain
           A ddychwel i'w addef;
        'Nol blino'n treiglo pob tref
        Teg edrych tuag adref.

(2)   Rhoes ei nerth a'i brydferthwch—tros ei wlad,
           Tros aelwydydd heddwch:
        Gyfoedion oll, gofidiwch!
        Lluniaidd lanc sy'n llonydd lwch.

168. Mair K. Davies has written an account of the genesis and nature of her husband's last poem of which these translated sentences are part: 'The poem was fashioned in a hospital, between two surgical operations, for inclusion in a series of poems written for radio, during the winter of 1951–2. It was from a few notes of his on paper, and from listening to my husband's spoken words line by line, that I set it down on paper, there by his bedside. Some, remembering the place and the time and Kitchener's death a few months after the broadcast, have seen a deep significance in the references to scalpel and needle-syringe and ether-meth and the cancer of anglicization writhing through Wales. But these are images—arising, admittedly, from specific circumstances—which are a part of the meditation upon *life*, on being a Welshman today, and tomorrow, and of the age-old experience of the individual . . . The poem follows a life's course, from the loving closeness of childhood at Cors Caron [Tregaron bog, in Cardiganshire, Dyfed], by way of the whole business of responsibility towards nation and society and kindred and family in the Rhondda, to the coming face-to-face with the traumatic choice between a life comfortable and pleasant and the blind pilgrimage of the martyr and the saint.'

175. A much-discussed poem by a visionary, patriot, pacifist, and good neighbour, who thought all men, whatever their race, creed, colour or class, 'the children of God and fellow-citizens of eternity'. He has offered a clue to its fuller understanding not only by his reference to a specific personal experience (in the footnote on p. 219), but in an article in *Y Faner*, 20 June 1956, where he quotes a verse of the Irish poet AE:

> Sometimes, when alone
> At the dark close of day,
> Men meet an outlawed majesty
> And hasten away

— and comments: 'There is nothing save this solitude that can bring us, through the medium of the Exiled King, to the right relationship between man and man.' This relationship cannot be achieved within the heart-chilling bounds of the sovereign state or the caesardom of the world, but through the felt and accepted presence of the Exiled King from whom man has come to live in such bleak estrangement.

187. First published in *The Times Literary Supplement*, 2 December 1955.

197. Lehrte Bahnhof, writes Alun Llywelyn-Williams, is the Berlin railway station 'where at the end of World War Two some of the many thousands of poor wretches were unloaded who were driven out of those lands in the east which Russia had given to Poland'. The Heledd of the poem is the Heledd who lamented the cruel aftermath of war in the elegy on Cynddylan (no. 7 and note). Inge is her modern counterpart. The eagle, like the eagle of Pengwern, is the ever-present functionary attendant upon death, destruction, and defeat.

199. The poem expresses the dilemma of a man standing between two cultures, in time and place, i.e. in a particular country, and even in a particular part of that country, in this case that region of South Wales which embraces the immemorial mountain and river country of the Brecon Beacons on the one hand, with all its associations of language, way of life, religion, and history over the ages, and on the other the changed valleys of industrial Glamorgan and the new city of Cardiff. Of the precise locale of the poem the poet has this to say: 'Pont y Caniedydd is a real bridge, two or three miles south of Brecon, in Cwm Seri in the foothills of the Beacons. It is, or used to be, a beautifully sequestered spot, and there is a track leading from it to Cwm Cynwyn and over the pass, Bwlch ar y Fan, to the Taf Fechan valley, where one is on the edge of the industrial area. I suppose the name means the Bridge of the Singer, but I know nothing of its history or its significance. It is a marvellous name for a marvellous place, and it suited me to take it ambiguously, for *caniedydd* can mean *poet*, and in the context of the poem it is the poet's wish to be a bridge of sorts.'

218. A prominent and much-metamorphosized figure in early Welsh vaticinatory poetry was Myrddin, better known to readers of Arthurian romance and pseudo-history as Merlin, of whom we are told that *c.* A.D. 575 he fought at Arfderydd (Arthuret, near Carlisle) for King Gwenddolau against King Rhydderch. Gwenddolau was slain, and Myrddin lost his reason during the fight. He fled to the forest of Celyddon (Caledonia), where to the wild things of the wood, and particularly to the sweet-apple tree and the little pig his companions, he confided his griefs, fears and trials, together with prophecies designed to harden Welsh (or British) resistance against the English and later the Norman oppressor.

228. The translation was made by the author for 'Dial a Poem', and appeared in *Poetry Wales*, VII, 1 (1971).

230. The investiture of Prince Charles as Prince of Wales took place on 1 July 1969 at Caernarfon Castle before a chosen assembly and a worldwide television audience. Not all Welshmen were enchanted with the occasion. 'Is there peace?' is the thrice-repeated ritual question asked before the crowning and chairing ceremonies at the National Eisteddfod of Wales. A sword is half drawn, and the audience has so far answered 'There is', whereupon the sword is sheathed and the crowning or chairing of the bard takes place.

INDEX OF AUTHORS

The references are to the numbers of the poems

INDEX OF TRANSLATORS

1. The translator's name is followed by the number and English title of the poem as it appears in this volume, e.g.

Bell, C. C.: 51, Mary's Dream.

2. All Welsh-language poems in copyright (they begin with 108) are given their Welsh title in italics, e.g.

Williams, Gwyn: 127, The Fox (*Y Llwynog*).

3. A reference P. followed by a number (i.e. P. 20) indicates that the Welsh original of a translation will be found wholly or in part in Thomas Parry's *Oxford Book of Welsh Verse* (1962). For convenience I have added the Welsh titles of all such poems up to 108 as well, e.g.

Clancy, Joseph P.: 231, Portrait of an Engine Driver (*Portread o Yrrwr Trên*, P. 334).

G. J.

INDEX OF TRANSLATORS

INDEX OF TRANSLATORS

INDEX OF FIRST LINES

References are to page numbers

INDEX OF FIRST LINES

INDEX OF FIRST LINES